Beyond the antislavery haven

Manchester University Press

Series editors: Anna Barton, Andrew Smith

Editorial board: David Amigoni, Isobel Armstrong, Philip Holden, Jerome McGann, Joanne Wilkes, Julia M. Wright

Interventions: Rethinking the Nineteenth Century seeks to make a significant intervention into the critical narratives that dominate conventional and established understandings of nineteenth-century literature. Informed by the latest developments in criticism and theory the series provides a focus for how texts from the long nineteenth century, and more recent adaptations of them, revitalise our knowledge of and engagement with the period. It explores the radical possibilities offered by new methods, unexplored contexts and neglected authors and texts to re-map the literary-cultural landscape of the period and rigorously re-imagine its geographical and historical parameters. The series includes monographs, edited collections, and scholarly sourcebooks.

To buy or to find out more about the books currently available in this series, please go to: https://manchesteruniversitypress.co.uk/series/interventions-rethinking-the-nineteenth-century/

Beyond the antislavery haven

Slavery in early Canadian print culture, 1789–1889

Eleanor Bird

MANCHESTER UNIVERSITY PRESS

Copyright © Eleanor Bird 2025

The right of Eleanor Bird to be identified as the author of this work has been asserted in accordance with the Copyright, Designs and Patents Act 1988.

Published by Manchester University Press
Oxford Road, Manchester, M13 9PL

www.manchesteruniversitypress.co.uk

British Library Cataloguing-in-Publication Data
A catalogue record for this book is available from the British Library

ISBN   978 1 5261 7429 1   hardback

First published 2025

The publisher has no responsibility for the persistence or accuracy of URLs for any external or third-party internet websites referred to in this book, and does not guarantee that any content on such websites is, or will remain, accurate or appropriate.

EU authorised representative for GPSR:
Easy Access System Europe, Mustamäe tee 50, 10621 Tallinn, Estonia
gpsr.requests@easproject.com

Typeset
by Deanta Global Publishing Services, Chennai, India

Contents

Figures	*page* vi
Acknowledgements	viii
Introduction: the construction of Canada as an antislavery haven in transatlantic print culture	1
1 The representation of slavery in Quebec's newspapers, 1789–93	25
2 Canada in the antebellum slave narrative, 1849–57	59
3 Thomas Jones in Nova Scotia and New Brunswick: a slave narrative in context, 1851–53	93
4 *Broken Shackles*: a narrative of slavery in the United States and Canada's first major book distributor, 1889	129
Conclusion	160
Bibliography	165
Index	183

Figures

1.1 Fugitive slave advertisement for Joe, a pressman at the *Quebec Gazette*, *Quebec Gazette*, 27 November 1777, p. 3, image credit Bibliothèque et Archives nationales du Québec. *page* 34

1.2 Fugitive slave advertisement for an unnamed 'young healthy negro woman', *Quebec Gazette*, 22 April 1790, p. 4, image credit Bibliothèque et Archives nationales du Québec. 35

1.3 William Wilberforce's speech to the House of Commons, *Quebec Gazette*, 13 August 1789, p. 2, image credit Bibliothèque et Archives nationales du Québec. 39

1.4 Report of the loss of a slave ship, *Quebec Gazette*, 24 November 1791, p. 2, image credit Bibliothèque et Archives nationales du Québec. 43

1.5 William Cowper's poem 'The negro's complaint', *Quebec Gazette*, 21 January 1790, p. 4, image credit Bibliothèque et Archives nationales du Québec. 48

1.6 'The negro's recital' poem, *Quebec Gazette*, 16 December 1790, p. 4, image credit Bibliothèque et Archives nationales du Québec. 50

2.1 Title page of the second edition of Austin Steward's *Twenty-Two Years and Slave and Forty Years a Freeman*, 1859, © British Library Board, shelfmark 10880.bb.15. 66

2.2 Title page of Frederick Douglass's *My Bondage and My Freedom*, 1855, © British Library Board, shelfmark 10880.bb.9. 68

Figures

vii

2.3 Illustration from Austin Steward's slave narrative
     of Williams fighting an overseer, British Library,
     © British Library Board shelfmark 10880.bb.15. 74

3.1 The title page of the New Brunswick reprint of
     Thomas Jones's slave narrative, J. and A. McMillan,
     1853, image acknowledgement: Book cover: *The
     Experience of Thomas Jones, Who Was a Slave for
     Forty-Three Years*. Source: Library and Archives
     Canada/OCLC 1006821943. 103

3.2 Thomas Jones's 'Card' in the *Weekly Chronicle*, 13
     June 1851, p. 3, reproduced with the permission of
     the copyright bureau at Library and Archives Canada. 106

3.3 The newsprint page with 'The Old Oak Tree'
     narrative, *Wesleyan*, 24 February 1853, p. 1,
     reproduced with the permission of the Nova Scotia
     Archives. 111

3.4 The newsprint page with 'Old Jeddy, There's
     Rest at Home', *Wesleyan*, 20 October 1853, p. 1,
     reproduced with the permission of the Nova Scotia
     Archives. 112

3.5 Advertisement for Thomas Jones's narrative in the
     Wesleyan, 21 June 1851, p. 5, reproduced with the
     permission of the Nova Scotia Archives. 116

3.6 Advertisement for Thomas Jones's narrative in the
     Presbyterian Witness, 21 June 1851, p. 3, image
     credit The Presbyterian Church in Canada Archives. 117

Acknowledgements

The research for this book began as part of a collaborative PhD in the School of English at the University of Sheffield and the British Library, funded by a scholarship from the University of Sheffield, awarded in 2018. I am grateful to the Eccles Centre for American Studies at the British Library for a fellowship that supported travel to conduct research with its newspapers and slave narratives. Grants from the British Association for American Studies and Nova Scotia Museum Board of Governors supported the research with newspapers in Nova Scotia and New Brunswick explored in Chapter 3, and I really appreciate their support.

Sections of this book have appeared in the *Journal of Transatlantic Studies* (2021) (reproduced by permission of Springer Nature) and *American Periodicals* (2024) (reproduced by permission of Ohio State University Press). I thank the editors and publishers for their kind permission to reuse them.

Introduction: the construction of Canada as an antislavery haven in transatlantic print culture

In the antebellum slave narrative, the arrival of the self-liberated person in Canada West, now known as Ontario, is a climactic moment that represents the end of their journey from slavery to freedom. The self-liberated Josiah Henson describes arriving in Canada and kissing the ground in his 1849 slave narrative *The Life of Josiah Henson, Formerly a Slave, Now an Inhabitant of Canada, as Narrated by Himself*: 'When I got on the Canada side [...] my first impulse was to throw myself on the ground, and giving way to the riotous exultation of my feelings, to execute sundry antics which excited the astonishment of those who were looking on.'[1] Henson is overjoyed because, by stepping onto Canadian soil, he has become a free man. Henson explains to a Canadian gentleman: 'I jumped up and told him I was free.' This marks a distinct political boundary between the slaveholding United States and the free (British) Canadian colonies. Henson reinforces the sense that, for self-liberated people from the United States, Canada is a place where they are liberated from slavery.

The image of Canada as an antislavery haven for self-liberated people was satirised within anti-*Tom* fiction. Anti-*Tom* novels, as Sarah Meer has suggested, were pro-slavery 'replies' to *Uncle Tom's Cabin* that tapped into the commercial success of Harriet Beecher Stowe's classic antislavery novel and attempted to contradict its central message.[2] In W. L. G. Smith's *Life at the South*, published in 1852, the self-liberated Tom is unable to recognise that he has arrived in Canada. He asks his Black guide to interpret his surroundings for him. 'Whar we cum to, captin'?' he asks. Tom's guide

2   *Beyond the antislavery haven*

replies: '"You don't know, do you? don't it look like Canady, you fool?" Tom looked around, after he stepped upon the beach, but as this was his first visit to that particular spot, he could not tell whether he was in the land of freedom or not.'[3] Tom's inability to recognise that he has arrived in Canada or to experience Canada as different from the United States undercuts the idea that the moment of arrival in Canada would be experienced instinctively as a moment of liberation. In Smith's pro-slavery novel, which wants to return Tom to slavery by his own choice, Tom is exploited, beaten, and treated inhospitably in Canada. Smith's text probably intended to parody the flight of Eliza, George, and Harry to Canada and their crossing of Lake Erie in *Uncle Tom's Cabin*, but it also recalls Henson's arrival in Canada, published a few years before Stowe's novel, which may have also been an influence on Stowe.[4] Alyssa MacLean has shown that Lake Erie crossings were a regular feature of Black autobiographical writing such as Henson's.[5] In Smith's text, the narrator relates that Tom is unable to tell by looking around whether 'that particular spot' is Canada or the United States because he has never been there before. This scene plays with the fact that the moment of arrival in Canada was a literary convention with a set of expectations for how it should unfold textually. Tom is not acting as he should, and by drawing the reader's attention to this, the novel reminds them that they are reading a literary work, suggesting that Canada as an antislavery space is little more than a well-worn literary convention.

As these extracts show, antislavery and pro-slavery writing in the nineteenth century competed over the meaning of Canada and its literary representation because it was bound up with debates about the institution of slavery in the United States. The dominant image of Canada today is the endpoint of the Underground Railroad, an antislavery space morally superior to the pro-slavery United States. It is seen as having a better historical record when it comes to slavery than the United States. As this extract from *Life at the South* suggests, anti-*Tom* literature undercuts a genre expectation for how the self-liberated person would perform their arrival in Canada in literary texts. Nineteenth-century readers saw Canada as a haven and a non-slaveholding space and considered that the arrival of a self-liberated person in Canada would be the endpoint of their exhausting journey. Today, Canada has a strong antislavery identity

Introduction 3

that comes from its history as a destination and home for thousands of self-liberated people from the United States in the mid-nineteenth century. The image of Canada as an antislavery utopia persists and resurfaces at moments within the popular historical narrative of Canada.[6]

This book sets out to answer two key questions. First, how has the image of Canada as an antislavery haven developed, given the earlier history of slavery in Canada and the presence of fugitive slave advertisements in Canadian newspapers? Second, how can we use a range of nineteenth-century texts to get beyond Canada's antislavery image and come to a more nuanced understanding of its relationship with slavery, and indeed its connection to transatlantic and Black Atlantic discourses of slavery and abolition? A central aim of this book is to get beyond Canada's idealised antislavery image and to show that a more complicated relationship between Canada and slavery, in Canada and the wider Americas, emerges when we explore slavery in early Canadian print culture between 1789 and 1889.

This book examines Canadian newspapers, and slave narratives related or written by self-liberated and free Black people from the United States. The texts examined were published between 1789 and 1889, starting with the fugitive slave advertisements and anti-slave trade sentiment printed in newspapers in the province of Quebec, and concluding in the final chapter with a book-length slavery narrative published by William Briggs, who is often celebrated as the first major book publisher in Canada. The texts explored in this study were published after the American Revolution (1775–83) following the loss of the thirteen American colonies by Britain, which saw the birth of the United States. They largely fall into a period before Canada was united into a single federal dominion by Confederation in 1867. This book uses the term 'Canada' throughout to refer collectively to the provinces that would later become what we now know by that name, but the nation state of Canada did not exist for much of the period covered by this book. However, the term 'Canada' was used in practice to denote different regions in North America. It was used by explorer Jacques Cartier to refer to a region around the St Lawrence River, and the term was used sometimes to refer to the French colony of New France. In 1791, the British Parliament divided the province of Quebec into Upper

4 *Beyond the antislavery haven*

Canada (Ontario) and Lower Canada (Quebec), and in 1840 reunited them as the United Province of Canada (between 1841 and 1867 they were known as Canada West and Canada East); throughout both periods, they were collectively known as 'The Canadas'.

The phrase 'beyond the antislavery haven' in the title of this book has several meanings. It reflects that the book goes beyond the dominant narrative of Canada as an antislavery utopia to explore a more complex account of Canada's relationship with slavery and freedom. The title is also meant to evoke the idea of going beyond the 'moment of arrival' in the slave narrative genre. It examines Black settlers' accounts of their experiences in Canada after crossing the border in mid-nineteenth-century slave narratives, which have been critically neglected. The book also gets beyond the antislavery haven by looking at how slave narratives circulated across the Canada–US border. Finally, the book moves beyond the haven trope by reading newspapers and slave narratives in their holistic print context and reading texts about slavery in Canada alongside abolitionist discourses. Canada's relationship with slavery is more complicated than as a slaveholding space or an antislavery haven. Canada is connected to all of these other places in its print culture, and this has been key to how Canadians and Canadian readers have fashioned their self-image in relation to the transatlantic slave trade and slavery.

In its aim to get beyond the idealised narrative of Canada, this book aligns with scholarship in Canadian Studies that has worked to draw attention to the history of slavery in Canada, the presence of racism in Canada, and its legacies. Challenges to the image of Canada as an antislavery haven began in the nineteenth century. In his 1855 narrative, the Black abolitionist Samuel Ringgold Ward identified Canada as a place of liberty but also of racism, which he described as 'Canadian Negro hate'.[7] Since James Walker's seminal study in the 1970s, scholars have engaged with the violent racism targeted at the Black Loyalists and the discrimination they faced in terms of the small, unprofitable plots of land they were granted (if any at all).[8] More recently, a flurry of works including the *Unsettling the Great White North*, *The Promised Land*, and *Harriet's Legacies* recognise the persistence of the idealised narrative of Canada as a haven at the end of the Underground Railroad, and seek to unsettle and complicate it.[9] *Unsettling the Great White*

Introduction 5

North questions the 'persistent' narrative of Canada as a benevolent haven by exploring histories of anti-Black racism and stories of Black resistance and resilience, to focus on Black contributions to the nation.[10]

Scholars have challenged the idea of a hard border between the United States and Canada, showing rich histories of cross-border Black antislavery activism and communities. Recent work on places around the Canada–US border uses a borderland and 'fluid frontiers' approach to show how people could have closer proximity to their neighbours across the national border than to people in their own nations.[11] Two borderland spaces defy the idea of a hard Canada–US border: southwestern Ontario and New York, and New England and Nova Scotia, which until 1784 included the modern New Brunswick. Afua Cooper examines the transnational activism of the self-liberated abolitionist and newspaper editor Henry Bibb in Ontario.[12] Karolyn Smardz Frost focuses on the Niagara River region, with its hinterlands in southwestern Ontario and New York, as a borderland for Black cross-border transnationalism and cooperation in assisting refugees from slavery.[13] She also considers slavery in the pre-American revolutionary period, showing that enslaved people were brought to Nova Scotia during the 1759–68 arrival of New England immigrants, known as Planters. Frost shows that vessels in Halifax harbour were connected to trade and familial networks in New England and traded with the Caribbean, continuing to import and trade enslaved people.[14] In *Fugitive Borders*, Nele Sawallisch examines five autobiographies by Black authors in Canada West, in what is now known as Ontario, during the mid-nineteenth century, arguing that they contributed to a sense of 'cross-border community belonging'.[15] Finally, Harvey Amani Whitfield studies the enslaved people who came to Nova Scotia (including what is modern New Brunswick) during the Loyalist exodus.[16] These studies alert us to the fact that, in terms of Black histories and texts, these borderland spaces were rich nexuses of cultural, familial, and economic exchange.

This book contributes a new model for how Canada's antislavery image was constructed during the eighteenth and nineteenth centuries, beyond other critical models scholars have used. The existing model suggests that the construction of Canada as an antislavery haven in printed texts was a mid-nineteenth-century invention in

6   *Beyond the antislavery haven*

the antebellum slave narrative, and that this overshadows slavery in Canada, which was present in its eighteenth-century newspapers. George Elliott Clarke was an early and important voice arguing that what have long been seen as African American slave narratives also belong to the Canadian literary canon.[17] Clarke's claim that the mid-nineteenth-century slave narrative obscured an earlier depiction of colonial Canada as a slaveholding space was a central point of departure for the research carried out for this book. In '"This Is No Hearsay"', Clarke argues that 'scholars must also address the mass of memoirs treating African slavery in pre-Victorian Canada' found in 'trial records, letters, [and] newspapers'.[18] Clarke states that 'the latter narratives are so rich with almost bombastic praise for Canadian/British "liberty", that the more negative, earlier accounts of white settler racism [contained in newspapers and Black Loyalist narratives] are obscured to the point of erasure'.[19] Clarke suggests that reading the slave narratives had led 'our Canadian ancestors' to 'forget that slave ships docked in Halifax, Montreal, Saint John and York (Toronto)'.[20] This book interrogates Canada as an antislavery space through close reading of four groups of texts at different moments, to expose the contradiction of Canadian slaveholding and antislavery present in each text. By placing these texts back into their full print cultural context, a more complicated view of Canadian attitudes towards its own slavery and slavery in the wider Americas emerges.

This book suggests a more complex model for Canada's textual engagement with slavery than either seeing Canada as an antislavery haven for enslaved people from the United States or as a slaveholding space. Slavery in Canada has been marginalised in Canada's national narrative. However, recovering Canada's history of slavery from its newspapers and taking this out of the wider print context of the colonial newspaper recovers half a memory, which does not allow for the complexity of the fact that contemporaries could hold two seemingly contradictory positions: holding people in slavery and thinking about themselves as antislavery at the same time. There was a form of 'doublethink' taking place in the newspapers.[21] If enslaved people in Canada have 'passed from the mind', they were once in the mind. Enslaved people in Canada were part of the collective memory of the nation, constructed through its printed media and particularly colonial newspapers. However, the

Introduction

Canadian reader could also imagine themselves as belonging to an antislavery community.

The reprinted nature of slavery in early Canadian print culture

Many of the Canadian texts explored here are reprints that came from other national contexts. It is a central premise of this book that these texts are also Canada's literature of slavery and that, because of their reprinted nature, the contexts in which they were reprinted, in newspapers and as books, need to be explored to analyse how Canadian readers and writers related to them. These texts have been marginalised within critical studies, reflecting a bias towards locating texts in their place of original publication and a tendency to value 'original' texts over reprints. Despite the turn to book-length slave narratives and fugitive advertisements in newspapers, critics of Black Canadian literature have not read these within the wider textual context of newspapers, which framed these in particular ways for their local readers.

Given that British anti-slave-trade texts were reprinted in Canadian newspapers, the wider discussion of British anti-slave trade print is an important critical context. Scholars have explored how this literature could produce national celebratory narratives for Britain, and have examined the rhetorical strategies that were most common in these texts, such as sentimental rhetoric.[22] Scholars have also noted that British slave-trade literature was mobile and reprinted in other abolition contexts, for example in Pennsylvania and New York.[23] However, there has been less exploration of how the meaning of print could change when it was placed into a new context in a newspaper and how its original meaning and its new context played out together. The nation-making aspect of the British anti-slave-trade and pro-slave-trade discourse that Srividhya Swaminathan identifies seems to have been less well considered when abolitionist print travelled across national borders, but critics assume the continuity of its antislavery message in its new context.[24] J. R. Oldfield shows that, in the late 1780s and early 1790s, American newspapers reprinted British anti-slave-trade texts, as well as, to a lesser extent, anti-slave trade texts from France. He argues that reprinting these texts represents a 'reliance on European

8 *Beyond the antislavery haven*

texts to make the case against American slavery'.[25] While scholars like Oldfield have furthered our knowledge of the wide reprinting of antislavery texts in the late eighteenth century, they have paid far less attention to the wider textual context of the newspapers in which these texts were reprinted and how reprinting these texts may have circulated other discourses. Given the fact that abolitionist discourses could be about more than slavery, examining the context in which abolitionist texts and slave narratives were reprinted in Canada is essential to exploring which discourses were given emphasis in the Canadian context.

This book focuses on printed material rather than unpublished manuscript materials because, firstly, print circulated widely, and is part of a broader literary transatlantic that this book investigates. Secondly, printed texts provide a way to explore the public consciousness of Canada and to examine how slavery in Canada has been recorded and constructed in the national mind (and then forgotten). This provides a way to examine the contradiction that Canada can think about itself today as having been an antislavery haven for self-liberated people from the United States, despite an earlier history of slavery in Canada. This book examines newspapers, which construct what Benedict Anderson has referred to as 'imagined communities', producing an image of a national community for its readers.[26] Thirdly, this book explores textual representations of enslaved people rather than the lived experience of enslaved people. Hence, it examines how their presence is constructed on the page in the wider printed context in which enslaved people in Canada were represented.

To recover and uncover a more nuanced account of Canada's relationship with slavery, a key task is to treat newspapers holistically as a literary form. This book considers what Gérard Genette has termed 'paratext', the material surrounding a main text in a book, including blank space and title pages, examining how these 'thresholds' invited contemporaries to approach text in different ways.[27] It is important too to look at how modern editions produce revisions of texts, which can shape how we read them. Rather than searching for 'authentic' Black Canadian voices, this book examines how a range of voices are present in slavery narratives in Canada. This approach draws support from recent scholarly approaches to texts such as slave narratives, which caution against seeking

Introduction 9

'authentic' Black voices in these texts and instead explore how the presence of white editors and framing texts were part of narratives that do not present a stable and fixed Black subject.[28]

This book contributes to the continuing discussion about Canada's place within Paul Gilroy's conception of the Black Atlantic. Gilroy pioneered the concept of the Atlantic as a 'single [...] unit of analysis' and his work challenges the exclusive focus on national parameters when analysing Black lives, experiences, and beliefs, and the cultures of Black people in the Atlantic world.[29] Gilroy sees the ship as the 'central organizing symbol' of the Black Atlantic, highlighting his focus on the Atlantic Ocean and the 'cultural exchanges' between places. The ship also reflects that, for Gilroy, the Black Atlantic has its origins in the Atlantic slave trade and plantation slavery, linking places in the Americas, Europe, the Caribbean, and Africa.[30] However, Gilroy did not include Canada in his discussion of the Black Atlantic.[31] Scholars have since invoked the Black Atlantic in relation to Canada.[32] For example, Winfried Siemerling's book *The Black Atlantic Reconsidered* surveys Black Canadian writing and thought and shows that these matter to existing understandings of the Black Atlantic.[33] Alyssa MacLean examines autobiographical slave narratives that depict refugees from slavery crossing Lake Erie, arguing that this can be read as a 'Black Atlantic site' and that these 'fresh-water nautical crossings' are linked to 'the maritime experiences of the Black Atlantic'.[34] In *Harriet's Legacies*, a study of the freedom-fighter and conductor of the Underground Railroad Harriet Tubman's activism and its legacies in Canada, Ronald Cummings and Natalee Caple suggest that Black Canadian histories and texts can complicate Gilroy's dominant chronotope of the ship, and argue for greater attention to be paid to flight and movement across land.[35]

Black-authored texts and histories in Canada are explored in this book, but it also explores white-edited newspapers and reprinted anti-slave-trade texts from the international abolition debate. Chapter 3 explores how Thomas H. Jones's slave narrative was framed for readers of religious newspapers in Nova Scotia. As such, it discusses Canada as part of the circulatory system of the Atlantic Ocean and as part of the land mass of North America. Analysing Jones's narrative in the local printed context of newspapers, it takes what David Armitage describes as a 'cis-Atlantic' approach to this Atlantic history by focusing on the particular location of Nova Scotia and New Brunswick in the Atlantic world and particular local reading communities in Canada, considered as part of a wider web of Atlantic connections.[36] This book is the first to use newspapers and recover the paratext that framed Black Atlantic texts in newspapers in Canada. It analyses how newspaper editors and readers responded to these in the Canadian and local context and the meanings that they accrued. The book thus argues that the culture of reprinting, recontextualisation, and the wide circulation of printed texts and people across national borders were central to discourses about slavery and freedom in the United States, France, Britain, Canada, and the Caribbean. Focusing entirely on where and when texts were first and originally printed obscures the deeply connected and yet also specific and local contexts of the broader international debates around slavery and abolition.

Slavery in colonial Canada

This is a pivotal time in the study of historical slavery in Canada. In the wake of the global Black Lives Matter protests and the murder of George Floyd, in 2020, thousands of participants took part in protests in all ten provinces of Canada, protesting against racism and police brutality. Two key new projects have launched, which over the next six years will alter our understandings of slavery and freedom in Canada: a new project to improve understandings of Black Canadian history, led by Dr Afua Cooper; and, led by Charmaine Nelson, the creation of the first research hub to focus on Canadian slavery.[37] Scholars at Canada's universities have started research on how their institutions have benefited financially from slavery and their legacies of slavery and racism. Several Canadian universities have joined the international Universities Studying Slavery (USS) network, which draws together universities, researchers, and community groups in Canada, Britain, and the United States. In October 2023, USS held their annual conference in Canada for the first time. An entire day of the conference was fully dedicated to foregrounding slavery in Nova Scotia and Canada within the Black Atlantic World. Scholars continue to work on underexplored aspects of Canada's slaveholding past and the histories of enslaved people in

Introduction

Canada. New studies are extending beyond slavery in Canada in the years after the American Revolution and the Loyalist exodus. Natasha Henry's observation that we still do not know about many people who were held in slavery in what is now Ontario and that there is a need for a database of enslaved people in Ontario demonstrates one aspect of the work still left to be done.[38]

The enslavement of African and some First Nations people took place in the colonies that later became Canada, including Nova Scotia, Cape Breton, New Brunswick, Upper Canada (Ontario), and Quebec. Slavery in Canada was not plantation slavery. Maureen G. Elgersman's study of enslaved women in Canada suggests most enslaved people were engaged in domestic rather than field work, 'in the absence of a staple or monocrop production system'.[39] As Frank Mackey notes, there was '[no] single crop production' of sugar and tobacco, for example, that required a system of plantation labour.[40] According to Ira Berlin's definition, the Canadian colonies were 'societies with slaves' rather than 'slave societies'. Although Berlin does not discuss Canada, he deploys the terms to describe the transformation of slavery from 'societies with slaves' to 'slave societies' in four regions in mainland North America following the 'plantation revolution'. Berlin defines 'societies with slaves' as those in which there was no ruling planter class, in which enslavers who held people in slavery were 'just one portion of a propertied elite', and where 'slavery was marginal to the central productive processes; slavery was one form of labour among many'.[41] By contrast, 'slave societies' had a strong ruling slaveholding class and slavery was 'at the centre of economic production'. As Berlin notes, patterns of slaveholding in 'societies with slaves' did not mean that slavery was 'milder' than in 'slave societies'. He writes, 'Slaveholders in such societies could act with extraordinary brutality precisely because their slaves were extraneous to their main business. They could limit their slaves' access to freedom expressly because they desired to set themselves apart from their slaves.'[42] Brett Rushforth has explored the enslavement of First Nations people in New France, demonstrating how this could function as a form of gift-giving between French colonists and First Nations peoples to consolidate friendships and alliances. He argues that the enslavement of some First Nations people in New France was characterised by 'creative cultural adaptations' between French

12 *Beyond the antislavery haven*

Atlantic slavery and an earlier tradition of slavery and slaveholding practices rooted in the cultures of First Nations people in New France.[43] Marcel Trudel's survey of slavery in what is now Quebec from the mid-seventeenth century to the early nineteenth century finds 1,443 Black enslaved people and 2,683 First Nations people who were enslaved described in the available unpublished records.[44] Rushforth, building on Trudel, identifies 1,814 enslaved Indigenous people in New France's records between 1660 and 1760.[45] In Cape Breton, Ken Donovan identifies 418 enslaved people living there between 1713 and 1815. In Montreal, enslaved people tended to work as domestics or in semi-skilled professions, for example as printers. Finally, in Nova Scotia, enslaved people largely worked in households, and Harvey Amani Whitfield describes the range of roles that people held in slavery undertook: 'They carved out roads, built houses, planted crops, washed clothes, cooked meals and provided childcare, and they moved easily between rural, urban, and seafaring work.'[46]

In New France, enslaved people likely lived in the household rather than in separate quarters.[47] Yet archaeological evidence suggests that in Nova Scotia there could have been a continuity in patterns of slaveholding with slavery in New England in the United States. Loyalists brought enslaved people with them as part of the exodus to Nova Scotia after the American Revolution. Catherine M. A. Cottreau-Robins's study of the Loyalist Timothy Ruggles suggests a 'continuity' of Loyalist enslaving practices between New England and Nova Scotia, as he tried to recreate the plantation he had 'lost'. Enslaved people in Nova Scotia may have lived in separate accommodation looked down on by the main house, echoing the geography of the United States plantation.[48]

Canadians participated in what Gregory E. O'Malley has described as the 'intercolonial slave trade', which were journeys made by enslaved people within the Americas after arriving on slave ships from Africa.[49] Whitfield notes that, prior to the end of the American Revolution, enslaved people in Nova Scotia came predominately from New England. Some sales of enslaved people can also be understood in the context of merchants who traded goods across the West Indies, the American colonies, and Halifax; enslaved people were part of a broader commodity trade.[50] Frank Mackey shows that, of the 390 Black people enslaved at some

Introduction   13

point in Montreal between 1760 and 1800, over half came from the thirteen colonies, or, from 1776, the United States, with a large proportion born in Quebec, in addition to many coming from the Caribbean and Saint-Domingue.[51] He describes the movement of Black enslaved people into Quebec as

> stragg[ling] in singly, in pairs, occasionally in a family or small group, as part of the baggage of military officers, ship captains landing at Quebec, Loyalists, and others who had spent time in the West Indies, the American colonies or other slave societies, as prisoners seized in raids in the American colonies, as purchases made by fur traders and other frontiersmen at various western ports, or as goods bought in New York or New England for personal use or as a speculation.[52]

Around three thousand Black Loyalists arrived in Nova Scotia following the American Revolution, and their poor treatment with regards to the small and unprofitable plots of land they were granted (if any at all), and the discrimination they faced, has been well documented.[53] The movement of the Black Loyalists was part of a larger exodus: sixty thousand Loyalists left the new United States for remaining British dominions and approximately thirty thousand Loyalists arrived in Canada. Maya Jasanoff estimates that around two thousand Loyalist-owned enslaved people also entered British North America, primarily in Nova Scotia.[54] Several hundred enslaved people arrived in Quebec held in slavery by Loyalists.[55] During a six-week voyage between January and March 1792, Clarkson helped convey approximately 1,190 Black Loyalists who were dissatisfied with their unfair treatment in Nova Scotia to Sierra Leone.[56]

   To understand the textual presence of slavery in colonial Canada, it is important to understand the legal status of slavery there. As Whitfield notes, slavery was 'legally insecure' in Nova Scotia and New Brunswick as, while it was recognised under common law, it had no statutory basis, such as a slave code.[57] Historians argue that slavery was effectively ended as an institution in Lower Canada and Nova Scotia by a series of court rulings in the late eighteenth century that did not order self-liberated people to return to their enslavers.[58] Mackey characterises abolition in Lower Canada as precipitated by 'a few Montreal slaves who, in seeking their freedom, put the courts on the spot'.[59] These court rulings created 'chaos', according

14   *Beyond the antislavery haven*

to Robin W. Winks.[60] This is reflected in several printed documents, in which Canadians asserted their slaveholding rights and called for a clearer legal position on slavery in Canada, such as the 1799 *Petition to the Legislative Assembly by Slaveholders in Montreal* and the *Petition of the Slave Proprietors in Annapolis County* (1807). Records for enslaved people in colonial Canada disappear in the printed records after the early nineteenth century. As Mackey notes, the last advertisement for a sale of an enslaved person and the last fugitive slave advertisement appeared in the *Montreal Gazette* in 1798, and the last court case in which an enslaver tried to reclaim an absconded slave in Quebec was in 1800.[61] The last known sale of an enslaved person in Nova Scotia was in 1807, according to Winks.[62] In 1833, an Act was passed by the British Parliament that abolished slavery in the British colonies, although it dictated that a system of apprenticeship should take its place until 1840 (this was later changed to 1838), and this included slavery in the provinces that would become Canada.

The only legislation to limit slavery passed in colonial Canada was in Upper Canada in 1793, entitled 'An Act to Prevent the Further Introduction of Slaves and to Limit the Term of Contracts for Servitude within this Province'. An Act was passed in Prince Edward Island in 1781 that stated that the baptism of enslaved people 'shall not exempt them from BONDAGE'.[63] The 1793 ruling in Upper Canada made it illegal to import enslaved people into the province and dictated that the children of enslaved mothers must be freed at the age of twenty-five. As Winks notes, the Act to limit slavery in Upper Canada received 'unanimous passage' in the House of Assembly and the Legislative Council, having first being raised in the Executive Council, and it was 'given the royal assent on July 9 [1793]'.[64] In the same year, an attempt to abolish slavery in the House of Assembly in Quebec was unsuccessful, reflecting a reluctance to end slavery elsewhere in colonial Canada.

Despite this Act to limit slavery in Upper Canada, Afua Cooper notes that advertisements selling enslaved people and fugitive slave advertisements were printed in Ontario newspapers during the early nineteenth century, suggesting that this Act did not represent an absolute end to slaveholding in the colony of Upper Canada.[65] This reflects the fact that the act did not free the people held in slavery at the time it was passed, and stipulated that the children of enslaved

Introduction 15

mothers in Upper Canada could remain legally enslaved until they were twenty-five. The existence of fugitive slave advertisements and advertisements selling enslaved people printed in the early-nineteenth-century Ontario newspapers supports Mackey's point that the act to limit the introduction of new people held in slavery sought to protect rather than abolish slavery in Upper Canada, in a climate of legal uncertainty. Mackey argues that, '[a]t its heart, gradual abolition could have no purpose but to prolong slavery's existence to safeguard the property rights of slaveholders'.[66]

Slavery in print: a specific Canadian identity

Canada's history of slavery in print was shaped by a print context that had both similarities to and differences from a broader print context in the Americas and Europe. The fugitive slave advertisements printed in eighteenth-century Canadian newspapers are similar to those printed in newspapers across the Americas, for example, in Pennsylvania, South Carolina and Jamaica.[67] Antislavery print circulated widely in the Atlantic world in newspapers, and it was similarly reprinted by editors in newspapers. For example, the antislavery poem 'The Negro's Complaint' by the British poet William Cowper had wide circulation in newspapers across England 'till it travelled almost over the whole island', but it was also printed widely in the English-speaking world, for example in the United States and, as research for this book has shown, in Quebec.[68]

Canadian newspapers circulated antislavery sentiment and slavery texts concurrently, but this was not a contradiction unique to Canadian print culture. Benjamin Franklin printed Quaker antislavery tracts (anonymously) and slave advertisements in Pennsylvania in the *Pennsylvania Gazette*, which he began printing in 1729. Franklin owned enslaved people and they probably worked at his newspaper and in his home.[69] He was also the president of the Pennsylvania Abolition Society from 1787, and a correspondent of leading international antislavery figures such as Granville Sharp. His newspaper printed slave advertisements in a colony that had a strong Religious Society of Friends that were increasingly shaping a coherent antislavery identity, but he was still printing slave

16   *Beyond the antislavery haven*

advertisements in this context, and Quakers such as the abolitionist Benjamin Lay subscribed to his newspaper.[70]

Canada's circulation of slavery in print had three key differences that set it apart from elsewhere in the Americas. Firstly, there were very few original publications about slavery produced in eighteenth-century Canada and the reprint culture was more central as a space for Canadians to self-fashion abolition discourses. The newly formed United States began a prolific original and reprint book trade after independence from Britain, but Canada's print culture was dominated by newspaper publishing and by recirculating books first published elsewhere until the late nineteenth century, when this study ends. In the mid-nineteenth century, Canada was still reprinting and recirculating abolition print such as slave narratives and newspaper accounts of slavery. Editions of slave narratives that were recirculated in Canada tended to be written for either a British or an American audience, and hence did not directly address or appeal to Canadian readers. By contrast, British and American editions of the same slave narrative could differ substantially and addressed their specific national audience.[71]

Secondly, the texts that circulated in Canada were very infrequently about Canadian slavery. In the eighteenth century, Britain produced hundreds of texts, poems and debates about slavery in the British Empire (although not about slavery in Canada). Canadian newspapers very rarely mention slavery in Canada, and the newspapers examined in this book for the periods outlined, do not contain any poems and narratives about slavery in Canada. Two important exceptions to this are the fugitive slave advertisements printed in newspapers, and the only known printed slave narrative by a Canadian enslaved person: that of Sophia Pooley née Burthen, which is contained in a collection of mid-nineteenth-century American slave narratives by Benjamin Drew titled *A North-Side View of Slavery: The Refugee or the Narratives of Fugitive Slaves in Canada*, published in Boston in 1856.[72] Sophia lived as an enslaved person in Canada, having been stolen as a seven-year-old from her parents in New York State, sold at Niagara to the Mohawk military leader Thayendanegea or Joseph Brant in 1778, and then sold to an Englishman called Samuel Hatt, before liberating herself and living in the Waterloo Township and later the Black settlement of Queen's Bush. Andrew Hunter draws out the significance of Sophia's life

Introduction 17

and her narrative as the only narrative about slavery in Canada in Drew's collection, providing a rich archival exploration of her life and identifying her first entry into the written record in the 1851 census.[73] The texts reprinted in Canadian newspapers from Britain, France, and the thirteen colonies did not focus on Canadian slavery either, so this reprinting produced a discourse about other slaveries. When printed material on slavery appeared in Canadian publications, these were reprinted poems about slavery in the Americas. The first Canadian-authored poems found as part of the research in this book show a continuity with an aesthetic and cultural interest in slavery elsewhere.[74] To date, with the two noted exceptions, there are no known book-length first-person narratives, poems, or fictional accounts describing Canadian enslavement published in the eighteenth and nineteenth century. In general, when Canadians read about slavery, excepting the slave advertisements, they read about slavery taking place outside the colonies that became Canada.

Thirdly, through recirculating abolition print, Canadians were able to share some of the 'moral capital' of antislavery sentiment, something Christopher Leslie Brown has explored in the British abolitionism context.[75] However, because readers in Canada were not part of the political context of antislavery campaigns and were rarely appealed to directly as a national audience, they stood apart from the national guilt that could circulate in abolition discourses, for example in Britain, and at the same time they could perform their own antislavery identity.

Canada's relationship with slavery is more complicated than seeing it as a slaveholding space, or as an antislavery haven. Canada is connected to the United States, France, Britain, and the Caribbean in its print culture, and this has been key to how Canadians and Canadian readers have fashioned their self-image in relation to slavery. Thus, this book aims to recover the contexts in which fugitive advertisements, poetry about slavery, and advertisements for slave narratives were published, by reading newspapers holistically, and to examine forgotten portions of slave narratives that represented lives in Canada after crossing the Canada–US border. Collectively, the chapters in this book contest the idea of Canada as an antislavery and non-slaveholding space, and examine what we may see as antislavery literature today within a frame that highlights its 'moral capital' for readers. Chapter 1 turns to the print in which

18 *Beyond the antislavery haven*

representations of slavery in Quebec were most present and disseminated in the colonial period: newspapers. These will be read within their full print context to understand how early Canadian readers could witness slavery in Canada while also seeing this as distinct from chattel slavery in the wider Americas. Chapters 2 and 3 focus on the slave narrative. Chapter 2 looks at how self-liberated and free Black people from the United States represented their lives in Canada after crossing the border. It argues that self-liberated people and free Blacks from the United States imagined Canada simultaneously as a haven for self-liberated and free Black people from the United States and as an exploitative capitalist space, which bound people into experiences that they depicted as a kind of re-enslavement. Chapter 3 explores the circulation of a single slave narrative in Nova Scotia and New Brunswick. Reading Thomas H. Jones's slave narrative in the context of the newspapers that advertised it for sale recovers the framing of this text within amelioration-ist (rather than immediate) calls for the abolition of slavery; it also highlights Jones's agency as he found ways to record and document his life in print and sell his narrative. Chapter 4 discusses *Broken Shackles*, which blends the slave narrative and American colour genre, published by William Briggs. This preserves the history of slavery in the United States and reproduces a narrative of Canadian antislavery after abolition. Comparing the 1889 edition to a 2001 reprint, which standardises Henson's dialect speech and makes other editorial changes, the chapter shows that the modern reprint remembers only one side of the Canadian attitude to self-liberated and free Black people who arrived from the United States – its antislavery stance – but not its simultaneously racist handling of the experiences of enslaved people.

Notes

1 Josiah Henson, *The Life of Josiah Henson, Formerly a Slave, Now an Inhabitant of Canada, as Narrated by Himself* (Boston: A. D. Phelps, 1849), pp. 58–59.
2 Sarah Meer, *Uncle Tom Mania: Slavery, Minstrelsy and Transatlantic Culture in the 1850s* (Athens: University of Georgia Press, 2005), p. 75.

Introduction

3 W. L. G. Smith, *Life at the South, or 'Uncle Tom's Cabin' As It Is, Being Narratives, Scenes, and Incidents in the Real 'Life of the Lowly'* (Buffalo: Geo. H. Derby, 1852), p. 455.

4 Jared A. Brock, 'The Story of Josiah Henson, the Real Inspiration for "Uncle Tom's Cabin"', *Smithsonian Magazine*, www.smithsonianmag .com/author/jared-brock/ (accessed 2 August 2023). See also Jared A. Brock, *The Road to Dawn: Josiah Henson and the Story That Sparked the Civil War* (New York: PublicAffairs, 2018).

5 Alyssa MacLean, 'Canadian Migrations: Reading Canada in Nineteenth-Century American Literature' (unpublished PhD thesis, University of British Columbia, 2010), Part 2, pp. 159–263, especially p. 170, and pp. 198–99.

6 Afua Cooper, 'Epilogue: Reflections: The Challenges and Accomplishments of the Promised Land', in Boulou Ebanda de B'béri, Nina Reid-Maroney, and Handel K. Wright (eds), *The Promised Land: History and Historiography of the Black Experience in Chatham-Kent's Settlements and Beyond* (Toronto: University of Toronto Press, 2014), pp. 194–95.

7 Ward's comment is discussed by Nina Reid-Maroney, 'History, Historiography, and the Promised Land Project', in de B'béri, Reid-Maroney, and Wright (eds), *The Promised Land*, p. 64. Samuel Ringgold Ward, *Autobiography of A Fugitive Negro: His Anti-Slavery Labours in the United States, Canada and England* (London: John Snow, 1855), p. 147 and p. 150.

8 James W. St. G. Walker, *The Black Loyalists: The Search for a Promised Land in Nova Scotia and Sierra Leone, 1783–1870* (London: Longman, 1976). Ruth Holmes Whitehead, *Black Loyalists: Southern Settlers of Nova Scotia's First Free Black Communities* (Halifax: Nimbus Publishing Limited, 2013).

9 Ronald Cummings and Natalee Caple (eds), *Harriet's Legacies: Race, Historical Memory, and Futures in Canada* (Montreal and Kingston: McGill-Queen's University Press, 2022). Michele A. Johnson and Funké Aladejebi (eds), *Unsettling the Great White North: Black Canadian History* (Toronto: University of Toronto Press, 2022). Nina Reid-Maroney, Boulou Ebanda de B'béri, and Wanda Thomas Bernard (eds), *Women in the 'Promised Land': Essays in African Canadian History* (Toronto: Women's Press, 2018). Marlene Epp and Franca Lacovetta (eds), *Sisters or Strangers? Immigrant, Ethnic, and Racialized Women in Canadian History* (Toronto: University of Toronto Press, 2016). Wayde Compton, *After Canaan: Essays on Race, Writing, and Region* (Vancouver: Arsenal Pulp Press, 2010).

20 *Beyond the antislavery haven*

10 Johnson and Aladejebi (eds), *Unsettling the Great White North*, pp. 6–7.

11 Afua Cooper, 'The Fluid Frontier: Blacks and the Detroit River Region: A Focus on Henry Bibb', *Canadian Review of American Studies* 30:2 (2000), 129–49, https://doi.org/10.3138/CRAS-s030-02-02. Karolyn Smardz Frost and Veta Smith Tucker (eds), *A Fluid Frontier: Slavery, Resistance, and the Underground Railroad in the Detroit River Borderland* (Detroit: Wayne State University Press, 2016).

12 Afua Cooper, 'Doing Battle in Freedom's Cause, Henry Bibb, Abolitionism, Race Uplift, and Black Manhood, 1842–1854' (unpublished PhD thesis, University of Toronto, 2000).

13 Karolyn Smardz Frost, 'The Cataract House Hotel: Underground to Canada through the Niagara River Borderlands', in Cummings and Caple (eds), *Harriet's Legacies*.

14 Karolyn Smardz Frost, 'Planting Slavery in Nova Scotia's Promised Land, 1759–1775', in Johnson and Aladejebi (eds), *Unsettling the Great White North*, p. 60.

15 Nele Sawallisch, *Fugitive Borders: Canadian Cross-Border Literature at Mid-Nineteenth Century* (Bielefeld: transcript verlag, 2019), p. 10.

16 Harvey Amani Whitfield, *North to Bondage: Loyalist Slavery in the Maritimes* (Vancouver: University of British Columbia Press, 2016).

17 George Elliott Clarke, '"This Is No Hearsay": Reading the Canadian Slave Narratives', *Papers of the Bibliographical Society of Canada*, 43:1 (2005), 7–32. https://doi.org/10.33137/pbsc.v43i1.18415.

18 *Ibid.*', 17, 18, n. 19.

19 *Ibid.*, 18, n. 19.

20 George Elliott Clarke, 'Introduction: Let Us Now Consider "African-American" Narratives as (African-)Canadian Literature', in Benjamin Drew, *The Refugee: Narratives of Fugitive Slaves in Canada* (Toronto: Dundurn Press, 2008), p. 11.

21 The Orwellian concept of 'doublethink' describes how a human mind can 'simultaneously' hold together 'two contradictory beliefs [...] accepting both of them [...] as equally valid'. George Orwell, *Nineteen Eighty-Four* (London: Penguin Books, 1949), p. 223. 'Doublethink, n.', *Oxford English Dictionary Online*, https://doi.org/10.1093/OED /6408439140 (accessed 2 January 2017).

22 On sentimental rhetoric and the British slave-trade debate, see Brycchan Carey, *British Abolitionism and the Rhetoric of Sensibility: Writing, Sentiment and Slavery, 1760–1807* (Basingstoke: Palgrave Macmillan, 2005); Stephen Ahern (ed.), *Affect and Abolition in the Anglo-Atlantic, 1770–1830* (Farnham: Ashgate, 2015); and Willie Sypher, *Guinea's Captive Kings: British Anti-Slavery Literature of the Eighteenth*

Century (Chapel Hill: University of North Carolina Press, 1942). On British national identity and the slave-trade debates, see Srividhya Swaminathan, *Debating the Slave Trade: Rhetoric of British National Identity, 1759–1815* (Farnham: Ashgate, 2009).

23 Dorothy Couchman, '"Mungo Everywhere": How Anglophones Heard Chattel Slavery', *Slavery & Abolition* 36:4 (2015), 704–20, 716. https://doi.org/10.1080/0144039X.2014.969581. For the reprinting of the British 'Epilogue' in the American newspapers, see, for example, 'From the Gentleman's Magazine … Epilogue to "The Padlock"', *Pennsylvania Packet and Daily Advertiser* (3 March 1788), p. 3.

24 Swaminathan, *Debating the Slave Trade*, pp. 3–4.

25 J. R. Oldfield, *Transatlantic Abolitionism in the Age of Revolution: An International History of Anti-Slavery, c. 1787–1820* (Cambridge: Cambridge University Press, 2013), pp. 57–59.

26 Benedict Anderson, *Imagined Communities: Reflections on the Origin and Spread of Nationalism* (London: Verso, 1991), pp. 5–7.

27 Gérard Genette, *Paratexts: Thresholds of Interpretation*, trans. Jane E. Lewin (Cambridge: Cambridge University Press, 1997), p. 2.

28 Sara Salih, '*The History of Mary Prince*, the Black Subject, and the Black Canon', in Brycchan Carey, Markman Ellis, and Sara Salih (eds), *Discourses of Slavery and Abolition: Britain and Its Colonies, 1760–1838* (Basingstoke: Palgrave Macmillan, 2004), p. 125.

29 Paul Gilroy, *The Black Atlantic: Modernity and Double Consciousness* (London: Verso, 1993), p. 15.

30 *Ibid.*, p. 4 and pp. 15–17.

31 George Elliott Clarke, 'Must All Blackness Be American?: Locating Canada in Borden's "Tightrope Time", or Nationalizing Gilroy's The Black Atlantic', *Canadian Ethnic Studies Association* 28:3 (2007), 56–71.

32 Clarke, '"This Is No Hearsay"', 20.

33 Winfried Siemerling, *The Black Atlantic Reconsidered: Black Canadian Writing, Cultural History and the Presence of the Past* (Montreal: McGill-Queen's University Press, 2015).

34 MacLean, 'Canadian Migrations', pp. 174–75.

35 Cummings and Caple (eds), *Harriet's Legacies*, p. 29.

36 David Armitage, 'Three Concepts of Atlantic History', in David Armitage and Michael J. Braddick (eds), *The British Atlantic World, 1500–1800* (New York: Palgrave, 2002).

37 '"A Black People's History of Canada" Set to Produce a Seismic Shift in Education about Canadian History', www.dal.ca/news/2021/04/09/-a-black-people-s-history-of-canada--set-to-produce-a-seismic-sh.html (accessed 20 June 2023). 'A Black People's History of Canada',

www.blackpeopleshistory.ca (accessed 2 November 2023). 'Charmaine Nelson Leading the Creation of the Institute for the Study of Canadian Slavery', www.ronfanfair.com/home/2020/7/22/a4sv9iwp3m9nm4f uya2q00llz2m75i (accessed 20 June 2023).

38 Natasha Henry, 'Where, Oh Where, Is Bet? Locating Enslaved Black Women on the Ontario Landscape', in Johnson and Aladejebi (eds), *Unsettling the Great White North*, p. 102.

39 Maureen G. Elgersman, *Unyielding Spirits: Black Women and Slavery in Early Canada and Jamaica* (London: Routledge, 1999), p. xiii.

40 Frank Mackey, *Done with Slavery: The Black Fact in Montreal, 1760–1840* (Montreal and Kingston: McGill-Queen's University Press, 2010), p. 112.

41 Ira Berlin, *Many Thousands Gone: The First Two Centuries of Slavery in North America* (Cambridge, MA: The Belknap Press of University of Harvard Press, 1998), p. 8.

42 *Ibid.*, p. 8.

43 Brett Rushforth, *Bonds of Alliance: Indigenous and Atlantic Slaveries in New France* (Chapel Hill: University of North Carolina Press, 2012), p. 10, p. 157.

44 Marcel Trudel, *Canada's Forgotten Slaves: Two Hundred Years of Bondage*, trans. George Tombs (Montreal: Véhicule Press, 2013), p. 76. Trudel identifies a further 59 enslaved people whose origins as Indigenous or Black people is unknown.

45 Rushforth, *Bonds of Alliance*, p. 398.

46 Ken Donovan, 'Forum: Slavery and Freedom in Atlantic Canada's African Diaspora: Introduction', *Acadiensis* 43:1 (2014), 109–15, 110. Mackey, *Done with Slavery*, p. 117. Whitfield, *North to Bondage*, p. 113.

47 Robin W. Winks, *The Blacks in Canada: A History* (Montreal and Kingston: McGill-Queen's University Press, 1997), p. 10.

48 Catherine M. A. Cottreau-Robins, 'Searching for the Enslaved in Nova Scotia's Loyalist Landscape', *Acadenisis* 43:1 (2014), 125–36, 132, 135.

49 Gregory O'Malley, *Final Passages: The Intercolonial Slave Trade of British America, 1619–1807* (Chapel Hill: University of North Carolina Press, 2014). O'Malley does not explicitly mention that Canada was part of the intercolonial slave trade.

50 Harvey Amani Whitfield, *Blacks on the Border: The Black Refugees in British North America, 1815–1860* (Burlington: University of Vermont Press, 2006), pp. 15–17.

51 Mackey, *Done with Slavery*, p. 103, p. 106.

52 *Ibid.*, pp. 116–17.

Introduction 23

53 Walker, *The Black Loyalists*, and Winks, *The Blacks in Canada*. Simon Schama, *Rough Crossings: Britain, the Slaves and the American Revolution* (London: Vintage Books, 2009).

54 Maya Jasanoff, *Liberty's Exiles: The Loss of America and the Remaking of the British Empire* (London: HarperPress, 2011), pp. 8–9. Whitfield provides an estimate of around 1,744 people, but notes that this could have been as high as 2,500 people in *North to Bondage*, pp. 119–20.

55 Jasanoff, *Liberty's Exiles*, p. 358, and Winks, *The Blacks in Canada*, pp. 32–33.

56 Winks, *The Blacks in Canada*, p. 73, n. 27.

57 Harvey Amani Whitfield, *Biographical Dictionary of Enslaved Black People in the Maritimes* (Toronto: University of Toronto Press, 2022), p. xxxii.

58 See Whitfield, *North to Bondage*, Chapter 5.

59 Mackey, *Done with Slavery*, p. 78.

60 Winks, *The Blacks in Canada*, p. 40.

61 Mackey, *Done with Slavery*, p. 40.

62 Winks, *The Blacks in Canada*, p. 105.

63 Whitfield, *North to Bondage*, p. 85.

64 Winks, *The Blacks in Canada*, p. 97, and see p. 96.

65 Afua Cooper, *The Hanging of Angelique: The Untold Story of Canadian Slavery and the Burning of Old Montreal* (Athens: University of Georgia Press, 2007), p. 87.

66 Mackey, *Done with Slavery*, pp. 68–70.

67 Billy G. Smith and Richard Wojtowicz (eds), *Blacks Who Stole Themselves: Advertisements for Runaways in the Pennsylvania Gazette, 1728–1790* (Philadelphia: University of Pennsylvania Press, 1989). Graham Russell Hodges and Alan Edward Brown (eds), *'Pretends to be Free': Runaway Slave Advertisements from Colonial and Revolutionary New York and New Jersey* (New York: Garland Publishing, 1994). Lathan A. Windley (ed.), *Runaway Slave Advertisements: A Documentary History from the 1730s to 1790, vol. 3. South Carolina* (Westport: Greenwood Press, 1983).

68 Thomas Clarkson, *History II*, quoted in J. R. Oldfield, *Popular Politics and British Anti-Slavery: The Mobilization of British Opinion against the Slave Trade, 1787–1807* (Manchester: Manchester University Press, 1995), p. 133. On the context in the United States, see John Oldfield, *Transatlantic Abolitionism in the Age of Revolution: An International History of Anti-Slavery, c. 1787–1820* (Cambridge: Cambridge University Press, 2013), p. 58.

24   *Beyond the antislavery haven*

69 David Waldstreicher, *Runaway America, Benjamin Franklin, Slavery and the American Revolution* (New York: Hill & Wang, 2004), p. 91 and p. 218.
70 *Ibid.*, p. 82.
71 See, for example, C. L. Innes, 'Introduction: Francis Fedric's Story: Historical and Cultural Contexts', in C. L. Innes (ed.), *Slave Life in Virginia and Kentucky: A Narrative of Francis Fedric, Escaped Slave* (Baton Rouge: Louisiana State University Press, 2010), pp. ix–xxxviii.
72 For an important exception, see the abolitionist pamphlet Rev. James MacGregor, *Letter to a Clergyman Urging Him to Set Free a Black Girl He Held in Slavery* (Halifax: John Howe, 1788).
73 Andrew Hunter, *It Was Dark There All the Time: Sophia Burthen and the Legacy of Slavery in Canada* (Fredericton: Goose Lane Editions, 2022), pp. 13–14, p. 33.
74 For an example of a mid-nineteenth-century Canadian authored poem about slavery that focuses on a slave from Saint-Domingue, see 'Eustache, the St. Domingo Slave', *Wesleyan* (16 December 1852), p. 1. Nova Scotia Archives, reel 8423.
75 Christopher Leslie Brown, *Moral Capital: Foundations of British Abolitionism* (Chapel Hill: University of North Carolina Press, 2006).

1

The representation of slavery in Quebec's newspapers, 1789–93

Newspapers are the key printed space in which to find the textualisation of slavery in Quebec that circulated in colonial Canada. There has been an emphasis on fugitive slave advertisements in Quebec's eighteenth-century newspapers as part of the recovery of Canada's marginalised slaveholding past. This chapter places fugitive slave advertisements from newspapers in Quebec in their full print context for the first time. By approaching the newspapers more holistically than previous scholarship, it challenges previous interpretations that have neglected or diminished the significance of anti-slave-trade sentiment in late eighteenth-century Canadian newspapers. It examines two of the most popular and longest-running newspapers in the province of Quebec, known as Lower Canada between 1791 and 1840: the *Quebec Gazette* (*QG*) and the *Montreal Gazette* (*MG*).[1] The focus is on the years 1789–93, which the research for this study identified as the most heterogeneous period in terms of the newspapers' handling of slavery. As was common editorial practice throughout the Atlantic world, the editors of the *QG* and *MG* selected and reprinted previously published texts in their newspapers and constructed particular worldviews for local audiences from these recycled parts.[2] Reading fugitive slave adverts is particularly important because it recognises that newspapers were multi-vocal forms that could contain a range of clashing voices that were not always entirely within the editor's control.[3] By reading newspapers in their entirety, the chapter examines the particular worldviews that editors constructed from reprinted materials for local audiences. It argues that during the period 1789–93, these editors created antislavery worldviews for their readers by reprinting

26 *Beyond the antislavery haven*

materials from the international abolition debate and excluding pro-slave-trade discourse from their newspapers. The editors carefully selected and edited copy from British and French newspapers to create a coherent antislavery consensus and silenced pro-slavery arguments. The *MG* and the *QG* presented different responses to the transatlantic debate, with the *MG* showing a tension between French and British perspectives.

This chapter uses the term 'pro-slavery' to refer to texts that, within the worldview of that individual text, advocated for or defended slavery, often in response to anti-slave-trade arguments, and especially texts that were part of the slave-trade debate and the relevant political movements in Britain and France. The pro-slavery texts discussed below do not include the many further examples of advertisements for goods from Caribbean plantations, such as sugar and rum, or fugitive slave advertisements. This is because these practices went unchallenged and uncommented on within the world-views of the newspapers. Readers, based on what can be gleaned about their perspectives, were not invited to read these texts as 'pro-slavery' or connect them with debates about the Atlantic slave trade. While we recognise today that these were also pro-slavery texts, a holistic reading of newspapers over several years illustrates a lack of connection between slaveholding practices in Quebec and their relation to slaveholding societies (through the purchase and consumption of goods) with the Atlantic slave trade, which is the specific focus of the abolitionist attack in both newspapers.

This chapter examines the textual presence of slavery in Canada in two eighteenth-century Canadian newspapers published while slavery was still legal in Canada and slave-trade debates were raging in Britain, France, and the newly formed United States. The newspapers were published during a period of Black and Indigenous people being held in slavery in Canada and the intensification of this following the end of the American Revolution. Trudel identifies that between the mid-seventeenth century and the early nineteenth, century unpublished records identify 1,443 Black enslaved people in Quebec.[4] Following the Loyalist exodus at the end of the American Revolution in 1783, several hundred enslaved people arrived in Quebec, held in slavery by newly arrived Loyalists.[5] The chapter analyses the anti-slave-trade texts reprinted from this international movement in the newspapers and how this relates to

The representation of slavery in Quebec's newspapers   27

the depiction of enslaved people in Canada. In response to the marginalisation of slavery within Canada's national narrative, scholars have described slavery in Canada as a lost history and the subject of national 'amnesia'.[6] This chapter examines the printed place where representations of slavery in Quebec were most present and disseminated in the colonial period: its newspapers. Reading fugitive slave advertisements, which are the main texts within newspapers wherein slavery in Quebec was represented, in their full print context shows that early Canadian readers could hold two images of themselves together at the same time: witnessing slavery in Canada but also seeing this as distinct from chattel slavery in the wider Americas. Canadian readers were aware of slavery in Canada, but also consumed reprinted texts that generated a sense of being part of an imagined community that shared anti-slave-trade sentiment. Canada's construction as an antislavery space has often been dated to mid-nineteenth-century depictions of Ontario in slave narratives, but this chapter suggests a longer history of Canadians viewing themselves as an antislavery haven, alongside an awareness of enslaved people in Quebec. Canadian newspapers, their editors, and their readers were far more engaged with transatlantic slave-trade debates than has previously been understood.

Slavery in New France before the newspapers

Indigenous and African slavery existed in what is now Canada long before the first newspapers were published in Quebec in 1764. The earliest examples of recorded Black voices are mediated court record transcripts and missionary records. Olivier Le Jeune's is the first known recorded enslaved African voice in what later became Canada. Olivier was probably born in Guinea or Madagascar and arrived as a child in Quebec in 1629, where his enslaver was Guillaume Couillard. He attended the school of the Jesuit missionary Le Jeune and was given the name Olivier following his baptism in 1633; his African birthname is not known. Olivier's recorded speech was related by the Jesuit missionary Le Jeune in the 1632 *Jesuit Relations*, published in Paris: 'You say that by baptism I shall be like you: I am black and you are white, I must have my skin taken off in order to be like you.'[7] There are

28   *Beyond the antislavery haven*

around a dozen extant unpublished trial transcripts that contain the mediated voices of enslaved people in Canada.[8] In particular, unpublished trial transcripts from the hearing of the Black enslaved woman Marie-Joseph Angelique, who was tried and executed for her alleged involvement in starting a fire in Montreal in 1734, have received recent critical attention, notably in Afua Cooper's *The Hanging of Angelique*.[9]

There were no newspapers in New France, and the first newspaper in the province, the *QG*, was founded at the start of a period of British colonial rule. Therefore, slavery in New France is not represented in newspapers.[10] There were no newspapers in Upper Canada until 1793.[11] The *QG* and the *MG* were part of a thriving eighteenth-century newspaper print trade, with hubs in Quebec and Nova Scotia, and newspapers were a key part of local print culture.[12] The *QG* and the *MG* were two of the longest-running and most successful newspapers in the province of Quebec in this period.[13]

Brett Rushforth's important study of slavery in the French colony of New France up to 1763 explores how Indigenous nations and the French colonial elite engaged in slavery and slaveholding and how this negotiated the practices and meanings of slavery in these cultures.[14] Rushforth identifies 1,814 enslaved Indigenous people in New France between 1660 and 1760.[15] He also notes that Indigenous slavery persisted under the British in Montreal into the 1790s. A search of newspapers in Quebec shows that self-liberated Indigenous people were not mentioned in newspaper advertisements during this period, which are about Black self-liberated people, in contrast to contemporaneous British and American newspapers that printed fugitive slave advertisements about Indigenous people.[16] Rushforth provides one answer to how Indigenous slavery in Canada has become marginalised from the national narrative, noting that after France ceded all its North American colonies to Britain and Spain in 1763 and following a 1767 royal declaration that Indigenous people could not be enslaved in the French Caribbean, some enslaved people in the French Caribbean attempted to pass as Indigenous to gain legal freedom from enslavement.[17] Rushforth argues that this overwrote a century of Indigenous slavery in the French Atlantic world (including New France, now known as Quebec), erasing it from historical memory.[18] Another reason for the marginalisation of

The representation of slavery in Quebec's newspapers 29

the history of Indigenous slavery in Quebec is the absence of fugitive slave advertisements for Indigenous enslaved people in Canada in its first newspapers: newspaper readers were not presented with an image of the Indigenous enslavement that was a reality in their communities.

The newspapers' early editors

The period under study, 1789–93, marked a particular moment in the editorial history of the *MG* and the *QG*. During this time, Fleury Mesplet was the owner and printer of the *MG*, as he had been since establishing the newspaper in 1785. Samuel Neilson took over as editor and owner of the *QG* in March 1789 and ran it until early 1793. As their brief biographies below show, the newspapers' early owners and editors were transatlantic travellers, part of a connected print history in terms of slavery, spanning locations in Barbados, Scotland, France, Virginia, and Philadelphia.

The *QG* was the first newspaper established in the province of Quebec. William Brown and Thomas Gilmore founded the newspaper between 1763 and 1764. They published the first issue in June 1764, and ran the newspaper together until Gilmore's death in 1773.[19] William Brown was born in Scotland in 1737 and lived in America with his mother's relatives from around the age of fifteen.[20] He studied at the College of William and Mary in Williamsburg, Virginia, and had experience of running a bookshop in Philadelphia.[21] His mentor and possibly his uncle, William Dunlap, sent him to set up a printing shop in Barbados. He lived there for two years, before being attracted to the prospects of establishing the first newspaper in Quebec.[22] Dunlap was instrumental in providing Brown and Gilmore with a loan to establish the *QG*. The men met at Dunlap's print shop where they each worked, and where Gilmore was an apprentice.[23] Samuel Neilson became the editor of the *QG* on 22 March 1789 following his uncle's sudden death, and he ran the newspaper from 1789 until his own death on 12 January 1793.[24] Neilson was born in Scotland and moved to Quebec in 1785.[25] Following Neilson's death, Alexander Spark managed the newspaper on behalf of Samuel Neilson's younger brother John. Spark was a Presbyterian minister at the Scotch Church in Quebec,

30 *Beyond the antislavery haven*

and Samuel Neilson had been a member of his congregation. Spark was in charge of the newspaper until 1796, when John Neilson took over the running of the *QG*.[26]

Fleury Mesplet owned and printed the *MG* in Montreal. Mesplet established the *MG* in August 1785 and ran it until his death in January 1794. Mesplet was the 'first French printer in Canada' and 'the first printer in Montreal'.[27] He was born in France in 1734.[28] He set up a printing shop in London in 1773 and travelled to Philadelphia the following year, setting out for Quebec in 1775. Mesplet attempted to set up a French language newspaper in Montreal to aid the American revolutionary presence, following the capture of Montreal in 1775 by Richard Montgomery. He received funds and support from the Continental Congress to establish his newspaper, but was unable to carry out his plans before the revolutionary presence dissipated on 15 June 1775. Mesplet ran *La Gazette* for a year, a French language newspaper edited by Valentin Jautard, before he was imprisoned because of its content between 1779 and 1782. Claude Galarneau notes that it is unlikely that Mesplet was the editor of the *MG*, which was probably edited by Valentin Jautard until 1787.[29] However, Mesplet was a skilled printer, and it is likely that he was involved in fashioning the *MG* in this capacity, and as its owner, he would have taken overall responsibility for the content of the newspaper.

The *QG* was published once a week. It was a bilingual newspaper with each page divided into two columns, English on the left and a translation in French on the right. In the 1760s, it was three or four pages in length, but by the late 1780s and early 1790s, it was usually six pages, including a two-page supplement of notices and advertisements. The newspaper focused on foreign affairs in Britain, America, and France, as well as those in European colonies like Saint-Domingue. It was rare for local news to be printed in the newspaper, but an exception was the announcements made by the colonial government in the province of Quebec, which were regularly printed. As John E. Hare notes, the *QG* had 'a privileged status since the government published all its official announcements in it a yearly contract price'; under Samuel Neilson, the colonial government was charged for each item published, according to a list he produced.[30]

The *MG* was also a bilingual newspaper, published weekly. Like the *QG*, most of the content was international news reprinted wholesale or presented within news summaries. The founding proposals of the *MG*, printed in the second issue, described the newspaper as reports on European and American affairs and invited readers to contribute their own letters and articles free of charge.[31] It informed its readers that the cost of inserting advertisements or information was one Spanish dollar for one, and two dollars for three. The *MG* gave regular updates on political affairs from a range of European cities, including London, Paris, Lisbon, Stockholm, and Rome; during the period under study, the newspaper focused on providing news from France, the West Indies, America, and Britain. An advertisement for the *MG* addressed new subscribers in the urban centres of Quebec and Three-Rivers (Trois-Rivières), and it was available to subscribers in Montreal, where it was printed, indicating that many of its readers resided in these three urban areas.[32]

The general readership had to be appealed to in order to maintain the number of paying subscriptions to the *MG* and the *QG*, which ensured their financial survival. Both newspapers were able to stay in print during a challenging period in newspaper publishing when many other newspapers in the province went out of business.[33] This indicates that the content of the newspapers was well-received by its general readership and that they saw it as worth the money they paid in annual subscription costs. The *MG* cost three Spanish dollars a year, and the *QG* cost three American dollars a year until 1800.[34] It has been estimated that there were three hundred subscribers to the *MG* and between four hundred and five hundred subscribers to the *QG*.[35] Gerard Laurence describes newspaper readership in eighteenth-century Quebec as follows: '[n]ewspaper customers were [...] mainly an elite, half of them anglophone, wealthier, better educated, and more concerned with the news because of their positions and activities [and] ... the other half were francophones, a modest professional and merchant class numbering several thousand'.[36] Evidence from within the newspapers reveals a socially privileged readership of merchant families, seigneurs, and members of the colonial elite who held government offices and had particularly strong ties to England. The coffee shops and clubs mentioned in both newspapers reminds us that they circulated to multiple readers and were available to view by non-subscribers. Given

32   *Beyond the antislavery haven*

this, it seems likely that the actual number of readers would have been much greater than the number of subscribers implies.

The editors who held people in slavery

The first editors of both newspapers claimed enslaved people as property, and these men worked at their printing offices.[37] Trudel notes that Fleury Mesplet held at least one person in slavery while he was the editor of the *MG*.[38] Enslaved people worked at the *QG* printing office 'at least from 1767', according to Trudel.[39] William Brown and Thomas Gilmore held a man called Joe in slavery, who worked as a pressman. He frequently escaped from them and the *QG* contained fugitive slave advertisements calling for assistance in his recapture.[40] Therese P. Lemay notes that many fugitive slave advertisements feature Joe, with the first printed in 1777, reflecting his repeated attempts to escape the newspaper office; Lemay identifies that, after 1785, reprinted versions of these advertisements appeared in the *MG*.[41] Robin W. Winks notes that William Brown and John Neilson both claimed people as property:

> Already William Brown [...] and his nephew and successor, John Neilson, erstwhile slaveholders both, had begun to attack slavery. Brown appears to have held no slaves after 1789, and Neilson seems to have sold his by 1793; from 1790 on the [*Quebec*] *Gazette* printed antislavery poetry, English- and French-language versions of slave-ship atrocity stories, and related material well calculated to decrease support for slavery.[42]

This analysis does not acknowledge that Samuel Neilson was the editor of the newspaper between March 1789 and January 1793. Winks notes that William Brown held no enslaved people as property after 1789, but Brown died in that year, and Frank Mackey has noted that his enslaved man, Joe, was part of his 'property' when he died.[43] Hence, it appears that Winks is probably incorrect in his view that Brown might have stopped purchasing enslaved people or liberated them. Winks argues that the newspaper became more anti-slavery, but as this chapter will explore, this peaked whilst Samuel Neilson was editor, and the antislavery stance did not continue after his death. It is unclear whether Samuel Neilson held people in

The representation of slavery in Quebec's newspapers   33

slavery himself. Trudel does not identify Samuel as someone who held people in slavery, but mentions that his uncle, William Brown, and brother, John Neilson, claimed people as property.[44] Scholars offer different views on what may have happened to Joe upon Brown's death. Lemay claims that Brown left Joe to Samuel in his will, but Joe seems to have run away soon after, and Samuel apparently made no attempt to reclaim him; Lemay claims that Samuel was driven by financial motives not to recover Joe, '[p]rofiting from his uncle's experience', which taught him that Joe would repeatedly run away.[45] Frank Mackey notes that, following Brown's death, Joe was possibly sold to a merchant, Peter Stuart, 'one of the three trustees of [Brown's] … estate'.[46] Given Neilson's antislavery attitudes, as revealed in this chapter, further historical research into his relationship with Joe is required to fill the gaps in Joe's story.

Fugitive slave advertisements in the newspapers

Looking at the newspapers published in Quebec between 1765 and 1810, Frank Mackey counts ninety-four notices 'concerning the sale of black slaves and the flights of black prisoners, ship deserters, servants, and slaves' printed in five newspapers.[47] He identifies that the *QG* printed by far the most notices at seventy-three, whereas the *MG* printed eighteen, the *Quebec Herald* seven, and two other newspapers (the *Mercury* and the *Courant*) one each.[48]

The Canadian fugitive slave advertisements and advertisements selling enslaved people were part of the same print genre and wider print network as advertisements printed in the wider Americas. This is reflected in the similarities in language and visual form of the advertisements. The language and structure of the fugitive slave advertisements printed in eighteenth-century Canadian newspapers were similar to those printed in newspapers across the Americas, in Pennsylvania, South Carolina, and Jamaica.[49] They included detailed descriptions of the enslaved people's appearance and clothing when they ran away. David Waldstreicher, looking at fugitive slave advertisements printed in newspapers in the mid-Atlantic American colonies during the eighteenth century, has noted that they demonstrate the agency of enslaved people and their resistance to slavery.[50] He notes that, when they ran away, enslaved people performed their

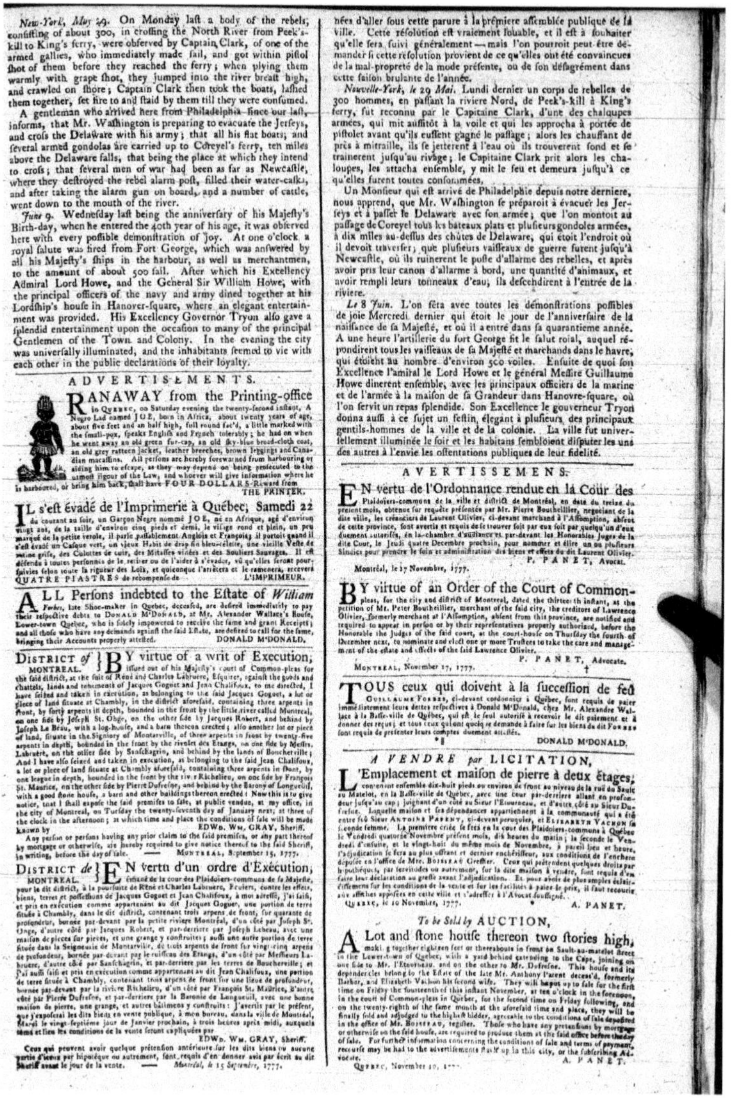

New-York, May 29. On Monday last a body of the rebels, consisting of about 300, in crossing the North River from Peek's-kill to King's ferry, were observed by Captain Clark, of one of the armed gallies, who immediately made sail, and got within pistol shot of them before they reached the ferry; when plying them warmly with grape shot, they jumped into the river breast high, and crawled on shore; Captain Clark then took the boats, lashed them together, set fire to and staid by them till they were consumed.

A gentleman who arrived here from Philadelphia since our last, informs, that Mr. Washington is preparing to evacuate the Jerseys, and cross the Delaware with his army; that all his flat boats, and several armed gondolas are carried up to Coreyel's ferry, ten miles above the Delaware falls, that being the place at which they intend to cross; that several men of war had been as far as Newcastle, where they destroyed the rebel alarm post, filled their water-casks, and after taking the alarm gun on board, and a number of cattle, went down to the mouth of the river.

June 9. Wednesday last being the anniversary of his Majesty's Birth-day, when he entered the 40th year of his age, it was observed here with every possible demonstration of joy. At one o'clock a royal salute was fired from Fort George, which was answered by all his Majesty's ships in the harbour, as well as merchantmen, to the amount of about 500 sail. After which his Excellency Admiral Lord Howe, and the General Sir William Howe, with the principal officers of the navy and army dined together at his Lordship's house in Hanover-square, where an elegant entertainment was provided. His Excellency Governor Tryon also gave a splendid entertainment upon the occasion to many of the principal Gentlemen of the Town and Colony. In the evening the city was universally illuminated, and the inhabitants seemed to vie with each other in the public declarations of their loyalty.

ADVERTISEMENTS.

RANAWAY from the Printing-office in QUEBEC, on Saturday evening the twenty-second instant, A Negro Lad named JOE, born in Africa, about twenty years of age, about five feet and an half high, full round fac'd, a little marked with the small-pox, speaks English and French tolerably; he had on when he went away an old green fur-cap, an old sky-blue broad-cloth coat, an old grey ratteen jacket, leather breeches, brown leggings and Canadian macassins. All persons are hereby forewarned from harbouring or aiding him to escape, as they may depend on being prosecuted to the utmost rigour of the Law, and whoever will give information where he is harboured, or bring him back, shall have FOUR DOLLARS Reward from

THE PRINTER.

IL s'est évadé de l'Imprimerie à Québec, Samedi 22 du courant au soir, un Garçon Negre nommé JOE, né en Afrique, agé d'environ vingt ans, de la taille d'environ cinq pieds et demi, le visage rond et plein, un peu marqué de la petite verole, il parle passablement Anglois et François; il portoit quand il s'est évadé un Casque vert, un vieux Habit de drap fin bleu-céleste, une vieille Veste de ratine grise, des Culottes de cuir, des Mitasses vinées et des Souliers Sauvages. Il est défendu à toutes personnes de le retirer ou de l'aider à s'évader, vû qu'elles seront poursuivies selon toute la rigueur des Loix, et quiconque l'arrêtera et le ramenera, recevera QUATRE PIASTRES de recompense de L'IMPRIMEUR.

ALL Persons indebted to the Estate of *William Forbes*, late Shoe-maker in Quebec, deceased, are desired immediately to pay their respective debts to DONALD M'DONALD, at Mr. Alexander Wallace's House, Lower-town Quebec, who is solely impowered to receive the same and grant Receipts; and all those who have any demands against the said Estate, are desired to call for the same, bringing their Accounts properly attested. DONALD M'DONALD.

DISTRICT *of* MONTREAL. } BY virtue of a writ of Execution, issued out of his Majesty's court of Common-pleas for the said district, at the suit of René and Charles Labruere, Esquires, against the goods and chattels, lands and tenements of Jacques Goguet and Jean Chalifoux, to me directed, I have seized and taken in execution, as belonging to the said Jacques Goguet, a lot or piece of land situate at Chambly, in the district aforesaid, containing three arpents in front, by forty arpents in depth, bounded in the front by the little river called Montreal, on one side by Joseph St. Ohge, on the other side by Jacques Robert, and behind by Joseph Le Beau, with a log-house, and a barn thereon erected; also another lot or piece of land, situate in the Signiory of Montarville, of three arpents in front by twenty-five arpents in depth, bounded in the front by the rivulet des Etangs, on one side by Messrs. Labruere, on the other side by Sanschagrin, and behind by the lands of Boucherville; And I have also seized and taken in execution, as belonging to the said Jean Chalifoux, a lot or piece of land situate at Chambly aforesaid, containing three arpents in front, by one league in depth, bounded in the front by the river Richelieu, on one side by François St. Maurice, on the other side by Pierre Dufresne, and behind by the Barony of Longueuil, with a good stone house, a barn and other buildings thereon erected: Now this is to give notice, that I shall expose the said premises to sale, at public vendue, at my office, in the city of Montreal, on Tuesday the twenty-seventh day of January next, at three of the clock in the afternoon; at which time and place the conditions of sale will be made known by EDWD. WM. GRAY, Sheriff.

Any person or persons having any prior claim to the said premises, or any part thereof by mortgage or otherwise, are hereby required to give notice thereof to the said Sheriff, in writing, before the day of sale. — MONTREAL, September 15, 1777.

DISTRICT *de* MONTREAL. } EN vertu d'un ordre d'Exécution, émané de la cour des Plaidoiers-communs de sa Majesté, pour le dit district, à la poursuite de Réné et Charles Labruere, Ecuiers, contre les effets, biens, terres et possessions de Jacques Goguet et Jean Chalifoux, à moi adressé, j'ai saisi, et pris en exécution comme appartenant au dit Jacques Goguet, une portion de terre située à Chambly, dans le dit district, contenant trois arpens de front, sur quarante de profondeur, bornée par-devant par la petite riviere Montréal, d'un côté par Joseph St. Onge, d'autre côté par Jacques Robert, et par-derriere par Joseph Lebeau, avec une maison de pieces sur pieces, et une grange y construites; aussi une autre portion de terre située dans la Seigneurie de Montarville, de trois arpents de front sur vingt-cinq arpens de profondeur, bornée par-devant par le ruisseau des Etangs, d'un côté par Messieurs Labruere, d'autre côté par Sanschagrin, et par-derriere par les terres de Boucherville; et j'ai aussi saisi et pris en exécution comme appartenant au dit Jean Chalifoux, une portion de terre située à Chambly, contenant trois arpens de front sur une lieue de profondeur, bornée par-devant par la riviere Richelieu, d'un côté par François St. Maurice, d'autre côté par Pierre Dufresne, et par-derriere par la Baronie de Longueuil, avec une bonne maison de pierre, une grange, et autres bâtimens y construits: J'avertis par le présent, que j'exposerai les dits biens en vente publique, à mon bureau, dans la ville de Montréal, Mardi le vingt-septiéme jour de Janvier prochain, à trois heures après midi, auxquels tems et lieu les conditions de la vente seront expliquées par EDWD. WM. GRAY, Sheriff.

Ceux qui peuvent avoir quelque prétension antérieure sur les dits biens ou aucune partie d'iceux par hipotéque ou autrement, sont requis d'en donner avis par écrit au dit Sherif avant le jour de la vente. — *Montréal, le 15 Septembre, 1777.*

nées d'aller sous cette parure à la premiere assemblée publique de la ville. Cette résolution est vraiement louable, et il est à souhaiter qu'elle sera suivi généralement — mais l'on pourroit peut être demander si cette résolution provient de ce qu'elles ont été convaincues de la mal-propreté de la mode présente, ou de son désagrément dans cette saison brulante de l'année.

Nouvelle-York, le 29 Mai. Lundi dernier un corps de rebelles de 300 hommes, en passant la riviere Nord, de Peek's-kill à King's ferry, fut reconnu par le Capitaine Clark, d'une des chalqupes armées, qui mit aussitôt à la voile et qui les approcha à portée de pistolet avant qu'ils eussent gagné le passage; alors les chauffant de près à mitraille, ils se jetterent à l'eau où ils trouverent fond et se trainerent jusqu'au rivage; le Capitaine Clark prit alors les chaloupes, les attacha ensemble, y mit le feu et demeura jusqu'à ce qu'elles furent toutes consommées.

Un Monsieur qui est arrivé de Philadelphie depuis notre derniere, nous apprend, que Mr. Washington se préparoit à évacuer les Jerseys et à passer le Delaware avec son armée; que l'on montoit au passage de Coreyel tous les bateaux plats et plusieurs gondoles armées, à dix milles au-dessus des chûtes de Delaware, qui étoit l'endroit où il devoit traverser; que plusieurs vaisseaux de guerre furent jusqu'à Newcastle, où ils ruinerent le poste d'allarme des rebelles, et après avoir pris leur canon d'allarme à bord, une quantité d'animaux, et avoir rempli leurs tonneaux d'eau, ils descendirent à l'entrée de la riviere.

Le 8 Juin. L'on fêta avec toutes les démonstrations possibles de joie Mercredi dernier qui étoit le jour de l'anniversaire de la naissance de sa Majesté, et où il a entré dans sa quarantieme année. A une heure l'artillerie du fort George fit le salut roial, auquel répondirent tous les vaisseaux de sa Majesté et marchands dans le havre, qui étoient au nombre d'environ 500 voiles. Ensuite de quoi son Excellence l'amiral le Lord Howe et le général Messire Guillaume Howe dinerent ensemble, avec les principaux officiers de la marine et de l'armée à la maison de sa Grandeur dans Hanovre-square, où l'on servit un repas splendide. Son Excellence le gouverneur Tryon donna aussi à ce sujet un festin, élegant à plusieurs des principaux gentils-hommes de la ville et de la colonie. La ville fut universellement illuminée le soir et les habitans sembloient disputer les uns des autres à l'envie les ostentations publiques de leur fidelité.

AVERTISSEMENS.

EN vertu de l'Ordonnance rendue en la Cour des Plaidoiers-communs de la ville et district de Montréal, en date du treize du present mois, obtenue sur requête présentée par Mr. Pierre Bouthellier, negociant de la dite ville, les créanciers de Laurent Olivier, ci-devant marchand à l'Assomption, absent de cette province, sont avertis et requis de se trouver soit par eux soit par quelqu'un d'eux duement autorisés, en la chambre d'audiance et par-devant les Honorables Juges de la dite Cour, le Jeudi quatre Decembre prochain, pour nommer et élire un ou plusieurs Sindics pour prendre le soin et administration des biens et effets du dit Laurent Olivier. P. PANET, Avocat.

Montréal, le 17 Novembre, 1777.

BY virtue of an Order of the Court of Common-pleas, for the city and district of Montreal, dated the thirteenth instant, at the petition of Mr. Peter Boutheillier, merchant of the said city, the creditors of Lawrence Olivier, formerly merchant at l'Assomption, absent from this province, are notified and required to appear in person or by their representatives properly authorized, before the Honorable the Judges of the said court, at the court-house on Thursday the fourth of December next, to nominate and elect one or more Trustees to take the care and management of the estate and effects of the said Lawrence Olivier. P. PANET, Advocate.

MONTREAL, November 17, 1777.

TOUS ceux qui doivent à la succession de feu GUILLAUME FORBES, ci-devant cordonnier à Québec, sont requis de paier immédiatement leurs dettes respectives à Donald M'Donald, chez Mr. Alexandre Wallace à la Basse-ville de Québec, qui est le seul autorisé à recevoir le dit paiement et à donner des requ[illegible]; et tous ceux qui ont quelque demande à faire sur les biens du dit FORBES sont requis de présenter leurs comptes duement attestés. DONALD M'DONALD.

A VENDRE par LICITATION,

L'Emplacement et maison de pierre à deux étages, contenant ensemble dix-huit pieds ou environ de front au niveau de la rue du Sault au Matelot, en la Basse-ville de Quebec, avec une cour par-derriere allant en profondeur jusqu'au cap; joignant d'un côté au Sieur l'Etourneau, et d'autre côté au Sieur Dufresne. Laquelle maison et ses dépendances appartiennent à la communauté qui a été entre feû Sieur ANTOINE PARENT, ci-devant peruquier, et ELIZABETH VACHON sa seconde femme. La premiere criée se fera en la cour des Plaidoiers-communs à Québec le Vendredi quatorze Novembre présent mois, dix heures du matin; la seconde le Vendredi d'ensuite, et le vingt-huit du même mois de Novembre, à pareil lieu et heure, l'adjudication se fera au plus offrant et dernier enchérisseur, aux conditions de l'enchere déposée en l'office de Mre. BOISSEAU Greffier. Ceux qui prétendent quelques droits par hypothéques, par servitudes ou autrement, sur la dite maison à vendre, sont requis d'en faire leur déclaration au greffe avant l'adjudication. Et pour avoir de plus amples éclaircissemens sur les conditions de la vente et sur les facilités à paier le prix, il faut recourir aux affiches apposées en cette ville et s'adresser à l'Avocat soussigné.

QUEBEC, le 10 Novembre, 1777. A. PANET.

To be Sold by AUCTION,

A Lot and stone house thereon two stories high, making together eighteen feet or thereabouts in front on Sault-au-matelot street in the Lower-town of Quebec, with a yard behind extending to the Cape, joining on one side to Mr. l'Etourneau, and on the other to Mr. Dufresne. This house and its dependencies belong to the Estate of the late Mr. Anthony Parent deceas'd, formerly Barber, and Elizabeth Vachon his second wife. They will be put up to sale for the first time on Friday the fourteenth of this instant November, at ten o'clock in the forenoon, in the court of Common-pleas in Quebec, for the second time on Friday following, and on the twenty-eighth of the same month at the aforesaid time and place, they will be finally sold and adjudged to the highest bidder, agreeable to the conditions of sale deposited in the office of Mr. BOISSEAU, register. Those who have any pretensions by mortgage or otherwise on the said house, are required to produce them at the said office before the day of sale. For further information concerning the conditions of sale and terms of payment, recourse may be had to the advertisements stuck up in this city, or the subscribing Advocate. A. PANET.

QUEBEC, November 10, 1777.

Figure 1.1 Fugitive slave advertisement for Joe, a pressman at the *Quebec Gazette*, *Quebec Gazette*, 27 November 1777, p. 3, image credit Bibliothèque et Archives nationales du Québec.

identities as free people using clothing, language, dialect, and stories.[51] In one advertisement printed in South Carolina, a former enslaver states: 'I suppose he will endeavour to pass for a free man.'[52] Similar advertisements were printed in Quebec: in one, the former enslaver notes that Pascal Puro 'calls himself a free man'.[53]

Scholars have undertaken significant research on Canadian fugitive slave advertisements in Quebec's newspapers.[54] However, they have overlooked texts that represent the broader Black Atlantic world within newspapers and reprinted texts from the international abolition movement. For example, George Elliott Clarke and Winfried Siemerling have encouraged hemispheric and rich readings of antebellum slave narratives, placing them within a Canadian literary canon, but their reading of eighteenth-century newspapers focuses narrowly on advertisements. Clarke argues that slave narratives in eighteenth-century Canadian newspapers (which he variously calls 'narratives', 'memoirs', and 'articles') pre-date the antebellum slave narratives that frame Canada as a haven and should be looked at as presenting an earlier history that has been exiled from the national narrative.[55] Siemerling's examination of Canadian literature and the Black Atlantic does not challenge the notion that advertisements and slave narratives are the best printed source for exploring Canada, the Black Atlantic world, and its legacies of slavery.[56] Historical studies of slavery in Quebec and Nova Scotia have similarly focused on fugitive slave advertisements in the

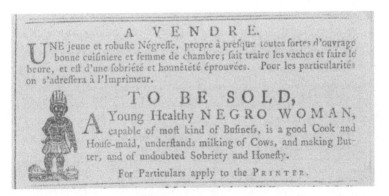

Figure 1.2 Fugitive slave advertisement for an unnamed 'young healthy negro woman', *Quebec Gazette*, 22 April 1790, p. 4, image credit Bibliothèque et Archives nationales du Québec.

36 *Beyond the antislavery haven*

newspapers.[57] Two early exceptions that look briefly at the antislavery texts in Quebec's newspapers may have shaped the disregard for these texts since. Trudel argues that '[t]here is not much point in trying to detect any coherent and orchestrated anti-slavery campaign in these writings ... there was nothing original about the antislavery press campaign and nothing relating to Canada'.[58] Winks identifies abolitionist texts in the *QG* and seems to imply that the newspaper editors of the *QG* grew increasingly critical of slavery in Canada from 1790, but he misses out the fact that these texts were about the transatlantic slave trade and reprinted from French and British newspapers.[59] Contextualising the newspapers in the wide circulation of abolitionist texts in the Atlantic world, this chapter will now explore how the newspaper editors in Quebec constructed a coherent anti-slave-trade stance for their local readers.

Anti-slave-trade sentiment in the newspapers, 1789–93

The years 1789–93 saw the most heterogeneous period of the newspapers' handling of slavery. An examination of the *QG* and *MG* during earlier periods, including the first year of each newspaper's publication (1763 and 1785 respectively, and in 1788, the year before this peak), shows that their editors did not print antislavery texts in their newspapers, but they did print fugitive slave advertisements. There was a marked increase in the anti-slave-trade materials printed in the newspapers between 1789 and 1793, which were printed alongside fugitive slave advertisements. Mackey counts twenty-five slave advertisements in Quebec's newspapers between 1789 and 1793, and twenty-three during the period 1784–88. The *QG* printed twenty-one in the period 1784–88 and eight between 1789 and 1793.[60] The *MG* printed two during the earlier period but ten in the later period, and the *Herald* also printed seven.[61] The editors of the *QG* and *MG* reprinted these texts during the peak of sentimental rhetoric in anti-slave-trade and some pro-slave-trade texts in Britain.[62] The *QG* contained twenty-three abolitionist texts and no pro-slavery texts between March 1789 and January 1793, while Samuel Neilson was its editor. There were no abolitionist texts published in the years immediately before or after this period when Neilson was editor. In the *MG*, there were eleven abolitionist

The representation of slavery in Quebec's newspapers   37

texts and four pro-slavery texts published over the same period, and there were no antislavery texts in its first year of issue, 1785 or 1788, immediately prior to the peak.

The period 1789–93 roughly corresponds to trends in British newspapers from which the *QG* derived much of its material. For example, Seymour Drescher shows that there was a peak in references to the slave trade in British newspapers starting in 1787, declining slightly in the early 1790s and then peaking again in 1793.[63] These years also correspond with the years that Samuel Neilson was editor of the newspaper, and in part, he seems to have driven a notably antislavery phase in the newspaper's history. An examination of the years immediately preceding and following his proprietorship reinforces the inference that Samuel Neilson was driving the emphasis on abolitionist discourses in the *QG*, and his presentation of these foreign debates shaped his newspaper in sympathy with these ideals. As Robin W. Winks has noticed, Samuel Neilson's proprietorship of the paper represents a more creative and literary phase for the *QG*.[64] Neilson's focus on antislavery sentiment may have been part of this new focus, including printing poems that were more international and seen to be of higher quality by contemporaries. His decision to reprint popular and esteemed antislavery poetry from the British context could reflect this wider shift.

The editors in Quebec reprinted anti-slave-trade texts from British and French newspapers in their own publications. They frequently provided the title of the British or French newspaper in which the reprinted texts first appeared. It has been possible in many cases to trace back these reprints to their source. Mesplet selected just two letters from an entire issue of the *St James's Chronicle, or the British Evening-Post* and reprinted them in his newspaper on 10 December 1789. In one of these letters, the writer voices pro-slavery views and implicitly fears that airing abolitionist ideas in the newspapers will incite rebellions led by enslaved people.[65] On 13 August 1789, Neilson reprinted the first speech that the British abolitionist William Wilberforce gave on the 12 May 1789 before the House of Commons, calling for the abolition of the slave trade, from the British newspaper, *The Diary, or, Woodfall's Register*.[66] This speech was part of an eighteen-year campaign to push the abolition of the slave trade through Parliament.[67] It dominated an issue of the *QG*, filling both left- and right-hand columns of pages two,

38   *Beyond the antislavery haven*

three, and half of page four, appearing in English only, and in much smaller print than usual. The following week and for the next three weeks, the speech appeared in French.[68] There was a three-month gap between when Wilberforce delivered the speech in May and when Neilson printed this version of the speech in the *QG*, and the three instalments of the French translation might have signified that it was taking time to translate the speech into French. This corresponds with the three months it usually took for newspapers from London to arrive in the newspaper's office in Quebec. Tracing these texts to source shows that the editors selected scraps of printed material from vast amounts of foreign printed material for reprinting in their newspapers.

Looking at the newspapers from which the editors in Quebec derived their anti-slave-trade content reveals that British newspapers also contained pro-slave-trade texts that Canadian editors chose not to reprint. The week after he published Wilberforce's speech to the House of Commons, delivered on 12 May, Neilson reprinted another antislavery text that probably came from *Woodfall's Register*: 'Wilberforce's Twelve Prepositions on the Slave Trade presented to the House of Commons'.[69] Neilson appears to have read issues of the British newspaper around this time, perhaps specifically looking for anti-slave-trade material. *Woodfall's Register* also contained pro-slave-trade ideas that Neilson did not select for reprinting in the *QG*, although its overall tone was sympathetic to anti-slave-trade feeling and legislation in Parliament. For example, in a letter to the newspaper's printer, Justinian states his objections to the abolition of the slave trade, seeing it as 'the old publick and patriotick cry of "Liberty and Property" that seems at present to have changed to that of "Liberty *against* property"'.[70] At the close of the letter Justinian states his intention to produce 'unanswerable objections to the abolition of the slave trade' and his confidence that they will be printed ('readily insert[ed]') in *Woodfall's Register* given the 'avowed impartiality' of that paper. A later letter printed in the paper, signed off by Terentius, adopted an anti-slave-trade stance. The letter challenged Justinian to state his objections against abolition clearly, implying that his letter has not made these obvious.[71] *Woodfall's Register* also printed petitions to the House of Commons from planters in the British West Indies stating their anxieties and desire for the slave trade to continue.[72]

Figure 1.3 William Wilberforce's speech to the House of Commons, *Quebec Gazette*, 13 August 1789, p. 2, image credit Bibliothèque et Archives nationales du Québec.

When the newspaper editors reprinted these texts, they selected them from other newspapers and layered them together in a new context, and in so doing, they created a local anti-slave-trade sentiment for local readers. The reprinted texts contained the original point of view, but by reprinting them in a new context and selecting them for inclusion in their own newspapers, the editors revoiced these texts. Through this lens, we see Samuel Neilson as one of Canada's first (anti-slave-trade) abolitionists. This understanding of the newspapers has come from close reading. There were no editorials in the period 1789–93 in which the editors explicitly stated an intention to create newspapers with anti-slave-trade worldviews. However, Samuel Neilson printed a text in 1792, in what may have been the voice of the editor, that predicted the local maple syrup trade would receive 'its almost certain advancement by the discontinuance of the African slave trade'.[73] The abolition of the slave trade is seen as offering economic success for Lower Canada, in terms of stimulating the local economy, rather than as a humanitarian success. It suggests that Neilson saw the abolition of the slave trade as very likely, based on the news he was receiving from Britain (the House of Commons passed the slave trade abolition bill in 1792, but it was rejected in the House of Lords). The study of the newspapers in 1789–93 revealed no letters from readers to the editors that discuss how local readers received the abolitionist and pro-slavery texts in the newspapers.

In the British context, Srividhya Swaminathan's examination of the rhetoric of the eighteenth-century British slave-trade debates has shown that they were part of a shared conversation, and that both the anti- and pro-slave-trade sides were about the formation of British national identity and not just abolition.[74] Debates about the slave trade were also concerned with defining the national character and the nature of the 'Briton'.[75] Swaminathan finds that both sides of the debate ultimately converged over a discursive terrain that constructed the view of the 'Briton' as commercial, moral, and white, and Swaminathan argues that this underpinned an imperial agenda for Britain in the nineteenth century.[76] In the newspapers in Quebec, editors selectively reproduced from one side of the British debate, and the absence of pro-slave-trade texts reflects their construction of an anti-slave-trade identity for their newspapers.

The representation of slavery in Quebec's newspapers   41

The newspapers sometimes presented fugitive slave advertisements near foreign anti-slave-trade texts. For example, one issue of the *QG*, dated 3 September 1789, contained news reports on the abolition of the slave-trade debates in France and Britain and a fugitive slave advertisement in French.[77] This, in part, reflects the multiplicity of voices that could appear together in newspapers. It also reflects a disparity between the way that editors could align their readers with anti-slave-trade sentiments in the more discursive and outward-looking parts of their newspapers, while advertisements for enslaved people were part of everyday business in the advertisement sections of the newspapers, paid for by members of the local community. The reprinted international texts focused specifically on the abolition of the slave trade and its horrors in the West Indies. It is possible that readers could have seen the abolitionist materials and fugitive slave advertisements and held those two seemingly contradictory views in their mind at the same time.

Through the act of reprinting, newspaper editors took on the voices of the texts that they reproduced. One item that appears in the London news summary of the *QG* in November 1791 is the account of the loss of a slave ship on the Middle Passage. An editorial voice, which could belong to Neilson (it is unclear), revoices the printed news of a slave ship being lost and goes on to criticise accounts that do not mention the loss of the lives of hundreds of enslaved African people:

> An African slave ship was lately lost on the middle passage: – the accounts say 'that the men were saved but the ship and cargo lost' – Lest the reader should mistake the nature of the cargo, he must know that it consisted of 230 of our fellow creatures: – found guilty of being born on the coast of Guinea, of black parents.[78]

The revoicing of the original text created a shock for the reader, focused on the words 'cargo' and 'men'. In the original text, 'cargo' is used to refer to the enslaved people, defining them as property, and the assumption in the 'accounts' is that the 'men' were saved, but this is narrowly defined as the crew of sailors. The editorial commentary invites the reader to feel disgust at this attempt to erase and categorise 230 enslaved African people ('fellow creatures') as 'cargo'. The lack of boundary between the news summary and the editorial voice of Neilson here produces the sense that Neilson

42   *Beyond the antislavery haven*

himself could be speaking the framing commentary, and that he is inviting his readers in Quebec to feel disgust at the definition of enslaved Africans as property.

Trudel's early discussion of some of the abolitionist texts in the *QG* and the *Quebec Herald* in *Canada's Forgotten Slaves: Two Hundred Years of Bondage*, originally published in 1960, is still the fullest critical discussion of this to date. Trudel argues that the editor of the *QG* did not provide any local editorial comment when they reprinted foreign abolitionist texts in news summaries, noting that he was unable to identify who wrote the abolitionist poems printed in the newspaper and whether or not these had Canadian authors.[79] Trudel's reading does not entirely account for the report of the lost slave ship. Neilson printed the report in the context of the abolitionist thrust of the *QG* that he developed. Moreover, there is ambiguity about whether Neilson reprinted the news or provided his own abolitionist commentary on 'accounts' he had received. What is significant is not whether this text was a reprint, but that its language exhibits ambiguity about who is speaking, and that it has the feel of a local editorial voice.

The Canadian newspaper editors may have reprinted texts from American newspapers (which were borrowing from British newspapers), picking through these to find British texts, but if this was the case, there is no trace of this in the Canadian newspapers. When reprinted British poems or political speeches were included, there was no reference to American newspapers. The absence of any reference to slavery in the United States in general in the newspapers is noteworthy, and indeed this differs from contemporaneous newspapers in Nova Scotia during this period, where abolitionist poetry and texts focused on depictions of slavery in the United States, probably originally published in the United States.[80] The editors in Quebec relied more on British than American newspapers when compiling their content on slavery.

French and British anti-slave-trade discourse in the *Montreal Gazette*

Mesplet similarly constructed an anti-slave-trade point of view in the *MG* through reprinting foreign abolitionist texts, but he created

The representation of slavery in Quebec's newspapers   43

SUNDAY, Aug. 28.

M. Humbert, deputed from the National Guard of Clermont, and in their name and the names of M. Bedu. and M. Carré, gives up to the nation the pecuniary recompence decreed to them for their conduct in stopping the King.

It was immediately decreed: that this act of patriotic generosity should be inserted in the journals,

The interview between the Emperor and the King of Prussia takes place on the 26th. of August, at Castle Plinitz in Saxony, where reports state, not improbably, they were joined by the Elector of Saxony.

The object of this meeting, once suspected to be for effecting a Counter Revolution in France, is in the first place to consult on the plan of a treaty proposed to be entered into for preventing the spreading of Liberty in Germany; for which purpose it is proposed to guarantee the possessions of each other, conformable to the ancient and present laws now existing.

What they may think of hereafter respecting France, is at present very little thought of

POLAND is certainly a great object of their consideration—for if the new Revolution in Poland is suffered to be permanent, these Monarchs may be said in some measure to be placed between two fires, and if the flames should spread, the conflagration, in all human probability, wouldbbecome general.

We cannot help confessing that the project, however salutary, is very dangerous, insomuch as it may create alarms where none existed; but we hope the joint wisdom of these Monarchs will agree in ameliorating the state of their peasantry so as to avoid any new commotions.

An African slave ship was lately lost on the middle passage :—the accounts say " that the men were saved but the ship and cargo lost." —Lest the reader should mistake the nature of this cargo, he must know that it consisted of 230 of our fellow creatures—found guilty of being born on the coast of Guinea, of black parents.

The Bishop of Ball has agreed to treat with M. Montmorin, the French Minister, and to accept of a compensation for the feudal rights of which he is deprived by the Revolution.

His example will be followed by the other German Princes, as soon as they find that they are not likely to be supported by arms in their demand of restitution.

The Commander of the Imperial troops at Luxembourg has found it necessary to call in the posts on the French frontier, on account of the frequent desertions.

To prevent the exportation of Coin from France, it has been proposed to inscribe on each piece the words—" TO LIVE FREE, OR DIE." " This," says the proposer, " will render our MONEY as much counterband in most foreign countries as our writings."

The business of a Poet Laureat is become extraordinary difficult, since Mr. Pitt's Administration, and Mr Pye should have it " considered in his wages." The country has been for some years in a sort of middle state, which defies all description. There has been a continual armament, so that he cannot sing the blessings of peace; yet there has been no military contention, to give him a topic in the glories of war !

The Cyclops of Birmingham swear, that if men are to be hanged for their loyalty and religion, they'll be d——d if they strike another stroke in defence of one or t'other: Church and K—— too,—say these heroes of the state, may see to themselves, for the devil a Birmingham blade will ever help 'em after this.

Striking Characteristicks of the People at Birmingham.   [By a Traveller.]

As these were written several months previous to the late riots, they must be acquitted of partiality, even supposing them to bear no internal marks of undisguised authenticity.

" Birmingham, says the author, is far from being distinguished by zeal in religion : what there is is among the Dissenters, and those who, adhering to Dr. PRIESTLEY, consider themselves as Philosophers; but the mass of people are ignorant and irreligious in the extreme! seldom, or never going to church, and spending their Sundays in their ordinary working apparel, in low debauchery. There is a great deal of trick and low cunning among the manufacturers in general (there are, no doubt, some exceptions), but this is partly owing to their universal barbarism and want of education, as, the moment the children are fit for any kind of work, instead of being sent to school, they are sent to a shop to earn sixpence, nine-pence, or one shilling per week ! and it has been known that many men have risen to opulence at this place without being qualified to read in a Common Prayer-book."

Such are those, with whom some calling themselves Churchmen, have proudly claimed the right-hand of fellowship, and whose sense and loyalty have been extolled by factious Prints as that of the nation in general !

Figure 1.4 Report of the loss of a slave ship, *Quebec Gazette*, 24 November 1791, p. 2, image credit Bibliothèque et Archives nationales du Québec.

44 *Beyond the antislavery haven*

a slightly different voice. Mesplet gave more space to French abolitionist texts and presented the slave-trade debate as unfolding simultaneously in Britain and France. The difference between the presentations of these texts in both newspapers underscores the need to contextualise the reprinted materials and to explore specifically how these transatlantic texts were framed when they were reprinted.

Mesplet achieved a balance between French and British calls to abolish the slave trade by alternating each week between French and British examples of abolitionist texts. Between August and October 1789, Mesplet reprinted anti-slave-trade texts originally printed in British and French newspapers during May 1789, spreading these across the *MG* for a longer period of three months. This had the effect of presenting these texts as part of an unfolding anti-slave-trade debate taking place in France and Britain. Mesplet printed these texts in both English and French, as was usual for political texts in the *MG*. Mesplet placed these debates under dated headings that indicated when the texts were originally published in the foreign newspapers. This presented the slave-trade debates as taking place simultaneously in France and Britain. On 20 August 1789, Mesplet printed a letter written by La Société des Amis des Noirs in Paris, and on the 27 August 1789, in the London news section under the date 'May 13', Mesplet printed 'pieces' sent by 'one of the opposers of slavery' in Britain 'in favor of that misfortunate portion of the human species'.[81] The following week, under the title 'Paris May 11 to 25', Mesplet printed texts about the opening of the Estates-General at Versailles on the 5 May 1789, including the speech of Louis XVI's finance minister Jacques Necker on the slave trade, in which he describes enslaved Africans as men 'similar to ourselves in the faculty of thought' and laments the cruelties of the French slave trade and indicates the need to 'mitigate it', noting that 'a distinguished nation has already given the signal' for its abolition, probably reflecting the anti-slave-trade discussions taking place in the British House of Commons.[82] On 10 September 1789, a text in which the Third Estate state their sympathy for the motion of abolishing the French slave trade is printed under the heading 'Paris 25 May'.[83] Then, on 1 October, Wilberforce's Twelve Prepositions, laid before the Privy Council, was printed in the *MG* by Mesplet in English and French in the London news section, headed with the date 'May 16'.[84]

The representation of slavery in Quebec's newspapers 45

Mesplet gave a greater focus than Neilson to French abolitionist arguments and texts that presented these as examples of French liberty and specialness. A letter from La Société des Amis des Noirs in Paris, addressed to those who send deputies to the Estates-General, 'established in France for the abolition of the Slave Trade', appeared in a London news summary.[85] This text appeared in French to the right-hand side, under the heading 'Londres, le 9th Mai. Commerce Des Noirs'. Mesplet reprints a copy of the letter that appeared in an unnamed London newspaper and appears to reproduce the introductory commentary to the letter given in the British newspaper. The introduction to the letter describes the likelihood of this issue being taken up by the National Assembly, and says this is evidence that will help 'to destroy the report which has been spread of the French having the intention to carry on the slave trade to a greater extent as soon as the British legislature will annihilate it'. The commentary suggests the letter is 'proof' that the French will not multiply 'that shameful traffic'. The letter contains the perspective of La Société des Amis des Noirs, who felt it hypocritical to proclaim their rights as Frenchmen but exclude enslaved people, who were also 'men', and to not extend the same rights to enslaved people in the French Empire. They exclaimed 'How dare we pronounce the word of rights, if we prove by our conduct that we do not look upon them as the same to all men', and they highlight the inconsistency of slavery in the French colonies given that 'we say that one man cannot become the property of another'. The language printed in the Amis des Noirs letter reads as potentially radical in its presentation of the specialness of French liberty. However, Mesplet printed this under a London news heading and reprints the British framing text saying it is a 'favourable time' to see the discussion taking place in France. This placed the text about French views on liberty within a more politically sensitive context of British abolitionism, while also enabling Mesplet to print anti-slave-trade sentiment that presented the distinctiveness of French liberty.

In contrast to the *QG*, the *MG* provided a greater coverage of the slave-trade debate in France and presented a growing slave-trade abolition movement in both Britain and France, showing that both countries shared in this discussion. Whereas in Britain the two sides of the debate that Swaminathan identifies as part of a shared conversation are the British pro-slavery and antislavery

46 *Beyond the antislavery haven*

sides, in the *MG*, the British and French anti-slave-trade arguments appeared as part of a shared conversion. The week after reprinting material 'in favour of that misfortunate portion of the human species' on 27 August 1789, Mesplet printed texts about the opening of the Estates-General at Versailles, which took place on 5 May 1789.[86] He printed the speeches of Louis XVI and his finance minister Jacques Necker, who had resumed his office in August 1788.[87] Necker focused on 'fiscal and budgetary matters'.[88] Necker described ways to 'mitigate' the slave trade as part of two changes that will make the Assembly 'immortal': the abolition of the Corvie, which required the lower classes to labour on public roads; and '[s]ome modifications … in favour of the Slaves in the West Indies'.[89] In the same issue of the newspaper, Mesplet also printed an 'Extract at large from Mr Necker's Speech which concerns the slave trade'. There were silences and omissions in the speeches reported in this issue of the *MG*. The text did not report on the Keeper of the Seals's speech ('The Keeper of the Seals spoke next, and after him Mr. Necker'), but presented Necker's speech about the slave trade.

Mesplet gave an air of importance to Necker's abolitionist speech, by choosing to reprint it. Necker's speech depicted enslaved African people as humans and as 'an unhappy race of men' that were 'coolly considered only as the objects of a barbarous traffic'. He placed the responsibility for this inhumane treatment of enslaved people not with the slaveholder or slave trader, but with the French nation and the men of the National Assembly: 'Men, nevertheless, whom deaf to their lamentations, we crowd, we heap in the holds of vessels, to convey them to a bondage that awaits them in our islands.' Necker closed his speech with two pieces of flattery. First, he appeared to praise the British abolition effort ('A distinguished nation has already given the signal'), and he then tied the possibilities for modifications to the slave trade to treating enslaved people as men in the French colonies with the renewed and enlightened sitting of the Assembly, capturing the mood of the Estates-General. Necker implied that the Assembly would bestow 'honor' on itself and promote a positive legacy for themselves 'in the midst of an Enlightened age' by appearing favourable to anti-slave-trade measures. He argued that this was especially the case within the context of the Assembly meeting at an important moment in which its chief aims (as Necker presented them) were to tackle the abuses of the

The representation of slavery in Quebec's newspapers 47

king and to be seen as reforming and liberating the French government. For Mesplet, the discussion was about more than abolition: it was about the national prestige and honour of supporting abolitionism.

Poetry about slavery in the Caribbean in the newspapers

The first poems about slavery printed in Quebec's newspapers came from British newspapers, and were circulated widely in the Atlantic world. The newspapers contained three poems calling for the abolition of the British slave trade between 1789 and 1793: Cowper's 'The Negro's Complaint'; Frank Sayers's 'The Dying African' (written around 1789–1790, and first published in Norwich in England); and an anonymous poem, an 'Epilogue to "The Padlock"'.[90] These texts were about the slave trade, reprinted from the international movement. They did not take issue with or depict slavery in Canada. This section discusses one of these poems and argues that the newspapers in the colonies that later became Canada participated in a shared Anglo-American abolitionist print culture during this period. It shows how, in specific local contexts, the colonies' newspapers participated in the shared culture of the information highway of abolitionist ideas, as well as a culture of slavery and slaveholding.

'The Negro's Recital', the title given to the 'Epilogue to "The Padlock"' in the *QG*, printed on 16 December 1790, was perhaps the first text printed in Quebec in which the reader could have envisaged themselves as part of an imagined community more sympathetic to the suffering of enslaved African people in the British Caribbean. This predated the construction of Canada West as a British land of liberty in the mid-nineteenth-century slave narrative. The text was first published in London in the *Gentleman's Magazine* in 1787 as an epilogue to Isaac Bickerstaffe's 1768 comic opera *The Padlock*, which had music by Samuel Didben, titled an 'Epilogue to "The Padlock"'. In the 'Epilogue', the Black enslaved character, Mungo, is imagined as stepping in front of the audience at the end of the play and addressing them. Brycchan Carey notes that the 'Epilogue' is clearly abolitionist and draws on 'emerging discourses about the rights of man' but that it also contains ameliorationist undertones.[91] He questions how this text would have been

The following beautiful and pathetic Lines

By Mr. COWPER, need no other introduction than the name of their Author.

FORC'D from home, and all its pleasures,
  Afric's Coast I left forlorn,
To increase a stranger's treasures
  O'er the raging billows borne,
Men from England bought and sold me,
  Paid my price in paltry gold;
But though their's, they have enroll'd me,
  Minds are never to be sold.

Still in thought as free as ever,
  What are England's rights, I ask,
Me from my delights to sever,
  Me to torture, me to task?
Fleecy locks, and black complexion,
  Cannot forfeit Nature's claim;
Skins may differ, but affection
  Dwells in White and black the same.

Why did all-creating Nature
  Make the plant for which we toil?
Sighs must waft it, tears must water,
  Sweat of ours must dress the soil.
Think, ye masters, iron-hearted,
  Sitting at your jovial boards;
Think how many backs have smarted
  For the sweet your cane affords.

Is there, as ye sometimes tell us—
  Is there One who reigns on high?
Has he bid you buy and sell us?
  Speaking from his Throne—the sky!

Ask him, if your knotted scourges,
  Fetters, blood extorting screws,
Are the means which duty urges
  Agents of his will to use?

Hark! He answers—Wild tornadoes,
  Strewing yonder sea with wrecks,
Wasting towns, plantations, meadows,
  Is the voice with which he speaks.
He, foreseeing what vexations
  Afric's sons would undergo,
Fix'd their Tyrant's habitations
  Where his whirlwinds ‡ answer—No!

By our blood in Afric wasted,
  Ere our necks received the chain;
By the miseries which we tasted,
  Crossing, in your barks, the main;
By our sufferings since you brought us
  To the man degrading mart,
All sustain'd, by patience taught us,
  Only by a broken heart.

Deem our nations brutes no longer,
  Till some reason you shall find,
Worthier of regard and stronger
  Than the colours of our kind.
Slaves of gold, whose sordid dealings
  Tarnish all your boasted pow'rs,
Prove that you have human feelings,
  Ere you proudly question ours.

‡ Alluding to the hurricanes so common in the West Indies.

Figure 1.5 William Cowper's poem 'The Negro's Complaint', *Quebec Gazette*, 21 January 1790, p. 4, image credit Bibliothèque et Archives nationales du Québec.

read within the context of the wider performance of *The Padlock* given that the play is not an antislavery text, noting that there is no evidence that this epilogue was ever performed as part of the wider play.[92] Nevertheless, according to Carey's survey of plays, the abolitionist thrust of the 'Epilogue' sets it apart from contemporaneous plays. Carey notes that plays tended to overstate their sentimental rhetoric and damage their antislavery power, and that they did not play a central role in supporting the political anti-slave-trade campaign or play a key role in the development of antislavery rhetoric in eighteenth-century Britain.[93]

In the *QG*, the 'Epilogue' is divorced from theatrical references and reads as a piece of verse. It is set out in stanzas and a new line is introduced as a title to the text: 'A Black is supposed to be

The representation of slavery in Quebec's newspapers 49

introduced to an English Audience after an Entertainment.'[94] The theatrical context of the text is lost because the title describing it as an epilogue to Bickerstaffe's play is not reproduced.[95] Moreover, the description of the text as the speech of Bickerstaffe's character, Mungo ('MUNGO speaks:'), is removed, and the *QG* presented the opening line in Standard English rather than non-Standard English as it was in the original text.

The 'Epilogue' is different to the poems and political texts reprinted by Neilson that imagine enslaved people calling for abolitionist sympathy from a foreign and exotic setting. Readers of the *Quebec Gazette* who were part of the British Atlantic world could have identified themselves as part of a broader British audience for the poem and seen themselves as an intended audience for the enslaved person's appeal for abolition of the slave trade. The more general appeal to those 'Britons' in 'British lands' outside Britain itself invites readers to make this leap. This poem was reprinted within Neilson's newspaper within a wider context of anti-slave-trade sentiment and creating sympathy for enslaved African people, who had been wrongly categorised as 'chattel' rather than 'men', reinforcing readers' sense that they were part of an anti-slave-trade reading community.

Readers in Quebec may have identified themselves as belonging to the 'Free born British lands' that the enslaved person addresses. The enslaved persona claims his 'English audience' should feel more abolitionist sympathy for enslaved Africans because they are British: 'My tale, in any place would force a tear/ But calls for stronger, deeper feelings here!' The 'here' referred to in 'The Negro's Recital' printed in the *QG* (the reprinted and edited 'Epilogue' text) was the audience in the English theatre (the 'English audience') and more broadly Britain and its citizens, who were appealed to directly ('I speak to BRITONS'). The enslaved persona appeals to a sense that the British were especially able to feel sentimental sympathy for the enslaved man and the sufferings he had related, or that they should have demonstrated this sympathy, given their love of liberty and sentimental natures. This invited readers in Quebec to imagine that they were listening in on an abolitionist speech, aimed at a small community of English listeners. This group of imagined listeners might have represented the British public, Parliament, or nation, but the terms used throughout are generic, such as 'English audience'

50 · *Beyond the antislavery haven*

THE NEGROE's RECITAL.

A Black is suppposed to be introduced to an English Audience after an Entertainment.

THANK you, my Masters—have you
   laugh'd your fill ?
Then let me speak, nor take that freedom ill.
E'en from *my* tongue some heartfelt truths
   may fall,
And outrag'd Nature claim the care of all.
My tale, in any place, would force a tear,
But calls for stronger, deeper feelings *here* !
For whilst I tread the free-born BRITISH land;
Whilst now before me crouds of BRITONS
   stand ;
Vain, vain that glorious privilege to me,
I am a Slave, where all things else are free!

Yet was I born, as you are, no man's slave,
And heir to all that liberal Nature gave !
My thoughts can reason, and my limbs can
   move
The same as your's ; like your's my heart can
   love :
Alike my body food and sleep sustain ;
Alike our wants, our pleasure, and our pain.
One sun rolls o'er us, common skies around ;
One grave supports us, and one grave must
   bound !

Why then am I devoid of all to live
That manly comforts to a man can give ?
To live—untaught Religion's soothing balm,
Or life's choice arts; to live—unknown the
   calm

Of soft domestic ease ; the sweets of life,
The duteous offspring, and th' obedient wife.
To live—to liberty, and rights unknown,
Not even the common benefits my own.
No arm to guard me from *Oppression's rod*,
My will subservient to a tyrant's nod !
No gentle hand, when life is in decay,
To sooth my pains, and charm my cares away ;
But, helpless, left to quit the horrid stage,
Harrass'd in youth, and desolate in age !

But I was born on AFRIC's tawny strand,
And you—in fair BRITANNIA's fairer land.
Comes freedom then from colour?—Blush with
   shame,
And let strong Nature's crimson mark your
   blame !
I speak to BRITONS—BRITONS, then, behold
A man by *Britons snar'd, and seiz'd, and sold* !
And yet no BRITISH statute damns the deed,
Nor do the more than murderous villains bleed !

O sons of Freedom ! equalize your laws,
Be all consistent—plead the Negro's cause ;
That all the Nations in your code may see
The British Negro, like the Briton, free !
But should he supplicate your laws in vain,
To break for ever this disgraceful chain,
At least, let gentle usage so abate
The galling terrors of its passing state,
That he may share the *Great Creator's* plan,
For though no Briton, *Mungo* is—*a man* !

SLAVE TRADE.

THE Africans, says the ingenious and humane Author of the HISTORICAL POCKET LIBRARY, just published, p. 92. are not, as the Americans were, in their rough and simple state of nature. They are in the most disgraceful situation of human degeneracy. Being daily exposed to the lions which dispute and divide with them the woods—they sell themselves and are sold for the most abject drudgery. Those who once taught learning to the world, and contended for its empire, with abilities that long balanced the glory and prosperity of conquering Rome, are now the slaves of the rest of the world, which is equally disgraced for thus trampling like tyrants on the common and natural rights of their fellow creatures.

Figure 1.6 'The Negro's Recital' poem, *Quebec Gazette*, 16 December 1790, p. 4, image credit Bibliothèque et Archives nationales du Québec.

and 'Free born British lands', and they could equally refer to any British colonial possession, including Quebec. Through reading the poem, Canadians could imagine themselves as part of a benevolent British community sensitive to the appeals of enslaved Africans and feeling abolitionist sympathy for the abolition of the slave trade and as part of a special transnational British community that valued

The representation of slavery in Quebec's newspapers 51

liberty. The direct address 'I speak to BRITONS – BRITONS, then, behold' merges the audience in the poem with the role of the reader who also occupies the role of audience. In a more general sense, the poem flatters the British national character, appealing to a sense of British specialness in depicting the British people as lovers of liberty. The description of the 'British lands' could equally have been a reference to the British American colonies. Rather than see this reprinted British anti-slave-trade poem, with what Carey describes as its ameliorationist undertones, as a foreign reprint, understanding it within the broader anti-slave-trade stance in the *QG* and examining how the readers/audience are addressed with the poem reveals that by reading this, Quebec readers could imagine themselves as belonging to a community with particular sympathies for the sufferings of enslaved Africans.

This chapter has argued that, during the period 1789–93, two newspaper editors in Quebec produced a local anti-slave-trade sentiment through reprinting materials from the international slave-trade debate and excluding pro-slave-trade texts. Rather than seeing these texts as foreign reprints that did not reflect local attitudes about slavery in the wider Americas and the Atlantic slave trade, it has shown that, through reprinting these texts and layering them together, the editors Neilson and Mesplet created particular responses to these debates. In the business and community sections of the newspaper, advertisements for enslaved people were part of everyday business, but in the outward-looking, discursive sections, the editors aligned their community with anti-slave-trade arguments. This contradiction was possible because the reprinted abolitionist texts focused on the Atlantic slave trade and slavery in the wider Americas and did not depict slavery in Quebec. The newspapers in the colonies that would later become Canada participated in a shared Anglo-American abolitionist print culture during this period. Further research is necessary to examine Canada within studies of the circulation of abolition and slavery print culture. The study of the two newspapers in this chapter has shown that Canadian newspapers, their editors, and readers were much more informed about, and in touch with, transatlantic slavery debates than previously acknowledged. Canada's self-image as an antislavery space and its participation in transatlantic slavery debates began in earnest in its newspapers, at the site where its most prominent printed accounts of slavery in Canada circulated. This predated the better-known depiction of Canada in Black Atlantic slave narratives as an antislavery space by several decades. It indicates that, to recover Canada's slaveholding past, scholars need to look for the early transatlantic voices and reprints in Canadian newspapers. They will need to continue to challenge how the original national place of publication of abolitionist texts is privileged and reprints are undervalued, and on examining newspapers more holistically.

Notes

1 For simplicity, this chapter uses the term 'Quebec' throughout to refer to the province of Quebec, although after 1791, when the colony of Quebec was divided into the two colonies of Upper Canada and Lower Canada, the newspapers under discussion here were published in what became Lower Canada.

2 David Copeland, 'America, 1750–1820', in Hannah Barker and Simon Burrows (eds), *Press, Politics and the Public Sphere in Europe and North America 1760–1820* (Cambridge: Cambridge University Press, 2002), p. 149. Hannah Barker, *Newspapers, Politics and Public Opinion in Late Eighteenth-Century England* (Oxford: Clarendon Press, 1998), p. 95, p. 97.

3 See Jared Gardner, *The Rise and Fall of Early American Magazine Culture* (Urbana: University of Illinois Press, 2012), pp. 3–4, and Benjamin Fagan, *The Black Newspaper and the Chosen Nation* (Athens: University of Georgia Press, 2016), p. 15, p. 3.

4 Marcel Trudel, *Canada's Forgotten Slaves: Two Hundred Years of Bondage*, trans. George Tombs (Montreal: Véhicule Press, 2013), p. 76.

5 Maya Jasanoff, *Liberty's Exiles: The Loss of America and the Remaking of the British Empire* (London: HarperPress, 2011), pp. 8–9; and Robin W. Winks, *The Blacks in Canada: A History*, 2nd edn (Montreal and Kingston: McGill-Queen's University Press, 1997), pp. 32–33. On the enslaved people who arrived in Atlantic Canada with their Loyalist enslavers, including in Nova Scotia, see Harvey Amani Whitfield, *North to Bondage: Loyalist Slavery in the Maritimes* (Vancouver: UBC Press, 2016).

6 Maureen Moynagh, '"This History's Only Good for Anger": Gender and Cultural Memory in Beatrice Chancy', in Joseph Pivato (ed.), *Africadian Atlantic: Essays on George Elliott Clarke* (Toronto: Guernica Editions, 2012), p. 100.

The representation of slavery in Quebec's newspapers   53

7 For Olivier Le Jeune's recorded voice in the original 1632 and 1633 editions of the *Jesuit Relations* published in Paris with an English translation, see Reuben Gold Thwaites (ed.), *The Jesuit Relations and Allied Documents, Vol. 5: Quebec, 1632–1633* (Cleveland: The Burrows Brothers Co, 1897), p. 63 and p. 198. For the trial testimony, see Archives du Séminaire de Québec, Documents Faribault, 20 August 1638, p. 17, cited in Trudel, *Canada's Forgotten Slaves*, pp. 16–17, p. 273, n. 2.

8 Brett Rushforth, *Bonds of Alliance: Indigenous and Atlantic Slaveries in New France* (Chapel Hill: The University of North Carolina Press, 2012), p. 393; Whitfield, *North to Bondage*, p. 83, p. 95. For an example of a court document relating to slavery in Nova Scotia, see the testimony of the enslaved woman Diana, in 'R. v. Andrews, 19 May 1801, Shelburne County Special Court of Oyer and Terminer', Nova Scotia Archives, African Nova Scotians in the Age of Slavery in Abolition, https://archives.novascotia.ca/africanns/archives/?ID=61 (accessed 15 March 2023).

9 Afua Cooper, *The Hanging of Angelique: The Untold Story of Canadian Slavery and the Burning of Old Montreal* (Athens: University of Georgia Press, 2007).

10 On the lack of newspapers in New France, see John Dickinson and Brian Young, *A Short History of Quebec*, 4th edn (Montreal: McGill-Queen's University Press, 2008), p. 92. On the point that slavery in New France is not represented in newspapers, see Rushforth, *Bonds of Alliance*, p. 291.

11 Robin W. Winks, *The Blacks in Canada: A History*, 2nd edn (Montreal and Kingston: McGill-Queen's University Press, 1997), p. 100.

12 Marie Tremaine, 'Newspapers', in *A Bibliography of Canadian Imprints, 1751–1800* (Toronto: University of Toronto Press, 1952), pp. 594–659.

13 The popularity and longevity of these newspapers is evident when compared to other newspapers in Quebec in the eighteenth century. See Tremaine's survey in 'Newspapers', pp. 594–659.

14 Rushforth, *Bonds of Alliance*.

15 *Ibid.*, p. 398.

16 *Ibid.*, p. 370. A search of Frank Mackey's Appendix and my own search of the *QG* and *MG* found that advertisements frequently described self-liberated people using terms that we now know to be offensive – 'negro' or 'mulatto', but not 'Indian' – or terms that might imply Indigenous heritage. See Frank Mackey, 'Appendix I: Newspaper Notices', in *Done with Slavery: The Black Fact in Montreal 1760–1840* (Montreal and Kingston: McGill-Queen's University Press, 2010), pp. 308–44. Eighteenth-century fugitive advertisements published in

Britain included Native American and African enslaved people, as indicated by a search of the database of the Runaway Slaves in Britain Project, 'Runaway Slaves in Britain: Bondage, Freedom, and Race in the Eighteenth Century', www.runaways.gla.ac.uk (accessed 15 March 2023).

17 Rushforth, *Bonds of Alliance*, pp. 378–82.

18 *Ibid.*, pp. 369 and 379.

19 Jean-Francis Gervais, 'William Brown', *Dictionary of Canadian Biography*, www.biographi.ca/en/bio/brown_william_4E.html (accessed 15 March 2023).

20 *Ibid.*

21 *Ibid.*

22 *Ibid.*

23 Mary D. Turnbull, 'William Dunlap, Colonial Printer, Journalist, and Minister', *The Pennsylvania Magazine of History and Biography* 103:2 (1979), 151–52.

24 For a contemporary notice regarding William Brown's death and Samuel Neilson's commencement as editor, see *QG* (26 March 1789), p. 3, British Library, reel BL.M.C.271.B. All subsequent references to the *QG* in this chapter will refer to this microfilm reel.

25 John E. Hare, 'Samuel Neilson', *Dictionary of Canadian Biography*, www.biographi.ca.en/bio/neilson_samuel_1771_93_4E.html (accessed 15 March 2023).

26 James H. Lambert 'Alexander Spark', *Dictionary of Canadian Biography*, www.biographi.ca/en/bio/spark_alexander_5E.html (accessed 15 March 2023).

27 Green, 'The British Book in North America', p. 594.

28 The biographical information in this paragraph is based on Claude Galarneau, 'Fleury Mesplet', *Dictionary of Canadian Biography*, www.biographi.ca/en/bio/mesplet_fleury_4E.html (accessed 15 March 2023).

29 *Ibid.*

30 Hare, 'Samuel Neilson'.

31 'Proposal for the Establishment of a New Gazette', *MG*, British Library, reel BL M.C.270. All subsequent references to the *MG* in this chapter are from this microfilm reel.

32 'Such Persons as are willing to Subscribe …', *MG* (6 October 1785), p. 4. For an early call for subscribers to sign their names in a book, see 'The Printer to the Public.' *MG* (25 August 1785), p. 1.

33 Tremaine, *A Bibliography*, pp. 594–659.

34 *Ibid.*, p. 630.

35 Gérard Laurence, 'The Newspaper Press in Quebec and Lower Canada', in Patricia Lockhart Fleming, Gilles Gallichan, and Yvan Lamonde

The representation of slavery in Quebec's newspapers   55

(eds), *The History of the Book in Canada, Volume One, Beginnings to 1840* (Toronto: University of Toronto Press, 2004), pp. 234–35.

36 *Ibid.*, p. 235.

37 Trudel, *Canada's Forgotten Slaves*, p. 110.

38 *Ibid.*, p. 110.

39 *Ibid.*, p. 110.

40 For example, see the advertisements in the *Quebec Gazette* 'Ran Away from the Printing-Office in Quebec' (27 November 1777), p. 3; and 'Advertisements. Ranaway from the Printing-Office in Quebec' (29 January 1788), p. 2.

41 Therese P. Lemay, 'Joe', *Dictionary of Canadian Biography*, www .biographi.ca/en/bio/joe_4E.html (accessed 15 March 2023).

42 Winks, *The Blacks in Canada*, p. 100.

43 Mackey, *Done with Slavery*, pp. 534–35, n. 28.

44 Trudel, *Canada's Forgotten Slaves*, p. 110.

45 Lemay, 'Joe'.

46 Mackey, *Done with Slavery*, pp. 534–35, n. 28.

47 See Mackey, 'Appendix I', p. 307.

48 *Ibid.*, p. 313. For examples of advertisements selling enslaved people and fugitive slave advertisements in the *Montreal Gazette*, see 'To Be Sold', *MG* (9 April 1789), p. 3; and 'Run Away on Thursday Morning Last from the Subscriber, a Mullatto Man Named TOM' (29 September 1785), p. 4.

49 Classic critical collections of fugitive slave advertisements are: Billy G. Smith and Richard Wojtowicz (eds), *Blacks Who Stole Themselves: Advertisements for Runaways in the Pennsylvania Gazette, 1728–1790* (Philadelphia: University of Pennsylvania Press, 1989); Graham Russell Hodges and Alan Edward Brown (eds), *'Pretends to be Free': Runaway Slave Advertisements from Colonial and Revolutionary New York and New Jersey* (New York: Garland Publishing, 1994); Lathan A. Windley (ed.), *Runaway Slave Advertisements: A Documentary History from the 1730s to 1790 Vol. 3. South Carolina*, 4 vols (Westport: Greenwood Press, 1983).

50 David Waldstreicher, 'Reading the Runaways: Self-Fashioning, Print Culture, and Confidence in Slavery in the Eighteenth-Century Mid-Atlantic', *William and Mary Quarterly* 56:2 (1999), 244, 247–48. https://doi.org/10.2307/2674119.

51 *Ibid.*, 253.

52 *Runaway Slave Advertisements*, comp. Windley, p. 532.

53 'Run Away from the Schooner Lucy', *QG* (5 June 1788), p. 5 and 'Eight Dollars Reward. Run Away from the Subscriber on Saturday Morning', *QG* (26 June 1788), p. 2.

56 *Beyond the antislavery haven*

54 For a substantial discussion of fugitive slave advertisements, see Charmaine A. Nelson, *Slavery, Geography and Empire in Nineteenth-Century Marine Landscapes of Montreal and Jamaica* (Abingdon: Routledge, 2016). Charmaine A. Nelson, '"Ran Away from Her Master ... a Negroe Girl Named Thursday": Examining Evidence of Punishment, Isolation, and Trauma in Nova Scotia and Quebec Fugitive Slave Advertisements', in Joshua Nichols and Amy Swiffen (eds), *Legal Violence and the Limits of the Law* (New York: Routledge, 2017). Charmaine Nelson, 'Servant, Seraglio, Savage or "Sarah": Examining the Visual Representation of Black Female Subjects in Canadian Art and Visual Culture', in Nina Reid-Maroney, Boulou Ebanda de B'béri, and Wanda Thomas Bernard (eds), *Women in the 'Promised Land': Essays in African Canadian History* (Toronto: Women's Press, 2018), pp. 43–74. Harvey Amani Whitfield, *Black Slavery in the Maritimes: A History in Documents* (Peterborough, ON: Broadview Press, 2018).

55 George Elliott Clarke, '"This Is No Hearsay": Reading the Canadian Slave Narratives', *Papers of the Bibliographical Society of Canada* 43:1 (2005), 17, 18, n. 19. https://doi.org/10.33137/pbsc.v43i1.18415.

56 Winfried Siemerling, *The Black Atlantic Reconsidered: Black Canadian Writing, Cultural History and the Presence of the Past* (Montreal and Kingston: McGill-Queen's University Press, 2015), pp. 33–37.

57 Maureen G. Elgersman, *Unyielding Spirits: Black Women and Slavery in Early Canada and Jamaica* (London: Routledge, 1999) and Harvey Amani Whitfield, *North to Bondage*.

58 Trudel, *Canada's Forgotten Slaves*, p. 235.

59 Winks, *The Blacks in Canada*, p. 100.

60 Mackey, 'Appendix I', pp. 325–37.

61 *Ibid.*, pp. 325–37.

62 For 1789–93 as the peak moment in sentimental rhetoric in the British slave-trade debates, see for example Brycchan Carey, *British Abolitionism and the Rhetoric of Sensibility: Writing, Sentiment and Slavery, 1760–1807* (Basingstoke: Palgrave Macmillan, 2005), p. 196.

63 Seymour Drescher, 'The Shocking Birth of British Abolitionism', *Slavery & Abolition* 33:4 (2012), 576. https://doi.org/10.1080/0144039X.2011.644070.

64 Winks, *The Blacks in Canada*, p. 35.

65 'Negroes: To the Printer of the St. J. Chronicle', *St James's Chronicle or the British Evening Post* (27–29 August 1789), p. 2. Burney Newspapers Collection.

66 'From Woodfall's Register, London May 13, House of Commons, Tuesday May 12, The Slave Trade', *QG* (13 August 1789), pp. 2–4. The

The representation of slavery in Quebec's newspapers   57

speech was originally printed in the *Diary or Woodfall's Register*, 'Slave Trade' (13 May 1789), pp. 2–4. Burney Newspapers Collection.

67 John Wolfe, 'William Wilberforce', *Oxford Dictionary of National Biography*, www.oxforddnb.com/view/article/29386 (accessed 13 March 2023).

68 'Chambre des Communes, LONDRES, Mardi le 12 Mai, 1789. Debat sur le Commerce D'esclaves' (20 August 1789), p. 4. This was continued on 27 August 1789, p. 4, and 3 September 1789, p. 4.

69 For the Twelve Prepositions, see 'The Diary, London, May 14, 1789', *Diary or Woodfall's Register* (14 May 1789), p. 2; Burney Newspapers Collection, and 'Correct and Authentic Copies of the Twelve Propositions Submitted on Tuesday Evening the 12th May Last, by Mr. Wilberforce ...', *QG* (20 August 1789), p. 3.

70 'To the Printer of *The Diary*: Slave Trade: Letter I', *Diary or Woodfall's Register* (16 May 1789), p. 2. Burney Newspapers Collection.

71 'Slave Trade, A Card', *Diary or Woodfall's Register* (18 May 1789), p. 3. Burney Newspapers Collection.

72 'Slave Trade: The Following Petition Has Been Presented to the House of Commons on Behalf of the Planters and Owners of Property in the Island of St. Christopher', *Diary or Woodfall's Register* (18 May 1789), pp. 3–4. Burney Newspapers Collection.

73 'Quebec, April 19', *QG* (19 April 1792), p. 2.

74 Srividhya Swaminathan, *Debating the Slave Trade: Rhetoric of British National Identity, 1759–1815* (Farnham: Ashgate, 2009), pp. 3–4.

75 *Ibid.*, p. 4.

76 *Ibid.*, pp. 215–16.

77 'Paris, May 25', *QG* (3 September 1789), p. 1; 'London, June 2 to 10', *QG* (3 September 1789), p. 2; and 'Il s'enfuit de Québec Lundi dernier matin', *QG* (3 September 1789), p. 3.

78 'Sunday, Aug. 28', *QG* (24 November 1791), p. 2.

79 Trudel, *Canada's Forgotten Slaves*, p. 234

80 For an example of American slavery and antislavery texts in Nova Scotian newspapers, see the poem titled 'From a Late New York Paper. Advertisement', *The Royal Gazette and the Nova Scotia Advertiser* (26 January 1790), p. 4, Nova Scotia Archives, reel 8163.

81 'London, May 9: Slave Trade', *MG* (20 August 1789), pp. 1–2; 'London, May 13', *MG* (27 August 1789), pp. 1–2.

82 'Extract at Large from That Part of Mr. Necker's Speech Which Concerns the Slave Trade', *MG* (3 September 1789), p. 2.

83 'Extracts from the Instructions of Some of the Bailiwicks Relating to the Abolition of the Slave Trade', *MG* (10 September 1789), p. 1.

84 'London, May 16: Correct and Authentick Copies of the Twelve Propositions Submitted on Tuesday Evening by Mr Wilberforce ...' *MG* (1 October 1789), pp. 1–3.

85 'London, May 9: Slave Trade', *MG* (20 August 1789), pp. 1–2.

86 'London, May 13', *MG* (27 August 1789), pp. 1–2. 'Extract at Large from That Part of Mr. Necker's Speech Which Concerns the Slave Trade', *MG* (3 September 1789), p. 2.

87 William Doyle, *The Oxford History of the French Revolution*, 2nd edn (Oxford: Oxford University Press, 2002), p. 86.

88 *Ibid.*, p. 101.

89 'Paris, May 11 to 25. His Most Christian Majesty's Speech at the Opening of the States General at Versailles, the 5th of May, 1789', *MG* (3 September 1789), pp. 1–2.

90 'Parnassian Flowers. The Negro's Complaint, A Song, To the Tune of Hosier's Ghost', *MG* (11 June 1789), p. 4. 'The Following Beautiful and Pathetic Lines by Mr COWPER Need Not Other Introduction Than the Name of Their Author', *QG* (21 January 1790), p. 4. 'Song. The Dying Negro', *QG* (21 June 1792), p. 2. For a modern reproduction of Sayers's poem, see James G. Basker (ed.), *Amazing Grace: An Anthology of Poems about Slavery, 1660–1810* (New Haven: Yale University Press, 2002), p. 401. For the 'Epilogue', see 'The Negro's Recital', *QG* (16 December 1790), p. 4.

91 Brycchan Carey, 'To Force a Tear: British Abolitionism and the Eighteenth-Century London Stage', in Stephen Ahern (ed.), *Affect and Abolition in the Anglo-Atlantic: 1770–1830* (Farnham: Ashgate, 2013), p. 122.

92 *Ibid.*, p. 120, p. 122.

93 *Ibid.*, p. 128.

94 'The Negro's Recital', *QG* (16 December 1790), p. 4.

95 'Epilogue to "The Padlock", From the Gentleman's Magazine', www.brycchancarey.com/slavery/padlock1.htm (accessed 1 November 2018).

2

Canada in the antebellum slave narrative, 1849–57

The Introduction showed that there was a textual expectation in nineteenth-century literature that the self-liberated person's arrival in Canada West, now known as Ontario, would be imagined as a moment of liberation, as they crossed the border and became free.[1] This chapter explores what happens in the slave narrative after that moment. In the 1850s, a new way of depicting Canada as part of the self-liberated and free Black person's experience developed. Several slave narratives from the 1850s present the lives of self-liberated and free Black people in Canada West.[2] There is a recurring pattern in how self-liberated people depict their lives in freedom in Canada West, focused on their experience of clearing, cultivating, and owning land. This chapter focuses on two book-length narratives that epitomise this focus on Canadian land: Benjamin Drew's edited collection *A North-Side View of Slavery: The Refugee: Or the Narratives of Fugitive Slaves in Canada* and Austin Steward's slave narrative, *Twenty-Two Years a Slave and Forty Years a Freeman*. *The Refugee* is a collection of over a hundred narratives transcribed and edited by Drew and published in 1856, in which free Black and self-liberated people living in Canada West relate their experiences of slavery and freedom. The narratives were collected by Drew as he toured the region in 1855, with the assistance of the Canadian Anti-Slavery Society. *Twenty-Two Years a Slave and Forty Years a Freeman* was first published in 1857. Steward was a self-liberated man, who had lived for many years as a free man in the United States and Upper Canada during the 1830s, when he came to write his experiences of slavery and freedom.

60   *Beyond the antislavery haven*

Drew and Steward complicate the image of Canada as an anti-slavery haven that we get if we focus exclusively on moments of arrival in the slave narrative. The Canadian wilderness in these narratives is presented as both a place where self-liberated and free Black people could forge new lives in freedom and an exploitative space, where fugitives could be 'obliged to lose all their labour' and where they could be bound into new exploitative relationships through labouring in the wilderness.[3] These narratives unsettle the border between slavery and freedom, and between the United States and Canada. They show a more porous boundary and a continuity of an experience of economic exploitation in North America, as it is textually constructed in the narratives. They problematise George Elliott Clarke's claim that the antebellum slave narrative presents an idealised image of Canada as an antislavery haven and that this has 'obscured' an earlier history of slavery in Canada.[4] These narratives present a far more complex depiction of Canada, which adds to the one-dimensional image of Canada that critics have identified in the British context. This develops Audrey Fisch's and Sarah Meer's finding that the representation of Canada in American slavery narratives that were circulated in Britain produced a nationalistic English discourse.[5] As the research in this chapter shows, this image was produced within a transatlantic context in which the representation of Canada was more varied and could criticise capitalist exploitation and English elites, while at the same time presenting an idealised image of Canada as an antislavery haven, as self-liberated people crossed the border.

Canadian literature shaped and was shaped by the slave narrative, which is something scholars have more fully explored for other national literary genres. Scholars have long acknowledged and explored how American and British literature was drawn on by authors of slave narratives to write into print their experiences of slavery, and these genres were shaped by the slave narrative in turn.[6] They have shown, for example, that the British Victorian novel influenced the slave narrative and the slave narrative shaped the form of some British Victorian novels; and that sentimental nineteenth-century American fiction was a key literary influence on slave narratives.[7] This chapter explores how Canadian literary genres have shaped the slave narrative, as well as British and American literary traditions, and it explores one way in which Canada has

Canada in the antebellum slave narrative

left its generic influence on the slave narrative by looking at the connections between slave narratives and Canadian female settler narratives. It does so through exploring the intertextual connection between Steward's text and the work of the canonical Canadian settler Susanna Moodie née Strickland, who also transcribed the slave narratives of Ashton Warner and Mary Prince, the latter being the first Black female autobiography published in Britain. Steward crafts a different narrative of the Canadian wilderness to many of the accounts in Drew's collection: his is not a story of Black emigrant success or of his own exploitation through land. Steward creates a middle-class narrative of thriving in the Canadian bush itself as unachievable, and appropriates Susanna Moodie's successful narrative of failed middle-class settlement, *Roughing It in the Bush*, first published in the United States and Britain in 1852 (and as a Canadian edition in 1871), in order to describe his experience and his return to the United States.

Equiano's *The Interesting Narrative*, 1789

Prior to the mid-nineteenth century, there are no precedents for representing Canada West in the slave narrative genre, and before the 1850s, the slave narrative stops as the self-liberated person crosses the border. However, there are earlier precedents for representing the lives of self-liberated people in Atlantic Canada in eighteenth-century Black autobiographical narratives. Two Black Loyalist narratives by Boston King and David George and the journal of the Black missionary John Marrant will be discussed in Chapter 3. Here, the focus is on *The Interesting Narrative of the Life of Olaudah Equiano, or Gustavus Vassa, the African, Written by Himself*, first published in 1789 in the context of the anti-slave-trade campaign in Britain, in which Olaudah Equiano depicts his experiences in Atlantic Canada. While an enslaved man to an officer in the British Navy during the Seven Years' War, Equiano describes being on board a boat with General James Wolfe in 1758 as part of the British seizure of the French port of Louisbourg, Cape Breton, which was tactically placed as a defence of the St Lawrence River, and his wider narrative represents his life after he gains his freedom in 1766.[8] In 1759, Wolfe led British troops to victory over the

62 *Beyond the antislavery haven*

French at the Battle of the Plains of Abraham, which resulted in the British capture of Quebec. Wolfe died in the battle and at the time of Equiano's writing was a celebrated war hero in Britain. Through depicting his presence at this moment of British military success and the capture and conquest of Canada, Equiano appeals to patriotic British sentiments and creates a point of identification between him and his British readers. As Brycchan Carey notes, Equiano's description of his presence at the Siege of Louisbourg (1758) gave him 'a certain amount of moral authority in the eyes of his contemporaries ... [and part of what] make[s] the end of this phase of the book, when Pascal sells him into plantation slavery, all the more shocking', revealing that these patriotic British moments were part of Equiano's anti-slave-trade political agenda.[9] Whilst there were early precedents for depicting Atlantic Canada in the slave narrative, it was another half-century before life in Canada West started to be represented textually.

Ending at the Canada–US border: the slave narrative before the 1850s

The Narrative of the Life of Henry Bibb, 1849

The Narrative of the Life of Henry Bibb is typical of how Canada is imaginatively constructed in the slave narrative prior to the 1850s. Henry Bibb moved to Canada West in November 1850, and continued to work for the American abolition movement, helping to establish two antislavery societies, and he set up his newspaper, *The Voice of the Fugitive*, before he died in Windsor in Canada in 1854.[10] Canada West does not feature as a narrative space in the *Narrative of the Life of Henry Bibb*, but it does occupy a dominant space in the narrative; it is mentioned forty-four times by Bibb, and provides a place of imagined safety and refuge for the fugitive from slavery in the text.[11] Throughout the narrative, Canada generates suspense and frustration as it functions as a goal and catalyst for action, inspiring Bibb to run away from slavery in the United States and providing him with a place to which he can escape. Bibb offers a humorous nod to this narrative back and forth after recounting

Canada in the antebellum slave narrative 63

his many thwarted attempts to reach Canada by the use of the word 'yet' in 'by which I might yet run away and go to Canada'.[12] His dream of reaching Canada is depicted as a quest akin to Homer's *Odyssey*. Bibb encounters delays and obstacles; he has to stop and earn money to get to Canada, and he returns for his wife and child when it looks as if he is just about to become free.

Canada West is presented as a political refuge for self-liberated people in Bibb's narrative. His preface conceives freedom as being legally defined as a 'human being' and not as 'chattel'.[13] Bibb presents Canada West as an ideal refuge for fugitives from slavery in the United States, as self-liberated people are legally recognised as men under British law. Bibb is told to make his way to Canada by a free Black man called Mr Dundy. Dundy describes Canada as a land 'over which waved freedom's flag, defended by the British government, upon whose soil there cannot be the foot print of a slave'.[14] The flag signifies an absolute boundary with the United States. His description of the impossibility of slavery existing in Canada creates an image of Canada as a non-slaveholding space. Bibb shows the tenuous status of fugitives from slavery as free people (rather than property) in the United States, and this reinforces a sense that Canada is special in its promise of a legal definition of 'human being' for fugitives. Bibb describes his attempts to run away with his wife and child as 'striving to make our way from slavery'.[15] This reflects the literal journey away from the plantation and the sense that, as fugitives from slavery in the United States, they are still to some extent experiencing slavery. He describes his recapture in Cincinnati, Ohio as having potential to 'change me back into property', highlighting that even in the free states, fugitives from slavery can be returned to his definition as property.[16]

Bibb's narrative expresses some tension that the longed-for anti-slavery haven of Canada may be in part a literary convention rather than a lived reality. Throughout his narrative, Bibb depicts Canada as the only place where he can imagine living as a free man. Yet at the end of his narrative, Bibb signs off from New York City.[17] This locates him as a free man in the United States, despite the strong imaginative pull of Canada as the site of freedom throughout his narrative.

64 *Beyond the antislavery haven*

Beyond the border: Canada in the mid-1850s slave narrative

Before the mid-1850s, slave narratives frequently ended with the self-liberated person's arrival in Canada West. After 1855, self-liberated people found new ways to narrate their experiences beyond the moment of arrival, reflecting a broader aesthetic struggle in the mid-nineteenth century to represent freedom. John Stauffer argues that, in the 1850s, the authors of slave narratives faced an aesthetic challenge when it came to representing their lives as free people.[18] Stauffer focuses on Frederick Douglass's second autobiography, *My Bondage and My Freedom*, published in 1855. He argues that Douglass faced a 'crisis of language and aesthetics'.[19] Stauffer provides a summary of the shift taking place in the aesthetics of the slave narrative genre in the mid-1850s:

> [prior to Douglass's 1855 autobiography] [n]arrators focused on their life in bondage and described the horrors of slavery in the hope of converting readers to abolitionism. The teleology of slave narratives centred around the moment of freedom. But narratives of freedom had not been developed.[20]

Stauffer highlights the newness of Douglass's attempts to narrate his life after slavery. He explains that, 'in writing *My Bondage [and My Freedom]*, he created a new genre that describes a life in freedom, rather than ending at the moment of freedom, as all previous slave narratives had done'.[21] Although Stauffer does not attend to the earlier context of eighteenth-century slave narratives that represent the lives of self-liberated people in freedom, he makes a useful distinction between 'the moment of freedom', the textual moment in which an enslaved person becomes free that typically signals the end of slave narratives prior to the mid-1850s, and 'narratives of freedom', in which an enslaved person attempts to construct a narrative of their life as a free person in the slave narrative genre. Stauffer does not specifically consider the implications of this 'crisis in aesthetics' for the presentation of Canada in the slave narrative, but the shift he sees in the aesthetics of the slave narrative genre in the mid-1850s provides a useful context in which to understand the imaginative depiction of Canada in the genre up until and during the 1850s, when Canada was used for the first time as a narrative space in which to explore the lives of self-liberated people living in freedom.

Canada in the antebellum slave narrative   65

In Drew's collection, the narratives are arranged into fourteen sections, corresponding to the locations in Canada West that Drew visited, such as Toronto, London, and Queen's Bush. In the introduction, Drew states that there are two reasons why he has transcribed and published oral interviews with fugitives from slavery in Canada: firstly, 'to collect, with a view to placing their testimony on record, their experiences of the actual workings of slavery'; and, secondly, to collect and publish 'what experience they have had of the condition of liberty'.[22]

Austin Steward's 1857 slave narrative, *Twenty-Two Years a Slave and Forty Years a Freeman*, develops a fuller account of his life and the lives of self-liberated people in Canada after the 'moment of freedom' and moment of arrival in Canada than previous slave narratives had done.[23] The first third of Steward's narrative presents his experiences of slavery in the United States, and, as Jane Pease and William Pease have noted, the majority of the narrative focuses on his life post-slavery: '[Steward] devoted two-thirds of it to his life as a freeman.'[24] Indeed, Steward depicts living in freedom in Canada in chapters 19–34 of his narrative. In these chapters, Steward recalls his time living in Canada between 1831 and 1837 as president of a Black settlement called the Wilberforce Settlement, a community of several hundred free Black and self-liberated people who fled from Cincinnati to Canada West in the early 1830s. Steward expands the generic constraints he inherited in his fuller representation of life in Canada after crossing the border.

Readers today could overlook the fact that accounts of post-slavery life in Canada West are a key part of the slave narrative genre in the 1850s. However, nineteenth-century readers may have been more sensitive to this. Title pages of slave narratives published in the 1850s indicate that authors and publishers invited readers to approach them as narratives of post-slavery lives in freedom as much as (or perhaps more than) narratives of slavery. Title pages contain large type to draw attention to the aspect of the narratives that related the life of fugitives from slavery after the moment of liberation. In this way, readers were invited to approach slave narratives not predominantly as accounts of bondage and escape but as narratives of freedom after slavery. For example, the title page of Austin Steward's slave narrative gives a greater focus to the text as an account of Steward's post-slavery life than in slavery. This is

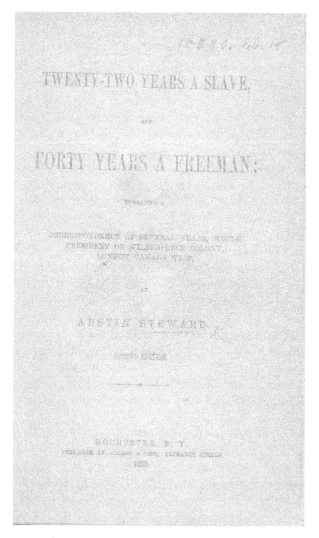

Figure 2.1 Title page of the second edition of Austin Steward's *Twenty-Two Years a Slave and Forty Years a Freeman*, 1859, © British Library Board, shelfmark 10880.bb.15.

reflected in the larger type of 'FORTY YEARS A FREEMAN' compared to that of 'TWENTY-TWO YEARS A SLAVE' on the original title page (Figure 2.1). Similarly, on the title page of Frederick Douglass's second slave narrative, *My Bondage and My Freedom*, an instant bestseller that sold fifteen thousand copies when

Canada in the antebellum slave narrative 67

published in New York in 1855, the words 'My Freedom' appear in much larger type than the words 'My Bondage' (Figure 2.2).[25] The balance this text attempts to achieve between these two parts of Douglass's life is reflected further in the description of the text as in two balanced parts: 'Part 1 – Life as a Slave' and 'Part II – Life as a Freeman'. Advertisements for Douglass's book, printed in his newspaper *Frederick Douglass's Paper*, also replicate this larger type being used for the words 'My Freedom', and this shows the wider circulation of the idea that the narrative's relation of Douglass's life as a free man is the most important part of this text.[26]

As readers today, we are often invited by front covers to read these narratives as accounts of experiences of slavery rather than as narratives of freedom. The cover of a recent edition of Austin Steward's 1857 slave narrative, published in 2004, reverses the emphasis given on the original title page upon the text being about Steward's life as a freeman by placing 'Twenty-Two Years a Slave' in the largest type and making 'Forty Years a Free Man' much smaller. This invites the modern reader to approach this text as a narrative of Steward's experiences of slavery rather than an attempt to present his life as a free man. This has implications for how modern readers may approach the narrative in which Steward recollects his life in Canada because it invites them to see these parts of the narrative as less important than depictions of Steward's life in slavery. It gives less emphasis to how slave narratives in the 1850s began to craft 'narratives of freedom' for self-liberated people in Canada West, whereas previously they had presented Canada as a point of arrival in 'moments of freedom'. Similarly, a modern edition of *My Bondage, My Freedom* edited by David W. Blight does not replicate the larger type for *My Freedom* when the book was originally published and advertised, but reflects the balance between these two aspects.[27]

Narrating Black settlement in Canada: liberty in the Canadian wilderness?

The amount of space given to describing lives in Canada varies across the texts in Drew's collection, with many people focusing on

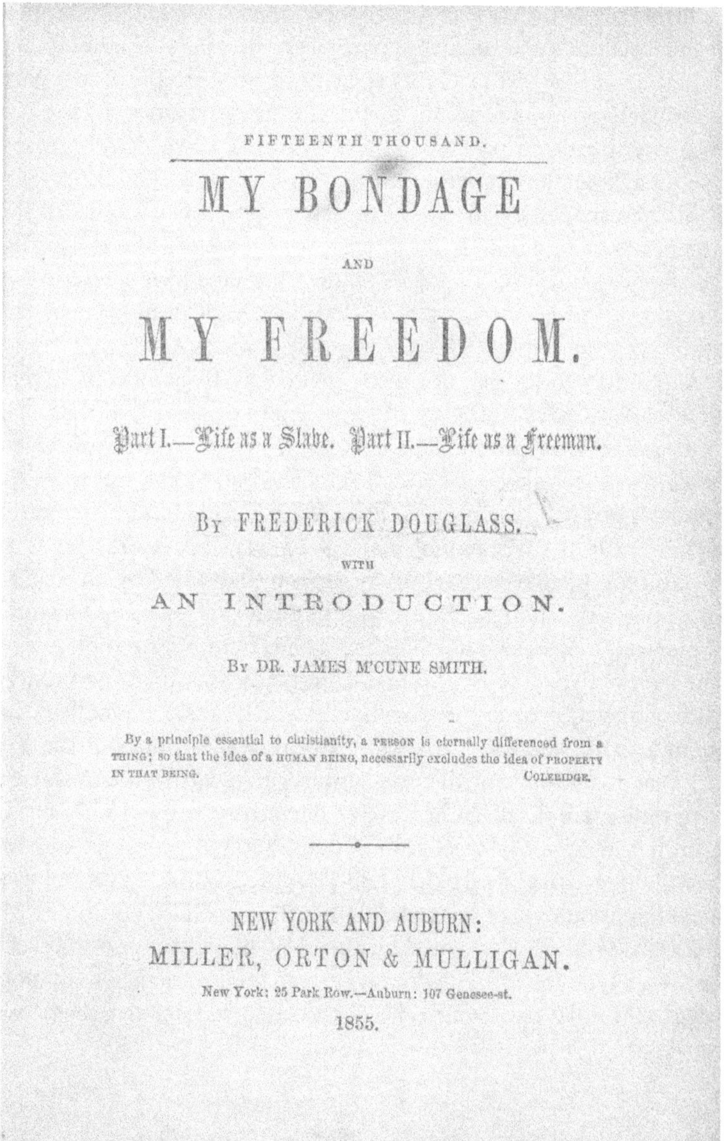

FIFTEENTH THOUSAND.

MY BONDAGE

AND

MY FREEDOM.

Part I.—Life as a Slave. Part II.—Life as a Freeman.

By FREDERICK DOUGLASS.

WITH

AN INTRODUCTION.

By DR. JAMES M'CUNE SMITH.

By a principle essential to christianity, a PERSON is eternally differenced from a THING; so that the idea of a HUMAN BEING, necessarily excludes the idea of PROPERTY IN THAT BEING.
COLERIDGE.

NEW YORK AND AUBURN:
MILLER, ORTON & MULLIGAN.
New York: 25 Park Row.—Auburn: 107 Genesee-st.

1855.

Figure 2.2 Title page of Frederick Douglass's *My Bondage and My Freedom*, 1855, © British Library Board, shelfmark 10880.bb.9.

Canada in the antebellum slave narrative 69

their experiences of slavery and giving just a sentence or two about their lives in Canada. David West's narrative focuses on his recollections of slavery and antislavery polemic. In the first few paragraphs, West describes his escape from slavery: 'When I left, I told my purpose to no one. I studied a plan by which I might get away and I succeeded.' In the next sentence, he switches to the present tense to describe his arrival in Canada: 'I am now in Canada doing well at my trade, and I expect to do yet better. My only trouble is about my wife and family. I never should have come away but for being forced away.'[28] West makes no further comment on his life in Canada, and instead reflects on the institution of slavery in the United States, which underpins the emotional impetus of his text.

The longest and richest descriptions of life after crossing the Canada–US border are contained in thirty narratives by self-liberated and free Black people that describe clearing and settling land or living in areas where cultivation was the basis of their livelihood. These settler stories were particularly fruitful spaces for the depiction of Black experiences in Canada. The narratives of Black settlement and ownership of land within Drew's collection draw upon the rhetoric of a white settler American dream in their depiction of Canadian wilderness, which is shown as a space in which self-liberated and free Black people are able to transform themselves into independent emigrants. They produce an image of the potential for self-liberated people to become independent Black yeoman farmers, and this image was one with an antislavery currency.

By contrast, narratives set in urban spaces in Canada West tend to focus on the possessions that have been attained rather than how the property was accumulated. A representative example is the narrative of Alexander Hamilton, who reached Canada in 1834. In his narrative, Hamilton relates that, since his arrival in Canada, he 'has made a good living', and he has become the owner of 'real estate in London':

> I reached Canada in 1834. I had only a dollar and a half. I had no need to beg, for I found work at once. I have done well since I came here: have made a good living and something more. I own real estate in London – three houses and several lots of land. It is a healthy country – Canada.[29]

70 *Beyond the antislavery haven*

The process of cultivating land is given space and focus in the two narratives of Mr and Mrs John Little, whose rags-to-riches story is enabled through taming the Canadian wilderness and rising through the social ranks to become a middling-status emigrant family. John Little's narrative is over nine thousand words and stretches across twenty-seven pages in the 1856 edition of Drew's text.[30] Little's narrative opens with him recounting his experience of slavery in North Carolina, where he was held in slavery by several enslavers, and his escape from slavery with his wife. He describes an incident in which he was denied a pass giving him permission to leave the plantation, and a scene in which he was whipped with the lash as a punishment and as an example to other enslaved people.[31] Little describes his and his wife's experience of clearing and settling land in Canada West. He recollects: 'we marched right into the wilderness, where there were thousands of acres of woods which the chain had never run round since Adam', depicting the place as ancient, spacious, remote, and untouched by man.[32] This conveys a sense of the Littles' energy and forcefulness through the term 'march[ing]', drawing on military language to depict them conquering the land. Through his narrative of the development of the land, John Little describes the transformation that contact with the wilderness has on the skills and personal qualities of himself and his wife. He describes himself and his wife as brave people who do not fear wolves, as resourceful in selling their labour at first to buy seeds, and as hardworking, spending all their time clearing the land: 'We went to chopping, day and night; there was no delay,' The repetition of 'we' and 'our hands' shows that it was a collective effort of Mr Little and his wife.[33]

The Littles' narratives present an image of the opportunities for self-liberated people to thrive as settlers in the Canadian bush. John Little gives a detailed account of the few possessions they took into the unsettled wilderness of Canada West and gives a dizzying list of items that they have accumulated at the time of him telling his story in 1851:

> I have one hundred and fifty acres of land: one hundred and ten of it cleared, and under good cultivation: two span of horses, a yoke of oxen, ten milch cows and young cattle, twenty head of hogs, forty heads of sheep; I have two wagons, two ploughs and two drags.[34]

Canada in the antebellum slave narrative   71

This is in stark contrast to their lack of possessions when they arrived in the woods fourteen years before. Little describes the gruelling task of clearing and cultivating the land and relates that they had no cattle or horses and he bought seeds using his own labour. He longs to encourage others in Canada West to settle in the bush:

> I would like to show it to those stout, able men, who, while they may be independent here, remain in the towns as waiters, blacking boots, cleaning houses and driving coaches for men, who scarcely allow them enough for a living. To them I say, go into the backwoods of Queen Victoria's dominions, and you can secure an independent support.[35]

Little describes the men working in urban spaces as 'independent', but also implies their dependence on others for their meagre wages. His patriotic outburst, and second-person address to Black labourers working in towns in Canada West to settle the land, labels the Canadian 'backwoods' as British, suggesting national British/Canadian superiority. On the surface, this seems to bolster Clarke's reading that Drew's text generates a pro-British/Canadian discourse. However, as this chapter explores, this view of the wilderness in Canada West appears alongside other voices that challenge representations of the Canadian wilderness as a fruitful haven for self-liberated people.

Most of the narratives contained in Drew's collection do not depict the moment of crossing the Canada–US border, but self-liberated people repeatedly mark Canada West out as special and antithetical to the United States through exclaiming they have arrived, reinforcing a sense of difference between life in Canada and the United States. Nancy Kang argues the narratives contained in *The Refugee* do not present the familiar imagery of fugitives from slavery crossing the border into Canada and this 'make[s] it difficult to register in time and place the shift from American to Canadian territory (and by extension, consciousness)', reflecting a sense of 'borderlessness' in the texts.[36] This is helpful in identifying the North American focus of these narratives rather than a narrower focus on the United States. The texts do not depict self-liberated people crossing the border, but reinforce the idea of Canada as a destination. For example, West locates himself in Canada in the present ('I am now in Canada').[37] The wilderness is seen as a liminal space for freedom

72   *Beyond the antislavery haven*

within its contexts in the United States and Canada; however, it is only in Canada that self-liberated people speak of clearing and settling the land, rather than moving through the wilderness to escape.

Steward's account of the self-liberated and free Black people who settled at the Wilberforce colony presents them as able settlers and valuable Black emigrants in their new society. Steward argues:

> the Wilberforce colony proves that the colo[u]red man can not only take care of himself, but is capable of improvement; as industrious and intelligent as themselves, when the yoke is taken off from their necks and a chance given them to exercise their abilities.[38]

He presents Canada as a special haven that transformed the settlers from the United States into strong, capable emigrants: 'the air of freedom so invigorated and put new life into their weary bodies, that the white people cannot deny soon became intelligent and thrifty'.[39] He uses the language of transformation to argue that the air and environment of Canada invigorated and improved the African American man, physically and intellectually.

Early on in his narrative, Steward presents his experience as an enslaved person in the northern frontier land outside New York. The violent overseer is depicted as unable to survive in the frontier land. This is reflected in his return to Virginia after his authority is tested in a scene in which his violent threats are turned back on him: he is violently beaten by an enslaved man. Williams gives the overseer 'such a flogging as slaves seldom get', grabbing the cowhide from the overseer and beating him with it, explicitly drawing attention to the subversion of power roles taking place as he is beaten.[40] This scene underscores the Black solidarity that was possible in the wilderness, as other enslaved people do not come to the overseer's aid despite his 'begging', and Williams is able to escape on a boat. Steward makes it clear that the excessive violence of the overseer will not be tolerated by the enslaved people now that they are in the northern wilderness. He comments that Williams 'thought as he was no longer in Virginia, he would not submit himself to such chastisement', and the overseer returns to Virginia, 'where he could beat slaves without himself receiving a cowhiding'.[41]

The depiction of the wilderness outside New York in Steward's narrative reflects what was common in many mid-nineteenth-century narratives: the northern states of America are imagined as

Canada in the antebellum slave narrative   73

a place of freedom, in contrast to the southern states, which are presented as morally defunct, violent, and oppressive. However, Steward's narrative goes further in its presentation of the thickly wooded wilderness in Canada West as a space for fugitives from slavery to become independent. Steward presents himself as a calm and adept settler, able to use his physical strength, enterprise, and ingenuity to protect the Wilberforce settlement from wild beasts. He shows how he is able to turn his encounters with the natural world into entrepreneurial successes. Steward relates how he caught and skinned two wolves in the wilderness of Canada West, in a chapter entitled 'Roughing it in the Wilds of Canada'. The title of this chapter is evocative of a wider genre of contemporary settler and emigration literature set in Canada about taming and surviving in the wilderness. Steward describes using his only bullet to kill a wolf and then ingeniously making a ball of wood for his rifle from a tree, developing an improvised shot with which he could kill a second wolf.[42] His detailed account describes preparing and selling the skins of the wolves for nine dollars, showcasing the profits to be made from the resources of the natural world and underscoring his entrepreneurial spirit. Steward describes how, with other settlers, he killed a bear that was roaming the Wilberforce settlement. He generates tension through exaggerating the physical threat of the bear, for example, describing its 'powerful paw' as sending a greyhound flying through the air.[43] He demonstrates his masculine prowess and abilities as a settler by describing the skillfulness of his aim – 'the second shot killed him on the spot' – and presenting himself, out of all the other unnamed 'half a dozen' settlers who were with him, as the one to fire the deadly shot.

The narratives contained in Drew's *The Refugee* and Steward's slave narrative borrow from an idea intrinsic to the making of white male settler identity in North American culture: that the emigrant can, through their own efforts in taming the wilderness, raise themselves up and become 'better Britons'. The transformative power of the wilderness to improve the emigrant has had a long tradition in emigration literature and culture. James Belich examines white settler society in New Zealand during what he describes as a period of 'recolonization' in the late nineteenth and early twentieth century; Belich uses the term 'better Britons' to describe a facet of white settler identity: 'Recolonisation consisted partly in the conviction

74 *Beyond the antislavery haven*

Figure 2.3 Illustration from Austin Steward's slave narrative of Williams fighting an overseer, British Library, © British Library Board shelfmark 10880.bb.15.

Canada in the antebellum slave narrative

that Australians, Canadians and New Zealanders were Britons too – indeed, in some respects better Britons than those of the homelands.'[44] The idea that land is a great equaliser and a space of meritocracy has deep roots in the American psyche. In J. Hector St John de Crèvecœur's *Letters from an American Farmer* (1752), a fictional farmer 'John' writes a series of letters discussing the characteristics of the American people and landscape. Crèvecœur's text is a foundational piece of emigration literature and an important intertext that provided a model for crafting the narratives of fugitives from slavery in Canada. In the third letter, Crèvecœur depicts the land as a space in which the new emigrant from Europe can seek liberty and independence. Central to Crèvecœur's vision of America is that the lowly and oppressed European emigrant can arrive without money or status and, through their own effort, build up their social status and wealth through land ownership. Crèvecœur is careful to stipulate that the successful European emigrant must be 'sober [...] honest, and industrious'.[45] The European immigrant is described as being 'naturalised' and being forged as an American ('he is now an American') through successfully owning land.[46] John sees American freeholders as experiencing a liberty unknown in Europe, and imagines them saying that 'for the first time in their lives', 'This is our "own grain, raised from American soil – on it we shall feed and grow fat, and convert the rest into gold and silver."'[47] American land is presented as a vehicle through which newcomers can achieve independence and a better life unencumbered by lords, masters, and princes, and their associated taxes and tithes, in Europe.

The low-status European emigrant is described as having a heavy spirit and as being kept in a 'mantle' by oppressive laws in Europe because of the system of renting and taxing land. By contrast, he is depicted as being elevated and experiencing a liberation in America, where he can purchase his own space: 'From nothing to start into being; from a servant to the rank of a master; from being the slave of some despotic prince, to become a free man, invested with lands, to which every municipal blessing is annexed!'[48] For example, the European settler Andrew is presented as being fearful that his rented land will be claimed by the king or the governor and he will be forced to quit it. John reassures him that this will not happen and it is all his 'own'.[49] Andrew's farm is shown as an abundant utopia, underscored by a table of all the property he has acquired over four

76   *Beyond the antislavery haven*

years of labour and its value in dollars, provided by Farmer John.[50] The narratives contained in *The Refugee* and Steward's slave narrative insert themselves into the existing discourse of white settler identity and European emigration rhetoric, presenting the development and ownership of land as a uniquely liberating experience.

Yolanda Pierce provides a model for thinking through the effect of Black emigrants using a discourse of white male settler identity in the slave narrative. Focusing on the slave narratives of Venture Smith and George White, Pierce examines two genres that traditionally make white male American settler identity: the captivity narrative and the spiritual autobiography, and how they intersect with the slave narrative. Pierce argues that both authors use and adapt these genres to craft an African American identity, 'revising and transforming conventional narrative forms'.[51] Pierce also notes that such borrowing can 'restore honour and worth to the status of the "African" in early American culture'.[52] Drew and Steward present self-liberated people in Canada West through this lens, conferring 'honour' and 'worth' on the African American subject, to fulfil an antislavery agenda.

Exploitation in Upper Canada (later Canada West)

Depictions of life after crossing the border give a more complicated picture of Canada. Drew and Steward do not simply offer a pro-Canadian and pro-British version of the Underground Railroad story. Drew's collection of narratives contains Mr Little's imperative to enjoy the riches of the Canadian wilderness, presenting Canada as a site of English liberty and voices of protest that see Ontario as an exploitative space. Drew and Steward suggest that Canada as a whole, and the wilderness in particular, is a place of liberty for the self-liberated person, but they also present Canada West as an anti-haven and the wilderness as a site of exploitation (this is overlooked by Clarke). These narratives acknowledge that the experience of fugitives from slavery in Canada West was also characterised by frustrations over land, exploitation, and anti-Black racism. Clarke argues that the antebellum slave narrative presents a very idealised view of Canada as an antislavery haven: 'rich with almost bombastic praise for Canadian/British "liberty"'.[53] In his introduction to Drew's *The Refugee*, Clarke claims that many of the stories

Canada in the antebellum slave narrative

contained in Drew's collection of narratives idealise Canada as a space of liberty: 'While Drew's interlocutors detail the savagery of slavery in the Great Republic, their ancillary effect is to paint [...] Victorian Ontario, as Paradise.'[54] Clarke teases out depictions of Ontario as a haven from Drew's collection of narratives. He reads Grose's narrative, for example, as presenting Canada as 'Eden' in his depiction of Black people in Quebec and Ontario – 'keeping stores, farming etc, and doing well' – and he uses a quotation from Henry Gowen's narrative that underscores his experience of racial equality in Canada: 'I am placed on an equality with him [with the white people legally].'[55] Clarke argues that Gowen's account of Canada supports a view of 'the superiority of British North America'.[56] He concludes that the poverty and racism experienced by self-liberated and free Black people in Canada are 'little mentioned' by the narratives.[57] However, he concedes that 'there are a few records herein of anti-black or other racism in Canada West', pointing to Sophia Pooley's narrative and others that present the failure of fugitives from slavery and their communities to prosper, but where this failure is blamed on the settlers themselves.

In the introduction to the Colchester section, one of the fourteen locations in Drew's collection, the Town Reeve, Peter Wright, notes that much of the cultivation of the area was done by fugitives from slavery, but that 'by the time they had made a good clearing, they were obliged to go somewhere else'.[58] The use of the word 'obliged' is ambiguous. It implies a potential for choice on the part of the settlers, but also highlights an unequal relationship in which they have to leave their land. A clear explanation of the power relationships in clearing is frustrated. Wright hints that one reason that the fugitives from slavery have lost their land is because of their own ignorance about the economic contract they have bound themselves into. Drew remarks: 'He pays $12 a year interest for ten years, supposing meanwhile that he is paying up the principal. *He don't understand it* – and when the ten years have come round he has not got the $200 and must leave his clearing.'[59] In this original edition, '*He don't understand it*' appears in italics, but this is edited out of the modern reprint by Dundurn Press, where it appears as 'He doesn't understand it.'[60] The dialogised heteroglossia of the free indirect speech in the 1856 edition '*He don't understand it*' blurs Drew's voice with that of the Black settler. The non-standard verb formation of 'he don't' in the 1856 edition produces a racist image of the settler, implying a stupid, uneducated, and baffled reaction to the loss of the land that he has been clearing and paying interest on. The original version suggests a confused settler who cannot understand the 'complicated' economic agreement, but David Grier, who describes himself as born free but leaving the United States to remove himself from the oppressive laws in the North, contradicts the framing white narrative. He claims that settlers were 'obliged' to leave the land they had cleared because white people deliberately 'took advantage of it to get the land cleared'. Moreover, he relates his own experience that he had cleared around seventy to eighty acres and 'got no benefit'.[61]

Philip Gould has found that 'the "loss" of the fruits of one's labour' is what constitutes slavery in a wider body of narratives, so that 'enslavement [is] understood in terms of the power one exerts over one's labour', although he does not consider this in the Canadian context.[62] Gould's observation is helpful because it invites us to explore texts that describe gradations of the lack of power over one's own body and its labour specifically, rather than fixating on a dichotomy of slavery and freedom. This wider perspective opens up the critical categories to explore narratives like Grier's alongside more traditional slave narratives, and also to allow an exploration of Canada within a wider culture of the economic exploitation of people.

John Francis explains that it has been a struggle to retain his land and that other self-liberated people have lost theirs.[63] He describes how exploitative land agents asking for high payments forced some to sell their land cheaply, and explains that the high repayments on loans are prohibitive and cause some settlers to lose their land. Robert Nelson, a settler writing from a farming region in Canada West, describes the fragile hold Black settlers had over their land in the role of clearers rather than owners of land:

> By the time they had got it cleared and removed some of the stumps, the lease was out. Then the white man said 'You can't have that piece anymore – you must go back in the bush.' They found they must do different from this. They began to work on the land for themselves, and to get farms of their own.[64]

Canada in the antebellum slave narrative 79

Nelson presents Black settlers as improving the land by pouring their labour into clearing it and removing the stumps of trees, which are characterised as stubborn, and then being forced off the territory. This presents Canadian land as a repository of one's labour and physical exertions, and the development of land as part of a cycle of exploitation, in which fugitives from slavery are kept in the low-status roles as clearers rather than owners of land. Nelson presents land as a site of racial inequality and tension, as the white disembodied voice sends the Black labourer back into the bush: 'you must go back in the bush'. Nelson relates how the settlers broke this pattern of exploitation by beginning to 'work on the land for themselves'. Mary Ann Shadd's *A Plea for Emigration to Canada West*, published in 1852, attempts to encourage Black emigrants to move to Canada. Uncleared woodland is described in terms of the dollars these trees will be worth once they are sold: 'Wood land will average seventy cords to the acre, every cord of which can be readily disposed of two and two and a half dollars, cash, in the towns.'[65] Shadd describes land as yielding profits to settlers with little effort, and it is silent on the exploitation and racial tension experienced in the wilderness explored in some of the narratives in Drew's collection.

Steward imaginatively links the exploitation of fugitives from slavery in Upper Canada in the 1830s with slavery in the United States. He presents the begging agents who sought funds in Britain and the United States on behalf of the Black settlers of the Wilberforce colony (and then squandered them) as being like the enslavers who live in oppressive luxury, profiting from their exploitation of others. Steward links Mrs N. Paul (the wife of the agent Nathaniel Paul, who raised funds for the Wilberforce colony in England but consumed most of the charity money raised through his expenses and pay) to Mr Helm's plantation in Virginia, and its oppressive luxury and exploitation. Mrs N. Paul is described as benefiting financially from the charitable donations collected for fugitives from slavery in Canada. She is described as sitting in one of the land agent's homes 'sparkling', with 'a gold chain encircling her neck' and in a sumptuous interior.[66] This echoes the depiction of the 'sparkling' and 'glittering' interior of the plantation, and it evokes a domestic, feminised, and sedentary interior. Like the people who held Steward in slavery, Mrs N. Paul grows rich from

80   *Beyond the antislavery haven*

others' labour. Steward describes the wedding of the daughter of
the planter, Mr Helm, to her Virginian cousin in a scene crowded
with 'glittering [...] diamonds', 'large mirrors', and 'sparkling wine'.
Helm is described as 'sparkling with jewels'.[67] The enslavers and
begging agents are linked through their role as a sedentary class
who grow rich from exploiting the labour of others. The semantic
links Steward crafts between the two spaces of Canada West and
the South present a broader geography of exploitation not so easily
confined to national borders.

Susanna Moodie, Mary Prince, and Austin Steward

Steward draws upon the conventions of the white female settler
narrative to tell his story of losing his wealth in Canada West and
his return to Rochester in the United States. Specifically, Steward
appropriates Susanna Moodie's narrative of failed settlements in
the Upper Canadian bush in the 1830s, *Roughing It in the Bush;
Or, Life in Canada*, to tell his story of failed middle-class philan-
thropy on behalf of these Black settlers. The evidence for her influence is that, firstly, the title of her bestselling work is appropriated
in chapter 21, 'Roughing It in the Wilds of Canada'. Secondly, the
structural form of the portion of his narrative set in Canada (chapters 19–34) closely resembles Moodie's narrative. These chapters
consist of short sketches of exciting incidents, such as meeting First
Nations people and encountering dangerous animals, and Steward
embeds the narratives of those he meets into his story in a third-
person voice, both of which have been identified as features of
Moodie's narrative.[68]

Moodie's *Roughing It in the Bush* was an instant 'best seller in
Britain and the United States' when it was first published in 1852
and is an example of Canadian female settler literature.[69] As Carole
Gerson notes, there was a gender bias in such accounts of Canada:
while immigration tracts and accounts of exploration tended to be
authored by men, the published 'literature of settlement' tended to be
written by women.[70] Moodie's narrative had a different tone to that
of contemporaneous female settler accounts. As Gerson notes, the
narrator of Susanna's sister Catherine Parr Traill's *The Backwoods
of Canada*, published in 1836, has a 'sunny temperament', which

Canada in the antebellum slave narrative 81

'contrasts sharply with the often regretful and emotional narrative of Moodie's *Roughing It in the Bush*'.[71] Gerson explains that Parr Traill writes from the perspective of a woman still living in the bush at the close of her narrative, whilst in contrast, Moodie speaks 'through the sagacity of hindsight' as one who has left the bush twenty years before she came to pen her narrative.[72] The ultimate message of Moodie's text, as others have noted, is that the middle-class emigrant cannot survive in the Canadian bush by working the land, and the Canadian wilderness is better suited to working-class labourers.[73] This can be seen in the closing lines of the second volume, where Moodie presents her thesis and attempts to deter genteel families from emigrating to the Canadian wilderness:

> If these sketches should prove the means of deterring one family from sinking their property, and shipwrecking all their hopes by going to reside in the backwoods of Canada, I shall consider myself amply repaid for revealing the secrets of the prison-house; and feel that I have not toiled and suffered in the wilderness in vain.[74]

Moodie shows that, even with an approach of middle-class thrift, industry, and godliness, her family is unable to successfully settle in the Canadian wilderness. Bush life is presented as consuming the resources they have brought with them to Upper Canada: her crockery is broken on the journey to their second bush farm and they are forced to sell their clothes in order to survive.[75] The second farm at the Douro township 'scarcely fed' Moodie and her young family, and they rely on John Moodie's wages from the militia.[76] Moodie makes this explicit in her assertion that without his wages they would 'plunge [...] into poverty'. Despite Susanna's 'Crusoe-like' efforts sowing and reaping a wealth of foodstuffs from her garden, making small paintings of 'birds and butterflies' on large mushrooms that she sells in Britain, and acquiring a commission to write, she is unable to make life in the bush sustainable for her family.[77]

The internal evidence of Moodie's narrative shows that the generic intertextuality and influence between it and the slave narrative does not just move one way. The Canadian female settler narrative was also shaped by the slave narrative. George Elliott Clarke has argued that Moodie's narrative can be read 'as a displaced "slave narrative" of a genteel, pioneer English woman, toiling in

82 *Beyond the antislavery haven*

the bush country of Upper Canada'.[78] The internal evidence from Moodie's narrative indicates she borrows from the conventions of the slave narrative to construct her account of her experience of the Canadian wilds. This is reflected in her description of the Upper Canadian wilderness as a 'prison-house' and her narrative as revealing its 'secrets', which evokes the convention within the slave narrative genre for first-hand insight into slavery in the South.[79] Moodie had already transcribed two slave narratives by Ashton Warner and Mary Prince by the time she penned *Roughing It*, prior to her marriage and under her maiden name Susanna Strickland. Moodie transcribed Mary Prince's narrative whilst a guest in the house of the Secretary of the Anti-Slavery Society in London, Thomas Pringle, between 1829 and 1830, and Prince was his domestic servant.[80] The term 'prison-house' refers to the slaveholding South. For example, this description is used in the introduction to Drew's collection of narratives: '[m]any, in spite of opposition, in the face of torture and death, will seek asylum in foreign lands, and reveal to the ears of pitying indignation, the secrets of the prisonhouse'.[81] Moodie uses the rhetoric of a self-liberated person whose place of suffering is the Canadian wilderness rather than southern slavery, reflecting a bleeding of intertextual discourse between the relevant genres.

Steward describes his experiences in the 1830s in Upper Canada, which was known as Canada West from 1841 to 1867 (now Ontario), in similar terms to those of the Black settlers who have been exploited, but he uses the wilderness land to craft a very different narrative for himself than that of the wider Black community of settlers. Steward frames his loss of land and experience of exploitation as a metaphor for his failed charitable efforts to help the Black settlers of the Wilberforce settlement. His account is primarily a middle-class narrative about the failure of his charitable efforts to help free Black people in Upper Canada, and he presents his experience of loss in Upper Canada (of money and reputation) as due to being betrayed by his social equal, Israel Lewis. Steward's narrative functions partly as a personal defence, a common rationale for writing an autobiography.[82]

Steward constructs a middle-class narrative that does not present him as being exploited in Canada through a desire to own land, but rather shows his philanthropic efforts to support self-liberated people in Canada as a failed settler dream, in which

Canada in the antebellum slave narrative   83

thriving in the Canadian bush is unachievable. Steward gives an account of the loss of his land, but this reads less as an account of his exploitation by a land agent than of the underhand dealings of his colleague and former friend, Lewis. Steward was bound up in legal proceedings with Lewis, who was one of the land colonists involved in the Wilberforce colony. Steward relates the cost of removing trees from his land to clear it, explaining his assumption that he legally owned the land in a way that is reminiscent of the exploited settlers in Drew's text: 'I commenced labo[u]ring on the wild land I had purchased; cleared some ten acres, which in consequence of it being so heavily timbered cost me at least twenty-five dollars per acre; built a house and a barn – supposing myself its legal possessor.'[83] This contrasts with Shadd's description of woodland in Canada West as a financial boon. In contrast to the emigration tract, Steward details the hard labour required to make a profit, rather than 'carefully concealing the toil and hardship to be endured in order to secure these advantages', a criticism Moodie made of contemporary emigrant guides.[84] Steward relates how Lewis sold him the land but then did not inform Steward when he received the money from the original owner, Mr Ingersoll, who had sold the land to somebody else. Steward's description of his loss of land is part of a wider discussion of the betrayal by his supposed friend and colleague. Steward describes facing trial because Lewis has accused him of stealing a promissory note. Steward's description of his friends encouraging him to leave Canada whilst he was awaiting trial frames his philanthropic labours in terms of land that he has expended his energies on, receiving no benefit in return: 'I was advised by different persons to flee from the country, which I had laboured so hard and so conscientiously to benefit, and received in return nothing but distraction and slander.'[85] Steward imagines this loss in terms of wasting his time and ruining his reputation. He is betrayed by his social equals, including Nathaniel Paul, who squanders the money he helps raise for the Black settlers in England, as well as Israel Lewis. Steward is betrayed by the same men whom he depicts as the sedentary class of exploitative men and women who profit from others' labour. Steward's description of Canada West as a hard wilderness unwilling to offer up its fruits posits it as the site of the failure of a middle-class code of Christian brotherhood.

84   *Beyond the antislavery haven*

The key thematic similarity between Moodie's *Roughing It* and Austin Steward's narrative of his post-slavery life in Canada is that both tell of failed settlement in the Upper Canadian bush from a middle-class emigrant perspective. Through appropriating and revising Moodie, Steward is able to write his own experiences into print and narrate the experiences of self-liberated people in Canada within a genre that had no precedent for representing the life of former slaves in Canada West before the 1850s. Steward tells the story of the failure of the Wilberforce settlement, framing his experience of Canada not as due to ineptness, idleness, or drunkenness but as the failure of a genteel family to survive in the bush. Steward uses this to craft his personal defence of himself. He describes the return of his family to Rochester in the United States following the 'disappointments' and 'difficulties' they have met in Canada. He depicts his family 'rejoic[ing]' at the prospect of returning home, explaining that they 'had experienced little less than care, labour and sorrow' in Canada.[86] He contrasts the possessions they had with them while travelling to Canada and when leaving Canada, five years later:

> I made preparation to take my family to Port Stanley, forty miles distant. But what a contrast was there between our leaving Rochester, five years before, and our removing from the colony! Then, we had five two-horse wagon loads of goods and furniture, and seven in family; now, our possessions were only a few articles, in *a one-horse wagon*, with an addition of two members to our household![87]

Steward's narrative does not end like Moodie's, with her leaving the wilderness and moving to the town of Belleville in Upper Canada, where she experiences a more comfortable life and her husband earns money from a colonial office. Steward revises the conventions of Moodie's settler narrative by presenting his family's, and, later in the narrative, his own, return to the United States. Steward's wife and family travelling by wagon to Rochester in New York State reproduces the image of the unsuccessful gentleman/gentlewoman settler of Moodie's female settler narrative. Steward presents his attempts to help the Black emigrants of Wilberforce as making him financially destitute, leading to his incarceration for debt. Steward depicts himself as having to use money from his Rochester bank account on behalf of the Wilberforce colony.

Canada in the antebellum slave narrative 85

Steward adopts and expands on Moodie's narrative of life in the Canadian wilderness. He pushes the boundaries of her account in several ways to write his own story of the exploited Black emigrants in Canada and his attempts to help them. Moodie depicts the decision to emigrate to Canada as made by her husband after he attended a talk about the 'advantages' of emigrating to Canada, delivered by William Cattermole, the author of the emigration tract *Emigration: The Advantages of Emigration to Canada in Britain*, published in 1831.[88] They are drawn by economic need, whereas Steward is convinced by Israel Lewis's account of the destitution of two thousand free Black people from the United States living in poverty. Steward recollects that he was 'affected deeply' by Lewis's description of the persecuted Black people from Cincinnati who settled in Upper Canada: 'eleven hundred persons were then in the dense woods of Canada in a state of actual starvation'.[89] Like the emigrant guides that artificially inflated the profits settlers could expect to obtain from wilderness land, Lewis's description of the Black settlers exaggerates the number of them living in Canada, as the actual figure was a few hundred people.[90] Steward makes plans to travel to Upper Canada to help the Black settlers and perform his Christian duty, reflected in his description that he decides to travel to Canada to 'try to do some good; to be of some little service in the great cause of humanity'.[91] If Moodie's thesis is that the middle-class emigrant cannot survive in the Canadian bush and that such an environment is more suited to the labouring classes, Steward's is a story of personal disillusionment.

The juxtaposition of Steward as a failed settler leaving Upper Canada with fewer goods than he arrived with, and the image of him demonstrating his masculine prowess as an able settler elsewhere in his narrative, reinforces the sense that Steward's decision to leave is not due to his own failings, or his inability to thrive outside of a system of enslavement, but rather the man-made corruption he has encountered in Canada. Mary Ann Shadd links the success of Black emigrants to their own efforts and energies in her representation of Canada as a fertile haven where Black emigrants are able to thrive, if they deploy a little skill and energy: 'I firmly believe that with an axe and a little energy, an independent position would result in a short period.'[92] Steward appropriates Moodie to craft an alternative narrative of a middle-class Black man who chooses to leave Canada because he does not thrive in his philanthropic labours, rather than because of his own personal failings or lack of energy and effort.

Isaac Mason's slave narrative, *The Life of Isaac Mason*, published in Worcester, MA in 1893, constructs Canada West as an exploitative anti-haven, and this represents the culmination of a tradition in the slave narrative that began with Drew and Steward in the mid-1850s. This reflects the simultaneous tradition in the slave narrative of presenting Canada as a space that bound fugitives from slavery into new kinds of exploitation and enslavement. Mason presents his brief experience in Canada in 1851 using the imagery of a failed settler whose financial resources are sucked out of him, describing a series of disastrous employment experiences. Mason describes his second role in Canada as a labourer chopping down trees in Queen's Bush. Mason depicts his labours as an entrepreneurial effort to make money, offered fifty cents a cord.[93] He describes how 'we went into the woods, cut down some logs and put up a log house'. He relates that he should have been paid thirty-five dollars at the end of the first week, but that each labourer, including Mason, was underpaid: 'instead of receiving that amount we only got fifty cents a piece; yes that was all we got'.[94] Mason is tricked into working for an additional week and is paid nothing for his labour. Mason finds out that the man employing him was not the owner of the land, but had been 'hired' by the owner to cut down the wood and deliver it. Mason approaches the owner of the land, but the owner absolves himself of responsibility for paying him, saying that he will not be able to pay them what he has already paid the agent who hired them: 'He told me if my companions and myself would go back to work chopping wood, he himself would see us paid, but we would have to be the losers of what he had already paid the agent.' Mason refuses to work for him again: 'Disgust and discouragement prevented me from labouring for a man who cheated me out of my just due.'[95] Mason writes to a friend in Worcester to ask for money so he can return to the United States. Like the Stewards, Mason returns to Worcester, MA having been 'rob[bed] of strength and labour', and just able to buy back his possessions with borrowed money.

This chapter has shown that looking at what happens to self-liberated and free Black people after their arrival in Canada in slave narratives offers a more complicated account of Canada as an idealised

Canada in the antebellum slave narrative 87

antislavery haven than when the focus is placed on the moment that they cross the border. The presentation of Canada West in the slave narrative after 1850 challenges the idea of a strong Canada–US border. Canada reads differently in these narratives after self-liberated and free Black people cross the border: as a less idealised space. In Steward's narrative and in many of the stories contained in Drew's text, Canada is presented as a more problematic space that unsettles its popular image as an antislavery utopia today: it contains exploitative land agents and the corrupt benefactors of the Wilberforce settlement who grew rich from the work of others. Steward links Canada West and the United States in his representation of men and women prepared to exploit the labouring classes in both places. His text shows that there are narrative precedents from the antebellum period for writing a very different, personal experience of Canada, and these could contest a one-dimensional image of that nation as a haven for self-liberated African American people. While Steward wrote his own story, Drew's text is a collection of narratives presented through his mediating presence as the amanuensis and editor of the stories. Drew's intrusions in the text only reflect the editorial role he wants his readers to see him take, and this leaves Drew's far greater role in shaping the texts as an interviewer and editor unseen. However, Drew's text does capture a range of voices and types of experience; he does not excise unflattering imagery of Canada or the angry accounts of settlers who felt they were exploited. His text contains very positive statements describing Canada as a place of liberty and criticising slavery in the United States, but overall it does not amount to Clarke's claim that it is a piece of 'anti-American [...] propaganda'.[96] In fact, the text attempts to place the United States and Canada West under the microscope. Canada West is presented in Drew's text as both a place of refuge and as a challenging new abode. Drawing on emigration rhetoric, slave narratives depict wilderness land in Canada West as a place for people to forge their freedom and independence from slavery, especially through settling the land, but they also present Canada as part of an exploitation narrative that challenges the idea of a strong Canada–US border. The experiences of exploited Black emigrant labourers in Canada and accounts of slavery in the United States were linked textually in slave narratives by both being depicted as losing one's labour at the hands of an exploitative class of landed gentry of slaveowners

88 *Beyond the antislavery haven*

and land agents. Mason's depiction of Canada as a capitalist space draws from earlier textual traditions. He shows that there was an alternative tradition of presenting Canada as an anti-haven in the slave narrative, not dissimilar to the depiction of Canada in the anti-*Tom* novel discussed at the start of this book. Mason's repetition of the representation of Canada as an anti-haven narrative in the late nineteenth century reflects that contemporaries recognised this aspect of earlier slave narratives. Rather than seeing the antebellum slave narrative as circulating a one-dimensional idealised view of Canada as an antislavery utopia, this chapter has shown that the representation of Canada in the mid-nineteenth century was far more complicated within abolitionist literature and Black autobiographies. This chapter has focused on book-length slave narratives published as part of a cross-border abolition movement and the textual representation of Canada in the slave narrative. The next chapter explores how one slave narrative by the Rev. Thomas H. Jones was circulated and framed for readers of religious newspapers in Nova Scotia and New Brunswick during his time there in the early 1850s, showing how abolitionist slave narratives could be framed within a range of texts and an ameliorationist response to slavery in the United States when they crossed the border. The chapter calls for a more expansive focus within African American print studies that examine slave narratives from a material, book history, and cultural circulation approach to push their discussion beyond the Canada–US border and see how slave narratives circulated in Canada, framing Canada as connected to a broader North American print space.

Notes

1 'Canada West' was the term used in 1841–67 for what is now known as Ontario.
2 A non-exhaustive list of first-person narratives by self-liberated people who, for portions of their narratives, depict their lives in Canada (in addition to Steward and Drew's texts) would include Josiah Henson, *Life of Josiah Henson, Formerly a Slave, Now an Inhabitant of Canada, As Narrated by Himself* (Boston: Arthur. D. Phelps, 1849); Thomas Smallwood, *A Narrative of Thomas Smallwood (Coloured Man) Giving an Account of His Birth – The Period He Was Held in Slavery*

Canada in the antebellum slave narrative 89

– His Release – and Removal to Canada etc, Together with an Account of the Underground Railroad Written by Himself (Toronto: printed for the author by James Stephens, 1851); Samuel Ringgold Ward, *Autobiography of a Fugitive Negro: His Anti-Slavery Labours in the United States, Canada and England* (London: John Snow, 1855); and Richard Warren, *Narrative of the Life and Sufferings of Rev Richard Warren (A Fugitive Slave)* (Hamilton: Christian Advocate, 1856).

3 Austin Steward, *Twenty-Two Years a Slave and Forty Years a Freeman* (New York: Dover Publications Inc., 2004), p. 166.

4 George Elliott Clarke, '"This Is No Hearsay": Reading the Canadian Slave Narratives', *Papers of the Bibliographical Society of Canada* 43:1 (2005), 18, n. 19. https://doi.org/10.33137/pbsc.v43i1.18415.

5 Audrey Fisch, *American Slaves in Victorian England: Abolitionist Politics in Popular Literature and Culture* (Cambridge: Cambridge University Press, 2000), p. 63. Sarah Meer, *Uncle Tom Mania: Slavery, Minstrelsy and Transatlantic Culture in the 1850s* (Athens: University of Georgia Press, 2005), pp. 141–42.

6 For this approach, see many of the essays in Audrey Fisch (ed.), *The Cambridge Companion to the African American Slave Narrative* (Cambridge: Cambridge University Press, 2007).

7 Julia Sun-Joo Lee, *The American Slave Narrative and the Victorian Novel* (Oxford: Oxford University Press, 2010). Cindy Weinstein, 'The Slave Narrative and Sentimental Literature', in Fisch (ed.), *The Cambridge Companion to the African American Slave Narrative*, pp. 115–34.

8 Olaudah Equiano, *The Interesting Narrative and Other Writings*, (Vincent Carretta (ed.) (New York: Penguin Books, 1995), pp. 72–76.

9 Olaudah Equiano, *The Interesting Narrative*, Brycchan Carey (ed.) (Oxford: Oxford University Press, 2018), p. xiii.

10 Afua Ava Pamela Cooper, '"Doing Battle in Freedom's Cause": Henry Bibb, Abolitionism, Race Uplift and Black Manhood, 1842–1854' (PhD dissertation, University of Toronto, 2000), pp. 1–3.

11 Henry Bibb, *Narrative of the Life and Adventures of Henry Bibb, An American Slave*, in Yuval Taylor (ed.), *I Was Born a Slave: An Anthology of Classic Slave Narratives* (Edinburgh: Payback Press, 1999), pp. 4–98.

12 *Ibid.*, p. 74.

13 *Ibid.*, p. 12.

14 *Ibid.*, p. 29.

15 *Ibid.*, p. 63.

16 *Ibid.*, p. 34.

17 *Ibid.*, p. 98.

18 John Stauffer, 'Frederick Douglass and the Aesthetics of Freedom', *Raritan: A Quarterly Review*, 25:1 (2005), 115.
19 *Ibid.*, 115.
20 *Ibid.*, 127.
21 John Stauffer, 'Frederick Douglass's Self-Fashioning and the Making of a Representative American Man', in Fisch (ed.), *The Cambridge Companion to the African American Slave Narrative*, p. 212.
22 Benjamin Drew, *The Refugee: Narratives of Fugitive Slaves in Canada* (Toronto: Dundurn Press, 2008), p. 28 and p. 39.
23 Stauffer, 'Frederick Douglass and the Aesthetics of Freedom', 127.
24 Jane H. Pease and William H. Pease, 'Introduction', in Steward, *Twenty-Two Years a Slave and Forty Years a Freeman*, p. x.
25 Frederick Douglass, *My Bondage and My Freedom* (New York: Miller, Orton & Mulligan, 1855) and Austin Steward, *Twenty-Two Years a Slave and Forty Years a Freeman*, 2nd ed. (Rochester: Allings & Cory, 1859).
26 For example, see 'The Great Plea for Freedom: Read It and You Cannot Resist It: My Bondage and My Freedom', *Frederick Douglass' Paper* (19 October 1855), p. 4.
27 Douglass, *My Bondage and My Freedom*.
28 Drew, *The Refugee*, p. 99.
29 *Ibid.*, p. 172.
30 *Ibid.*, pp. 198–224. For John Little's experience in the Canadian wilderness, see pp. 216–19.
31 *Ibid.*, p. 202.
32 *Ibid.*, p. 204.
33 *Ibid.*, p. 205.
34 *Ibid.*, p. 206.
35 *Ibid.*, p. 206.
36 Nancy Kang, '"As If I Had Entered a Paradise": Fugitive Slave Narratives and Cross-Border Literary History', *African American Review* 39:3 (2005), 444–45.
37 Drew, *The Refugee*, p. 99.
38 Steward, *Twenty-Two Years a Slave*, p. 124.
39 *Ibid.*
40 *Ibid.*, p. 38.
41 *Ibid.*
42 *Ibid.*, pp. 118–19.
43 *Ibid.*, p. 129.
44 James Belich, *Paradise Reforged: A History of the New Zealanders from the 1880s to the Year 2000* (Albany: Penguin Books, 2001), p. 11.

Canada in the antebellum slave narrative 91

45 J. Hector St John de Crèvecœur, *Letters from an American Farmer* (London: Thomas Davis, 1782), p. 89.

46 *Ibid.*, p. 78.

47 *Ibid.*, p. 94.

48 *Ibid.*, pp. 79–80.

49 *Ibid.*, p. 112.

50 *Ibid.*, p. 118.

51 Yolanda Pierce, 'Redeeming Bondage: The Captivity Narrative and the Spiritual Autobiography in the African American Slave Narrative Tradition', in Fisch (ed.), *The Cambridge Companion to the African American Slave Narrative*, p. 97.

52 *Ibid.*, p. 97.

53 Clarke, '"This Is No hearsay"', p. 18, n. 19.

54 Clarke, 'Introduction: Let Us Now Consider "African-American" Narratives As (African-) Canadian Literature', in Drew, *The Refugee*, p. 10.

55 *Ibid.*, p. 15.

56 *Ibid.*, p. 16.

57 *Ibid.*, p. 12.

58 Drew, *The Refugee*, p. 330.

59 Benjamin Drew, *A North-Side View of Slavery: The Refugee or Narratives of the Fugitive Slaves in Canada* (Boston: J. P. Jewett & Co., 1856).

60 *Ibid.*, p. 332.

61 *Ibid.*, p. 335.

62 Philip Gould, 'The Economies of the Slave Narrative', in Gene Andrew Jarrett (ed.), *A Companion to African American Literature* (Oxford: Wiley-Blackwell, 2010), p. 98.

63 Drew, *The Refugee*, pp. 187–89.

64 *Ibid.*, p. 334.

65 Mary A. Shadd, *A Plea for Emigration: Or, Notes of Canada West*, Richard Almonte (ed.) (Toronto: Mercury Press, 1998), pp. 51–52.

66 Steward, *Twenty-Two Years a Slave*, p. 160.

67 *Ibid.*, p. 53.

68 Michael A. Peterman, 'Introduction', in Susanna Moodie, *Roughing It in the Bush*, Michael A. Peterman (ed.) (New York: W. W. Norton & Company, 2007), p. xiii.

69 *Ibid.*, p. vii.

70 Carole Gerson, 'Literature of Settlement', in Coral Ann Howells and Eva-Marie Kroller (eds), *The Cambridge History of Canadian Literature* (Cambridge: Cambridge University Press, 2009), p. 87.

71 *Ibid.*, p. 87.

72 *Ibid.*, p. 94 and p. 103.

73 As others have noted, for example, D. M. R. Bentley, 'Breaking the "Cake of Custom": The Atlantic Crossing as a Rubicon for Female Emigrants to Canada?', in Moodie, *Roughing It*, p. 466.

74 Moodie, *Roughing It*, p. 330.

75 *Ibid.*, p. 180 and p. 243.

76 *Ibid.*, pp. 285–86.

77 *Ibid.*, p. 283 and p. 281. The term 'Crusoe-like' is used by David Stouck, '"Secrets of the Prison-House": Mrs Moodie and the Canadian Imagination', in Moodie, *Roughing It*, p. 425.

78 Clarke, '"This Is No hearsay"', 13.

79 Moodie, *Roughing It*, p. 330.

80 For these biographical details, see Moira Ferguson, 'Introduction', in Moira Ferguson (ed.), *The History of Mary Prince, A West Indian Slave, Related by Herself* (London: Pandora, 1987), p. 10.

81 Drew, *The Refugee*, p. 29.

82 William Andrews, *To Tell A Free Story: The First Century of Afro-American Autobiography* (Urbana: University of Illinois Press, 1986), pp. 1–2.

83 Steward, *Twenty-Two Years a Slave*, p. 118.

84 Moodie, *Roughing It*, p. 10.

85 Steward, *Twenty-Two Years a Slave*, p. 144.

86 *Ibid.*, p. 162.

87 *Ibid.*, pp. 163–64.

88 Moodie, *Roughing It*, p. 48.

89 Steward, *Twenty-Two Years a Slave*, p. 109.

90 *Ibid.*, p. 109, editorial note.

91 *Ibid.*, p. 110.

92 Shadd, *A Plea for Emigration*, p. 52.

93 Isaac Mason, 'Life of Isaac Mason as a Slave', in B. Eugene McCarthy and Thomas L. Doughton (eds), *From Bondage to Belonging: The Worcester Slave Narratives* (Amherst: University of Massachusetts Press, 2007), pp. 245–85 (p. 275).

94 *Ibid.*, p. 276.

95 *Ibid.*

96 Clarke, 'Introduction: Let Us Now Consider', p. 14.

3

Thomas Jones in Nova Scotia and New Brunswick: a slave narrative in context, 1851–53

The previous chapter looked at neglected portions of slave narratives: the accounts that self-liberated and free Black people gave of their lives after crossing the Canada–US border. It examined the textual construction of Ontario in the slave narrative as both a haven and an exploitative capitalist space. This chapter takes a case study approach and explores the circulation of a single slave narrative in Canada. It examines Thomas H. Jones's slave narrative in the context of the newspapers that advertised it for sale, recovering its framing within ameilorationist rather than immediate calls for the abolition of slavery in the United States. The chapter aims to better understand Jones's time in New Brunswick and Nova Scotia by using newspapers published in Canada to recover new texts about him and his narrative, adding to what we know about his cross-border antislavery activism and Christian preaching in Canada.

Slave narratives, pamphlets, and letters by self-liberated and free Black people who depicted their experiences of moving from the United States to Canada in the antebellum era are increasingly being read as part of a cross-border literary history within the United States, and within discussions of Black diasporic mobilities.[1] In *Fugitive Borders*, Nele Sawallisch discusses the autobiographies of four self-liberated men from the United States who settled in Canada West (now known as Ontario) and argues that they textually constructed a community across the Canada–US border, building on historical explorations of Ontario as a borderland space.[2] Marcy J. Dinius shows how Paola Brown's unauthorised reprinting of an altered version of David Walker's *Appeal* changed its textual content for circulation amongst its Canadian audience.[3] Winfried

94 *Beyond the antislavery haven*

Siemerling's *The Black Atlantic Reconsidered* was the first book-length study of Canada within the Black Atlantic world and provides an exploration of Black Canadian history and the eighteenth-century Black Nova Scotian slave narratives of John Marrant, Boston King, and David George.[4] However, the general scholarly approach to date reads slave narratives in their Canadian context as literary texts rather than material objects, and does not explore how slave narratives circulated or were framed for readers in newspapers.

This chapter builds on recent developments in African American print culture studies, for example, those by Teresa Goddu, Michaël Roy, Eric Gardner, Bryan Sinche, and Lori Leavell, which suggest that we need to move away from the previous emphasis on close readings of textual content to look at how slave narratives circulated, were framed, and received, particularly in a regional context in the United States, to unpack their meanings. Underpinning this approach is an acknowledgement that antislavery texts, including slave narratives, were cultural commodities and material objects, and this helps to account in part for their appeal.[5] Scholars are now exploring how these accounts travelled, to acknowledge the many forms that life stories took (including as letters, newspaper articles, and lectures), and to develop deep and detailed accounts of individual narratives. They are increasingly examining the multiple editions of specific slave narratives and the economic conditions of their circulation. This moves away from previous readings focused on rhetoric and generic influences or that traced how these stories shaped other literary genres.[6] Teresa A. Goddu's 'The Slave Narrative as Material Text' argues that scholars need to examine the slave narrative 'as a material artifact'.[7] For Goddu, researching the specific material and publishing histories of many more slave narratives will produce 'a more detailed map of the slave narrative' that highlights its 'geographical diversity' and 'varied publishing and distributional practices'.[8] Michaël Roy argues that scholars have long focused on bound-book narratives, overlooking pamphlets, newspapers, and the recirculation of narratives of slavery 'in all forms and formats'.[9] Roy sees lectures, performances, and children's books as forms of narrative circulation.[10] Roy argues that slave narratives were 'fugitive texts'; their lives did not end with their pages, and their popularity came from 'their capacity to shift between formats and media'.[11] Finally, Eric Gardner notes that scholars' knowledge of

Thomas Jones in Nova Scotia and New Brunswick 95

North American slave narratives is still 'miniscule' and argues that we can use biographical and textual research to compile the writing and personal records of authors to '(re)create archives in and surrounding slave narratives'.[12]

From the point of view of these studies, narratives of enslavement and self-liberation represent a complex and heterogeneous genre across material forms and national contexts. Scholars have begun to complicate assumptions about the popularity of the slave narrative genre, moving the discussion beyond a small number of what are assumed to be 'representative' narratives, such as Frederick Douglass's 1845 text *Narrative of the Life of Frederick Douglass, an American Slave*.[13] In 'Cheap Editions', Roy takes a book history approach to three narratives by James Williams, Frederick Douglass, and Solomon Northup to argue that approaching them from a focus on their publication and circulation shows that '[e]ach occupied a different position in antebellum print culture' and 'belonged to different social worlds'.[14] Bryan Sinche in 'The Walking Book' explores Aaron's slave narrative, *The Light and Truth of Slavery: Aaron's History*, in its multiple editions as a 'supplicant text' sold commercially by Aaron, and a 'record of supplication' that reflects his 'years-long writing and selling journey[s]'.[15] From this reading, slave narratives could be more about an economic transaction than liberating 'self-expression'.[16] Following these studies, every slave narrative must be approached as an 'entity in its own right'.[17]

Newspapers were central in the recirculation of slave narratives in the United States. Newspaper editors sometimes reprinted them in their entirety, as in the *Narrative of James Williams*, printed in *Zion's Watchman* in 1838.[18] Lori Leavell's examination of the recirculation of Walker's *Appeal* (1829–30) moves beyond the three Boston editions of the antislavery pamphlet to explore two newspapers published in New York and Philadelphia, which reprinted excerpts of the text and several articles that discussed it. Leavell sees newspaper articles discussing the *Appeal* as part of the 'fragmentary forms of recirculation' of the pamphlet that shaped later responses to the text, noting that many of the *Appeal*'s readers would have encountered his text 'by proxy' in newspapers.[19]

The existing scholarship in African American print studies, which takes a material, book history, and cultural circulation approach to slave narratives, stops at the Canada–US border. Thomas H. Jones was a self-liberated Wesleyan preacher and abolitionist whose *The Experience of Thomas Jones, Who Was a Slave for Forty-Three Years* was first published in Massachusetts in 1849, but circulated and reprinted in Nova Scotia and New Brunswick, where he travelled and lived between 1851 and 1853. Jones published a series of letters in Garrison's *Liberator* about this time in Canada. He placed a card in the *Weekly Chronicle*, a newspaper published in New Brunswick soon after his arrival in June 1851, and his narrative was advertised for sale in two newspapers in Nova Scotia (the *Presbyterian Witness* and the *Wesleyan*), and copies of his narrative were printed in New Brunswick in 1853. Using Jones as an example, this chapter proposes that we explore North America as a connected space for Black print culture through a study of the circulation and reception of slave narratives.

What follows here is a response to the critical silence around Jones's slave narrative in Atlantic Canada, reading Jones's narrative within the particular context of two religious newspapers in Nova Scotia. It uses Gérard Genette's conception of the 'paratext': the material that surrounds a text, such as prefaces, title pages, and illustrations, that function as 'threshold[s]' to texts and a 'zone between text and off-text'.[20] The chapter reads the newspapers as paratextual thresholds that shaped how readers of the religious newspapers approached Jones's text. This chapter first explores Jones's literary antecedents and eighteenth-century models for depicting Black lives in Nova Scotia and New Brunswick, and then examines the two evangelical newspapers and how they handle slavery in the United States before examining the notices for Jones's narrative and how the newspapers invited readers to approach it. This context is used to offer a close reading of the narrative, suggesting that, in order to unpack the cultural meanings of narratives of liberation in Canada, they need to be explored in their specific contexts, requiring an examination of how readers in Canada encountered these texts in newspapers.

Black Nova Scotian narratives: Thomas H. Jones's literary antecedents

As the previous chapter showed, the tradition for depicting what became known as Ontario in the slave narrative had its origins

Thomas Jones in Nova Scotia and New Brunswick 97

in the 1850s, but three Black autobiographical narratives repre-sent an earlier textual tradition for depicting Black experience in Nova Scotia and New Brunswick. These are the Black missionary John Marrant's *A Journal of the Rev. John Marrant, From August the 18th, 1785 to the 16th March, 1790*, published in London in 1790; and the Black Loyalist narratives of the Methodist mission-ary Boston King, *The Life of Boston King*, and the Baptist minister David George, *An Account of the Life of Mr David George, from Sierra Leone in Africa; Given by Himself in a Conversation with Brother Rippon of London and Brother Pearce of Birmingham*. They are antecedents to Thomas H. Jones's antebellum slave narra-tive and linked through the genre of Black spiritual autobiography.

Marrant was born a free Black man in New York, and on 18 August 1785 he left London for Nova Scotia to preach the gospel as a minister of the Countess of Huntingdon's Connexion of Calvinist Methodism. Marrant's *A Narrative of the Lord's Wonderful Dealings with John Marrant, a Black (Now Gone to Preach the Gospel in Nova-Scotia), Born in New York, in North-America* first published in London in 1785 covers the time up until Marrant left for Nova Scotia. He relates a letter from his brother in Nova Scotia: 'Her ladyship having seen the letter from my brother in Nova Scotia, thought Providence called me there: To which place I am now bound, and expect to sail in a few days.'[21] The sixth edition of the narrative contains a short postscript written in the third person, probably by his 'Editor', Rev. Mr Aldridge, that provides an update on his time in Nova Scotia: 'Mr. Marrant has travelled through that province, preaching the Gospel, and not without success … he has undergone much fatigue, and passed through many dangers; that he has visited Indians in their Wigwams, who, he relates were disposed to hear and receive the Gospel.'[22] The contents of this postscript are said to come from letters that Marrant sent to various people in Britain. Marrant's *Journal* picks up the story roughly where his pre-vious narrative ended. It starts with his ordination on 15 May 1785 and the start of his journey to Nova Scotia, as reflected in the inclu-sion of the date that he leaves London on his way to Nova Scotia in the title, on 18 August 1785. The *Journal* provides a detailed diary-style account of his time spent preaching and converting souls in Nova Scotia that at times reads as a list of places visited and people preached to, with Biblical references providing a record of

98 *Beyond the antislavery haven*

what he preached and occasionally expanding into fuller narrative sketches of the people he met and experiences he had, such as losing his son and helping to convert a destitute woman who (it is implied) resorted to prostitution during the late American Revolutionary war. Marrant travels around locations such as Halifax, Preston, Shelburne, Birchtown, and Ragged Island. The date 16 March 1790 in the title presumably reflects when Marrant arrived back in London; he relates that he arrived on 7 March in Londonderry, Ireland. The London edition of 1790 includes two sermons at the end: the funeral sermon of Mr Jonathan Lock of Ragged Island and another delivered on St John's Day in June 1789 to the African Masonic Lodge in Boston.

The preface in Marrant's *Journal* starts with a defence of his reputation, stating that the rumours that he had been given more money than he had at Bristol were untrue, and describing the loss of wealth and energy he experienced during the 'ferryings' between places in Nova Scotia and New Brunswick. He describes having to sell his jacket and sending back repeatedly to the Countess of Huntingdon for money but being giving no assistance and being forced to return to London, revealing an early critical account of Canada as a space that consumes one's imported resources. Marrant describes being an advocate for Black Loyalist settlers at the Black communities of Birchtown and Preston and relaying their requests to the governor in Halifax, with success. Marrant's travels in Nova Scotia conclude because he does not hear from the Countess or receive further funds, initially travelling to Boston, where he starts preaching. However, with the discovery of a plot against his life and still not hearing from the Countess, he departs.[23] While Marrant celebrates the successes he has had, listing a number of people whom he had brought to God, including Mr Jonathan Lock, he describes his experiences as 'my sufferings', makes it clear that he and his child experience a loss of wealth in Nova Scotia: 'I and my boy were bare-footed and covered with rags.' He also drops the word 'wonderful' from his previous title when describing his experiences in Nova Scotia: 'I have been giving my readers a large account of God's dealings with me in Nova Scotia.'[24] The trip may have been a Christian success but without financial support from a patroness back in England, it is ultimately unsustainable and comes at a personal and physical cost.

The narratives of Boston King and David George depict their experiences in Nova Scotia and New Brunswick after the American Revolution. Both King and George had been born enslaved and their narratives give accounts of being held in slavery as children, in South Carolina and Virginia respectively. King enlisted with the British in Charlestown, which had been under British control since 12 May 1780. King and his wife Violet set sail from New York to Shelburne, Nova Scotia, aboard the *L'Abondance* on 31 July 1783.[25] King depicts his life in Nova Scotia, including his wife's experience of religious conversion and his own salvation. King describes that his lack of belief in God drove him out to 'the woods, when snow lay on the ground three or four feet deep', and he reached a crisis point where he felt he was 'the most miserable creature upon the face of the earth'.[26] After listening to sermons and preaching, King describes experiencing 'God's pardoning love': 'Every thing appeared to me in a different light to what they did before; and I loved every living creature upon the face of the earth.'[27] King built salmon boats, went fishing, and preached to a Black Wesleyan congregation in Preston. He describes how the famine affected white and Black settlers in Nova Scotia, with some Black Loyalists having to sell themselves to merchants for periods of indentured labour.[28] He describes his experience of labouring amongst the people in Birchtown and Preston, Nova Scotia, to bring them to God and later being driven by a concern for the spiritual welfare of 'my poor brethren in Africa'. He also relates journeying to Sierra Leone to continue his efforts in converting others to God. As his narrative relates, King later spent 1794–96 in Britain receiving an education at Kingswood School, a Methodist establishment founded by John Wesley, before returning to Sierra Leone to work as a schoolmaster. His narrative was originally published in Britain in the *Methodist Magazine* in instalments between March and June 1798.[29]

George describes preaching and performing baptisms as a Baptist minister in Nova Scotia and New Brunswick, and the racism he encountered there. George narrates a race riot and violent mob destroying his family's house, beating him with sticks and driving him into a swamp. He also relates the resistance that local white people made to the Black Loyalists' plan to depart for Sierra Leone: 'The White people in Nova Scotia were very unwilling that we should go, though they had been very cruel to us, and treated

100   *Beyond the antislavery haven*

many of us as bad as though we had been slaves.'[30] The language George uses blurs the boundary between freedom and slavery as experienced by Black Loyalists in Nova Scotia. George encapsulates the cruelty and poor treatment many Black Loyalists experienced at the hands of white people in Nova Scotia, as many scholars, including James W. St. G. Walker, have discussed. As his narrative relates, George later relocated to Sierra Leone and travelled to Britain, where his narrative was published.[31]

The Black Loyalist narratives of George and King and Marrant's *Journal* depict the experiences of self-liberated and free Black people from the United States in Atlantic Canada as part of a broader Black Atlantic world. Two editions of Marrant's *Narrative* published in 1812 and 1813 in Halifax by J. Nicholson have sometimes been mistaken as being published in Nova Scotia, although more frequently scholars do not comment on the national location of the Halifax mentioned.[32] However, the Black Loyalist narratives were not reprinted or published in Canada, and were written in Britain, and published in Britain and the United States. Marrant's *Narrative* was published by J. Nicholson who was based in Halifax in West Yorkshire, England, and who also published Equiano's narrative (in 1808, 1812, and 1813), as well as in 1814 together with the poems of Phillis Wheatley.[33] An examination of contemporary newspapers in Nova Scotia and Quebec has not uncovered any evidence that these texts were advertised for sale or circulated in Canada in the eighteenth century. However, they were important literary antecedents to Jones's nineteenth-century depiction of his time in Nova Scotia and New Brunswick.

Thomas Jones in North America

Like many self-liberated and free Black people in the antebellum period, Thomas Jones moved between and around the United States and Canada. He travelled around Nova Scotia and New Brunswick, and between 1851 and 1853 he circulated and reprinted his slave narrative in both locations. Thomas H. Jones (1806–87) was born into slavery near Wilmington, NC. Whilst he was enslaved, Jones preached to congregations in Wilmington. After he bought his second wife's freedom, she travelled with their children to New York,

Thomas Jones in Nova Scotia and New Brunswick 101

and Jones joined them there in August 1849. After securing his freedom that year, Jones lectured as part of the antislavery movement in Connecticut and western Massachusetts and settled in Salem, where he preached at the Wesleyan church. The first edition of his narrative, *The Experience of Thomas Jones, Who Was a Slave for Forty-Three Years*, was published in Worcester, MA in 1849. As David A. Davis notes, the character of 'Jones' the narrator is best understood as a joint creation between Jones and his amanuensis, who transcribed and edited it.[34] Jones went to Canada to avoid recapture, following the passage of the 1850 Fugitive Slave Law. He travelled around New Brunswick and Nova Scotia between May 1851 and August 1853, apparently motivated by both religious and antislavery ideas, as he spent time preaching, lecturing against slavery, and selling subscriptions to the *Liberator*.[35]

Jones's decision to travel from New England to New Brunswick and Nova Scotia shows him moving around a borderland that had strong historical, cultural, and economic links. For example, Harvey Amani Whitfield has explored the continuity of slaveholding practices in Nova Scotia and New Brunswick following the Loyalist exodus at the end of the American Revolution.[36] During the same period, Black Loyalist settlers arrived in Nova Scotia and New Brunswick. Atlantic Canada was an important site of historical Black migration, for example, with the arrival of Black Refugees there following the War of 1812.[37]

Critics have typically seen Jones's narrative as purely abolitionist and firmly situated in cultural politics in the United States. Davis situates Jones's narrative in the abolitionist context of the 1840s, when the genre was 'at its commercial zenith' in the United States, and narratives such as Frederick Douglass's 1845 text were shaping its conventions.[38] He argues that 'the antebellum publication of *The Experience of Rev. Thomas H. Jones* had an overt political agenda: to publicize the inhumane treatment of slaves in order to arouse support for the abolitionist movement', and sees it as 'almost a textbook example' of slave narratives of the period.[39] Others have noted sentimental elements in Jones's narrative, such as a heavy focus on the family.[40] Jones's narrative was published just before a shift in the form. Although he does not discuss Jones's narrative, William L. Andrews sees the 1850s as key in the development of the slave narrative form, when it became more flexible as a format for telling stories

102   *Beyond the antislavery haven*

about the African American experience, characterised by experimentation, greater novelisation of the narrator's voice, and realism, moving 'beyond earlier restrictions and dictates of the genre'.[41]

Jones's narrative continued to sell well after the abolition of slavery in the United States, speaking to a wider appeal of his narrative than can be explained by an antislavery context. William L. Andrews notes that this narrative was one of the 'most long-lived' of the nineteenth century.[42] Roy identifies that an 1850 edition of Jones's narrative was sewn, together with other pamphlets, into a volume entitled 'Pamphlets on Slavery' in the Houghton Library at Harvard.[43] This is an example of the afterlife of this narrative and its placement within a political abolitionist context, alongside its adaptability as a pamphlet to be collected with others. The enduring popularity of Jones's narrative before and after abolition suggests it was valued for Jones's family-oriented and Christian account of his life story in addition to its abolitionist purposes, especially since the text changed very little in the reprintings in 1855, 1857, 1862, 1868, and 1871.[44] The 1880 edition expanded the 1862 edition, which was under copyright, and added a new section, 'Part Second', which contained further descriptions of Jones's life while enslaved and his time in Nova Scotia and New Brunswick.[45] There was a reprinted version of the expanded 1880 text in 1885. Andrews argues that the 1885 narrative adopts a 'mid-1880s vantage point' that focuses on Jones's preaching and 'takes pride in his gospel labours' while also highlighting his experiences of racism.[46]

Jones's narrative was reprinted in Saint John, New Brunswick, in 1853 by J. & A. McMillan, a leading bookselling and printing business, at that time owned and run by James McMillan Sr. (1810–86).[47] This is the only reprint of Jones's text listing a print location in Canada. The only known surviving copy of the text is 18 cm long and 10.6 cm wide, with an orange paper cover and a modern library binding, suggesting the narrative circulated in the form of a light, portable pamphlet.[48] Two recent collections of slave narratives that contain Jones's narrative do not discuss the Canadian reprint of it in New Brunswick nor the circulation of his narrative in Atlantic Canada, instead situating Jones's work in a collection of slave narratives in Worcester, MA, and North Carolina.[49] My research discovered *The Experience of Thomas Jones* circulated in Halifax, Nova Scotia in 1851, and was advertised for sale in two religious

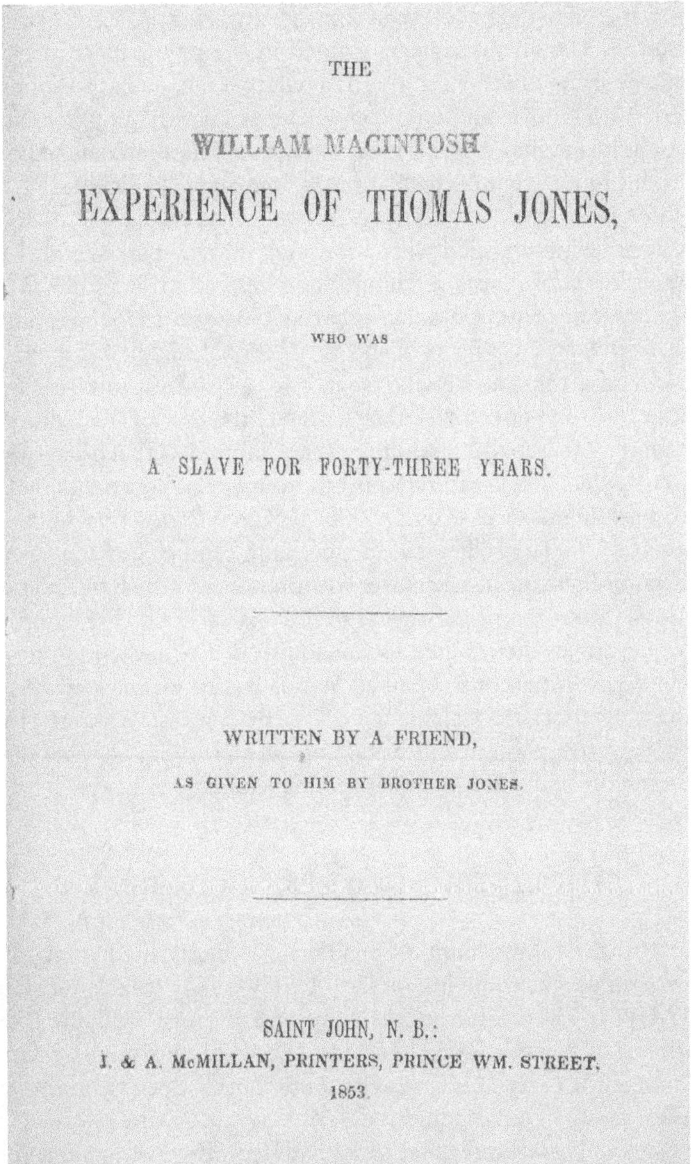

Thomas Jones in Nova Scotia and New Brunswick 103

THE

WILLIAM MACINTOSH

EXPERIENCE OF THOMAS JONES,

WHO WAS

A SLAVE FOR FORTY-THREE YEARS.

WRITTEN BY A FRIEND,

AS GIVEN TO HIM BY BROTHER JONES.

SAINT JOHN, N. B.:

J. & A. McMILLAN, PRINTERS, PRINCE WM. STREET.

1853.

Figure 3.1 The title page of the New Brunswick reprint of Thomas Jones's slave narrative, J & A McMillan, 1853, image acknowledgement: Book cover: *The Experience of Thomas Jones, Who Was a Slave for Forty-Three Years.* Source: Library and Archives Canada/OCLC 1006821943.

104   *Beyond the antislavery haven*

newspapers in June that year: the *Presbyterian Witness* and the *Wesleyan*. The advertisements printed in the newspapers in Nova Scotia describe Jones's narrative as a pamphlet that costs a shilling.[50] There is no known surviving copy of Jones's narrative with a Nova Scotia imprint, and it seems most likely that Jones recirculated copies of his narrative published in the United States in Halifax.[51]

Jones published his narrative during what Meredith L. McGill has identified as a period when reprinting (in newspapers and cheap reprints of books) was a 'culture' and central to literature in the United States.[52] She argues that between 1834 and 1853, literature in the United States was regional and transnational, and newspapers and books had a very close relationship. The early 1850s saw structural changes to the book trades that hastened the end of the culture of reprinting.[53] In Canada, reprinting culture lingered, with reprinted texts in newspapers and cheap reprints of international books dominating until the late nineteenth century. Eli MacLaren argues that American editions of books proliferated in nineteenth-century Canada, and its first major literary publishers were distributors of British or American editions rather than the original publishers of books.[54] Editions of slave narratives recirculated in Canada tended to be written for an audience in Britain or the United States, and hence did not directly address or appeal to Canadian readers. By contrast, editions of the same narrative published in Britain or the United States could differ substantially and addressed their specific national audiences.[55]

Thomas Jones in Saint John, New Brunswick

Upon his arrival in Atlantic Canada, Jones first visited Saint John, New Brunswick, sometime before 5 May 1851. In a letter dated 10 May 1851, printed in the white abolitionist William Lloyd Garrison's *Liberator*, Daniel Foster, a Massachusetts minister acting as an agent of the Massachusetts Anti-Slavery Society, introduces a letter from Thomas Jones dated 5 May and written from New Brunswick. Foster states that Jones had 'recently fled' to Saint John from Salem.[56] Jones's 1880 expanded edition summarises the many churches where he preached in New Brunswick.[57] Later, Jones is described as being 'of St. John' in a notice in the *Liberator* (elsewhere in that newspaper, he is described as a resident of the British

Thomas Jones in Nova Scotia and New Brunswick   105

Provinces).[58] We get the sense that Jones spent some time in Saint John, and this was also where the Canadian edition of his narrative was reprinted in 1853. In an unprinted letter to Garrison in February 1854, writing from New Haven, CT, Jones describes his intention to return to New Brunswick, and comments, 'I have just got up 4 thousand copies more of my books', suggesting his text was selling well.[59]

Jones left a fragmented record within the Saint John newspapers during his time there. A complete search of three newspapers between 1851 and 1854 (the *Morning News*, the *New Brunswick Courier*, and the *Weekly Chronicle*) revealed one notice placed there by Jones.[60] No advertisements for the Canadian edition of his narrative were found. These newspapers had large readerships and printed materials about slavery in the United States, taking a broadly abolitionist stance. The newspapers reprinted excerpts from slave narratives published in newspapers and book-length slave narratives, reflecting how these texts moved across the Canada–US border.[61] The newspapers also reported on the arrival of self-liberated people in Canada, local fundraising events to raise money for them, and abolitionist lectures.[62] These newspapers contributed to the idea that slavery did not exist in Canada.[63]

On 13 June 1851, William Durant's *Weekly Chronicle* (also known for part of the period examined for this chapter as the *St. John Chronicle and Colonial Conservative*) printed a 'card' written by Jones describing his imminent departure for Halifax, Nova Scotia. This is the first known reference to Jones in a Canadian newspaper. It emphasises Jones's role as a preacher and his membership of religious networks, suggesting that he was particularly involved with these during the earliest days of his trip. This reminds us that Jones, like fellow self-liberated intellectuals and writers in the Black Atlantic world, was not singularly focused on abolitionist causes but held diverse interests as members of complex networks. Jones's card does not mention his narrative, but thanks and names members of his Christian network, as well as thanking the citizens of Saint John:

CARD. THE REV. THOMAS H. JONES, on his departure from the City of St. John, feels it a pleasing duty to tender his best thanks to the citizens generally, for their cordial support and sympathies, but he especially thanks the Rev. Mr. Robinson, the Rev. Mr. Casewell, the Rev. Mr. Very, the Rev. Mr. McLeod, the Rev. Mr. Irvine, and the Rev. Mr. McKay, and their respective flocks, for the many Christian and brotherly favours received at their hands, hoping to meet them all on his return from Great Britain, he now bids them an affectionate farewell, in the spirit of truth and fellowship. June 13.[64]

The choice of a 'card' is interesting, given that between 1851 and 1854, the *Weekly Chronicle* only printed a few notices described this way, alongside many hundreds of notices and advertisements. Unlike other types of notices, cards like this one did not ask their readers to do anything. Jones inserts himself into the public life of Saint John and this reading community. Titling his notice as a 'card' within the ephemeral newspaper designed to be read and discarded evokes the more permanent material form of a thank-you card. Within the space of the newspaper page and the recognised form of the card, Jones creates a memory of his presence within his community and writes himself into local public life.

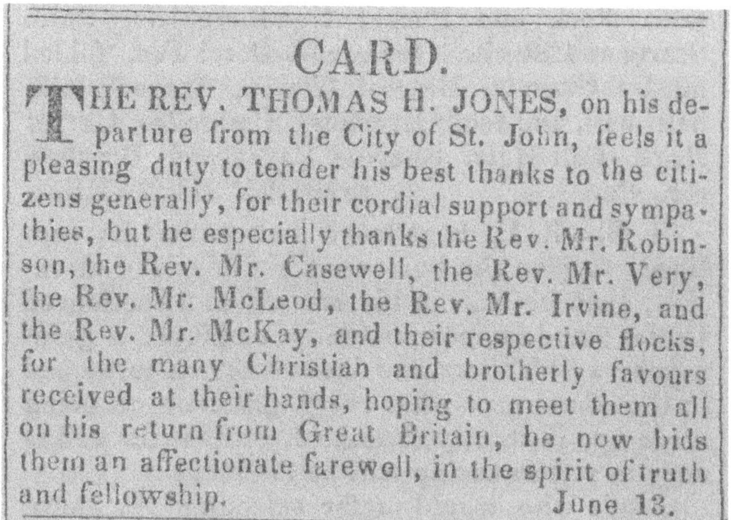

CARD.

THE REV. THOMAS H. JONES, on his departure from the City of St. John, feels it a pleasing duty to tender his best thanks to the citizens generally, for their cordial support and sympathies, but he especially thanks the Rev. Mr. Robinson, the Rev. Mr. Casewell, the Rev. Mr. Very, the Rev. Mr. McLeod, the Rev. Mr. Irvine, and the Rev. Mr. McKay, and their respective flocks, for the many Christian and brotherly favours received at their hands, hoping to meet them all on his return from Great Britain, he now bids them an affectionate farewell, in the spirit of truth and fellowship. June 13.

e011782773_s1

Figure 3.2 Thomas Jones's 'Card' in the *Weekly Chronicle*, 13 June 1851, p. 3, reproduced with the permission of the copyright bureau at Library and Archives Canada.

Jones's narrative

The title of Jones's narrative, *The Experience of Thomas Jones*, invites the reader to read the narrative as primarily about his religious 'experience'.[65] The *OED* glosses 'experience' as 'A feeling or state of mind forming part of one's religious or spiritual life' and as the experiences Methodists shared at meetings.[66] Today we can miss the religious meaning of 'experience' in the title of Jones's narrative. Similarly, on the front cover of the 1853 reprint, the way the title is arranged emphasises Jones's text as an account of his religious experience (Figure 3.1).

Jones's narrative closely resembles the structural form of the Wesleyan Methodist spiritual autobiography. Ted A. Campbell argues that the genre told the lives of prominent Methodists, and was 'a powerful means to disseminate Wesleyan and Methodist understandings of the Christian faith' and 'of Christian life'.[67] Jones's narrative begins with an account of his pre-conversion life, then relates his conversion to Christianity and the struggles of his soul after conversion, and ends with him answering his calling to be a preacher. Jones's narrative relates his experience of first attending a meeting at a Methodist church and later a Quaker meeting. Jones describes his journey towards God as beginning with learning to read. He recollects that he then began to pray, read the Bible, and attend religious meetings, where he was guided to confess his sins to God. Jones relates how he then went through a cycle of facing up to his sins and asking God for forgiveness.

The theme of spiritual conversion that animates Jones's narrative has a long tradition in the literature of the Black Atlantic. In his survey of texts published in the eighteenth century, Vincent Carretta states that 'virtually all the African-British publications in prose took the form of spiritual autobiographies' and underscores that the writers were largely 'beneficiaries and/or agents' of the evangelical Christian movement headed by Methodist or Baptist missionaries in the British Atlantic world.[68] Jones's focus on his spiritual life enables him to mount a Christian attack on slavery. His narrative presents slavery as precipitating despair in Jones, which endangers his religious health. Two aspects of slavery bring about Jones's loss of faith in the text: seeing that people are not obeying the Golden Rule, and the loss of his family and home.[69] After his first wife and

108   *Beyond the antislavery haven*

three children are sold into slavery, Jones describes his struggles: 'A deep despair was in my heart, such as no one is asked to bear in such cruel crushing power as the poor slave severed forever from the objects of his love, by the capacity of his brother.'[70] The loss of his family is described as precipitating a crisis of faith: Jones describes his home as becoming 'darker'.[71]

Jones in the Halifax newspapers: prioritising the spiritual health of readers

By 21 June 1851, it appears that Jones had arrived in Halifax, Nova Scotia. Two religious newspapers, the *Presbyterian Witness* and the *Wesleyan*, advertised his narrative. We will return to Jones himself later. First, this section will explore how the newspapers provided different paratexts, or thresholds, for the circulation of Jones's narrative, and describe how both prioritised their readers' spiritual health.

James Barnes edited and published the *Presbyterian Witness* in Halifax, Nova Scotia, in 1848–83.[72] The newspaper was a Free Church Presbyterian paper but became 'more generally Presbyterian'.[73] William Cunnabell published the Wesleyan Methodist newspaper the *Wesleyan*, and the Rev. Alex W. Macleod edited it, in Halifax, in 1849–52. Both were family denominational newspapers. The full title of the *Wesleyan – A Family Paper Devoted to Religion, Literature, General and Domestic News, etc* – identifies the family as a key audience of the paper. The *Wesleyan* presents itself as suitable for Wesleyan Methodist readers, stating its hopes to circulate 'generally among kind friends who bear the same distinguishing name'.[74] The *Presbyterian Witness* identifies its readers as Presbyterian families. In an article penned by its editors, Presbyterian ministers are asked to encourage every Presbyterian family in their congregation to subscribe to the newspaper.[75]

An examination of their handling of American slavery between 1851 and 1853 shows that the *Presbyterian Witness* is broadly antislavery, while the *Wesleyan* advocates for the amelioration of slavery but is not abolitionist. This reflects what we might expect from Presbyterian and Wesleyan Methodist churches in Canada, as in general the evangelical Protestant denominations in Canada

Thomas Jones in Nova Scotia and New Brunswick   109

were antislavery. Slavery was one of the 'worldly amusements' targeted by the middle-class 'moral crusades' undertaken by evangelical churches, as Marguerite Van Die suggests.[76] However, the Presbyterian Free Church and the Wesleyan Methodist church in Canada responded differently to chattel slavery in the United States. Van Die notes that the Presbyterian Free Church in Canada was particularly active in the Anti-Slavery Society in Canada.[77] Allen P. Stouffer's study of the Presbyterian Free Church in Canada West shows that it was 'strongly antislavery virtually from its inception [in the 1840s]'.[78] The Wesleyan Methodist church in Canada was in principle against slavery, but fell short of supporting abolition, according to Stouffer, who finds that, although the Wesleyan Methodists in Ontario initially supported abolition in the 1830s and sometimes made it clear in their newspaper that they did not in principle agree with slavery, they opposed immediate emancipation, and in the late 1830s took up a position of 'neutrality' on chattel slavery in the United States.[79]

The *Wesleyan* reprinted stories first published in newspapers in the United States featuring fictional enslaved African American characters that use slavery as a backdrop for religious tales. The many stories reprinted in the newspapers created a print environment marked by the interaction of religious and abolitionist messages, and introduced readers to a range of sympathetic African American characters suffering under enslavement. Appearing in the context of a newspaper designed to aid the religious practice of readers by delivering the truth of the gospel, encouraging missionary activity, and keeping the souls of the *Wesleyan* readers healthy, we can imagine that readers approached the stories with an eye on how they could help them practice their Christian faith. Three stories in the *Wesleyan* ('Old Jeddy, There's Rest at Home', 'The Old Oak Tree', and 'Old Moses') feature enslaved people whose religious enthusiasm is shown to fit within the institution of slavery in the world of the narrative.[80] The fictional stories printed in the *Wesleyan* use recognisably racist tropes and racialised stock characters to condone slavery and present the apologist position that chattel slavery in the United States was a peaceful system that supported the religious health of enslaved people, presenting a sanitised, unrealistic image of Southern United States plantations. The fictional enslaved characters in the *Wesleyan* are in the tradition that George Boulukos explores as developing in

110 *Beyond the antislavery haven*

eighteenth-century British writing, circulated widely in the transatlantic world. He argues that such tales were seemingly sympathetic to enslaved people, but 'always contained two central elements: an ameliorative view of slavery, and [the] suggestion of racial difference'.[81] These tales do not attempt to prompt readers to antislavery action, but rationalise enslavement in order to deliver a religious message. These stories are about saving white souls and present the reader with images of irreligious white people who exemplify the opposite of the missionary ideal of helping bring others to God by attempting to restrict the Christian practices of enslaved people.

In contrast, the *Presbyterian Witness* is outspokenly antislavery. In 1852, James Barnes reprints a text that he entitles 'A Real Uncle Tom'. This tells the story of a woman who attends a Methodist church in Kentucky and hears a sermon about an enslaved martyr who is whipped to death because he will not renounce his Christian faith. The embedded narrative of the enslaved Christian man forms the bulk of this text. The textual history of this story before it reaches Barnes is revealing: it was first published in antislavery newspapers in the United States, in Jane Grey Cannon Swisshelm's *Pittsburgh Saturday Visiter* and William Lloyd Garrison's *Liberator*. Barnes adjusted the text when he reprinted it, adding an opening paratextual sentence inviting his readers to read it as antislavery: 'The *Pittsburgh Saturday Visiter* gives the following horrible illustration of slavery as it exists in some of the States.'[82] The enslaved person who dies is described in the text as a 'martyr' and an 'old disciple', underscoring that his death and refusal to give up his faith is celebrated in the worldview of the Methodist sermon.

Barnes cuts over three hundred words from the version of 'Uncle Tom' that appeared in the *Liberator*. He does not reproduce the *Liberator*'s description of the Methodist minister and his congregation's response to the story of the enslaved martyr.[83] Rather, in the *Liberator*, the female narrator remarks on the effect that the narrative of the martyr had on the Methodist minister and his congregation. She relates that the preacher delivered the narrative of the enslaved person 'with many tears', and that his congregation cried in response to the story, overjoyed at his steadfastness and interpreting the story as one of Christian faithfulness and the strength of an enslaved person's religious faith. Their tears are a Christian 'sign of redemption'.[84] The story of the enslaved person's murder, and the sight of the congregation joyfully hearing this story, provokes 'horror' in the narrator and her friends. The narrator states that the

Thomas Jones in Nova Scotia and New Brunswick 111

Figure 3.3 The newsprint page with 'The Old Oak Tree' narrative, *Wesleyan*, 24 February 1853, p. 1, reproduced with the permission of the Nova Scotia Archives.

moral of the story of the persecuted enslaved person was lost on the preacher and his congregation: 'Our pulses all stood still with horror, but the speaker did not appear to dream that his story had any bearing against the institution with which he was surrounded.' The narrator implies that the congregation are led in their reaction

Figure 3.4 The newsprint page with 'Old Jeddy, There's Rest at Home', *Wesleyan*, 20 October 1853, p. 1, reproduced with the permission of the Nova Scotia Archives.

by the minister, who delivers the narrative of the Christian enslaved person within the context of a sermon, in which believers sought meaning for their own lives and Christian experience. In contrast, the female narrator and her companions are able to look beyond this frame and read the narrative differently.

Thomas Jones in Nova Scotia and New Brunswick   113

Barnes does not include this criticism of the story being used to stimulate joyful religious feelings. In editing this section, he also removes the image of the Christian congregation responding to the story and refuses to reproduce the text's depiction of joy in reaction to the suffering of the martyr. This section of the text proposed the martyr as a figure who could be interpreted from an antislavery perspective or from the perspective of white Christian ideology. Barnes cuts these lines, and his insertion of the framing paratext urging the reader to see this as an antislavery text performs a similar function, layering the original narrative with a secular antislavery frame that invites his readers to approach it with horror rather than joy. The title he provides ('A Real Uncle Tom') and the additional line describing how the narrative shows the horrors of slavery reflect the ideas expressed in the lengthier text. The version printed in the *Liberator* argues that there are 'thousands of real Uncle Toms' in America, and Barnes attempts to pick up on this in his title 'A Real Uncle Tom'.

Reading Jones's narrative in isolation reinforces an antislavery reading of Canada that sees it as a space for abolitionist print culture and stories of Black liberation. However, Jones advertised his narrative in newspapers that reprinted a wider set of white-authored narratives about slavery that contained racist stereotypes, and proslavery and ameliorationist arguments. The newspaper narratives with their offensive views about enslaved people show that narratives about slavery were used to reinforce 'Christian' teachings, often starkly at odds with abolitionist agendas. The narratives were reprinted from newspapers in the United States, and this represents the continuity of this kind of storytelling about slavery across the Canada–US border, challenging an idealised account of Canada as an antislavery reading space. This also shows the print world that Jones had to navigate when advertising his narrative to the readers of these two newspapers.

The notices as different thresholds

In 1851, Jones advertised his narrative in two religious newspapers in Halifax; the discovery of these notices reveals for the first time that his narrative was likely read in Nova Scotia. The religious newspapers seem to have provided a space for the advertisement

114 *Beyond the antislavery haven*

of Jones's narrative that contemporaneous secular newspapers did not. His narrative was not mentioned in a leading secular paper in Halifax that month, the *Acadian Recorder*.[85] The narrative's advertisements in the two religious newspapers suggest that the newspapers' editors identified the narrative as likely to interest and benefit their readers. The notices were not simply advertisements placed by the author or publisher to generate sales for their books, but part of a regular literature review section in both newspapers, apparently written by the newspapers' editors. Reviews were occasionally printed in which the editor laments that they have not been able to finish reading the text and saying that they will give a short review that week and a fuller one the following week.[86] The newspaper editors were both pastors, and their newspapers were seen as assisting in their readers' religious health. It seems likely that the books reviewed in the newspapers would have been seen as recommended reading for their readers.

Newspaper notices are a key space in which readers in Nova Scotia were addressed and told how to approach Jones's narrative. In the New Brunswick reprint, Jones did not alter his narrative for a Canadian audience; he did not insert a new preface to address readers in Canada. Of the known extant copies, the 1853 New Brunswick reprint of Jones's narrative is most like the 1857 edition printed by Henry J. Howland in Worcester, MA, and addresses an imagined audience of readers in Massachusetts.[87] Jones speaks as if residing there: 'Oh that these happy, merry boys and girls, whom I have seen in Massachusetts since my escape from slavery, whom I have so often met rejoicing in their mercies since I came here, only knew the deep wretchedness of the poor slave child!'[88] The final place of arrival mentioned in the text is Boston, MA: 'I came on to Springfield, and from thence to Boston, where I arrived penniless and friendless.'[89] The letters of introduction in the 1853 text are the same as in earlier editions published in the United States; all come from people in New England and imply a broad geographical reach of New England readers. They are signed from Exeter, NH; North Danvers, Essex County, MA; and Boston. In this context, the notices printed in the *Presbyterian Witness* and the *Wesleyan* and written in the voice of the newspapers' editors represent a key space for directly addressing religious readers in Atlantic Canada and inviting readers in Halifax to read the text in specific ways.

Thomas Jones in Nova Scotia and New Brunswick 115

The advertisement in the *Wesleyan* (Figure 3.5) presents Jones's 'mission' as a Christian one and does not explicitly present Jones's cause as antislavery.[90] It positions Jones as a Black Christian, rather than a man invested in a political cause. The notice does not clearly state that Jones's aim is to abolish slavery in either his visit to Halifax or in selling his narrative but introduces him as both a self-liberated man and a pastor of a Black church in Salem. His status as a pastor is mixed in the closing lines of the advert that describe a missionary appeal: 'he hopes to be furthered in the object of his mission'. The notice states that Jones deserves the 'benevolent sympathies' of those in Halifax, and suggests that by reading and buying the narrative, they can help 'one who needs your sympathy and aid'. The notice claims that readers will get a 'more fervent conviction of the necessity and blessedness of toiling for the desolate members of the one great brotherhood' by reading the narrative, detaching it from its antislavery political agenda.

The notice uses language that highlights the narrative as a classic abolitionist text, as reflected in the title 'Narrative of a Refugee Slave', but there is greater emphasis on the narrative as an account of Jones's religious experience and a story about him and his family. The review prioritises the religious aspect of Jones's narrative, drawing attention to the family element of the narrative by highlighting the escape of Jones's wife and children. Jones's flight is described as an act of divine intervention, reflected in the description of the 'providential escape' of his family.[91] This is not a major part of the narrative, and it probably reflects the fact that the writer of the review, who was most likely the editor, felt this would appeal to his readers.

The notice in the *Wesleyan* adapts an address that Jones makes to his reader in his narrative. The newspaper version changes the text in Jones's narrative and downplays the antislavery polemic of the original. Jones uses religious language such as 'friends' and the 'members of the one great brotherhood' and emotive words such as 'despairing' and 'desolate' to describe the suffering of enslaved people as a Christian crisis.[92] He uses a variety of theological concepts and discourses to deliver his antislavery polemic, such as eschatological language, the Golden Rule, and the jeremiad. Jones uses the theological tenant of the Golden Rule, that Christians should treat each other as they wish to be treated ('Whatsoever ye would that

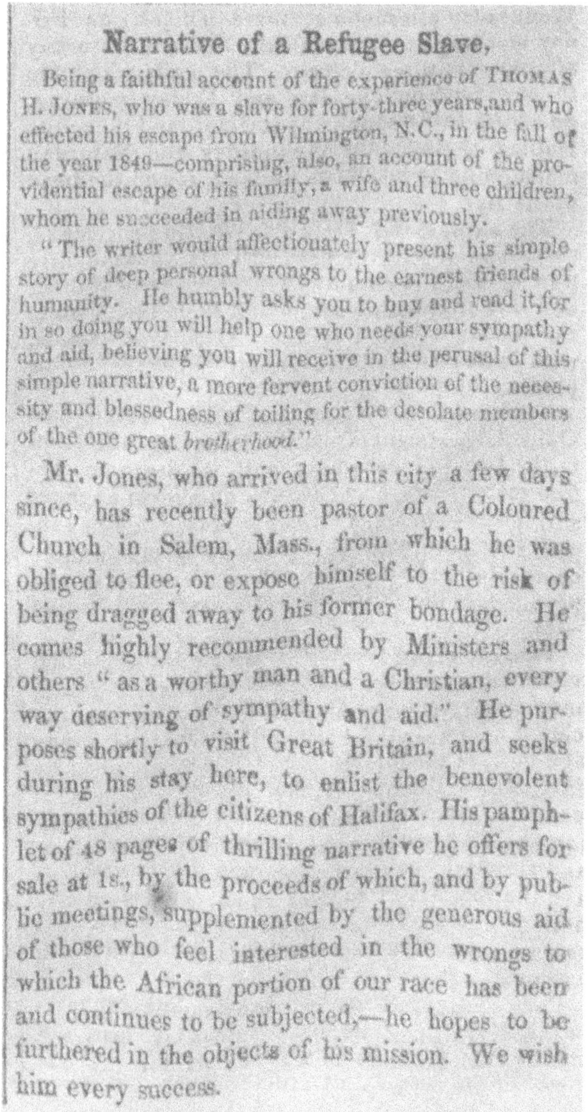

116 *Beyond the antislavery haven*

Narrative of a Refugee Slave.

Being a faithful account of the experience of THOMAS H. JONES, who was a slave for forty-three years, and who effected his escape from Wilmington, N.C., in the fall of the year 1849—comprising, also, an account of the providential escape of his family; a wife and three children, whom he succeeded in aiding away previously.

"The writer would affectionately present his simple story of deep personal wrongs to the earnest friends of humanity. He humbly asks you to buy and read it, for in so doing you will help one who needs your sympathy and aid, believing you will receive in the perusal of this simple narrative, a more fervent conviction of the necessity and blessedness of toiling for the desolate members of the one great *brotherhood.*"

Mr. Jones, who arrived in this city a few days since, has recently been pastor of a Coloured Church in Salem, Mass., from which he was obliged to flee, or expose himself to the risk of being dragged away to his former bondage. He comes highly recommended by Ministers and others "as a worthy man and a Christian, every way deserving of sympathy and aid." He purposes shortly to visit Great Britain, and seeks during his stay here, to enlist the benevolent sympathies of the citizens of Halifax. His pamphlet of 48 pages of thrilling narrative he offers for sale at 1s., by the proceeds of which, and by public meetings, supplemented by the generous aid of those who feel interested in the wrongs to which the African portion of our race has been and continues to be subjected,—he hopes to be furthered in the objects of his mission. We wish him every success.

Figure 3.5 Advertisement for Thomas Jones's narrative in the *Wesleyan*, 21 June 1851, p. 5, reproduced with the permission of the Nova Scotia Archives.

men should do unto you, do ye also unto them').[93] Quaker antislavery discourse frequently used this argument in Pennsylvania from the mid-seventeenth century on.[94] The passage also has echoes of eschatological language concerned with the destiny of individual souls and God's judgement. The combined effect is an uncompromising tone that chastises readers for not doing enough to help enslaved people. The *Wesleyan* excises parts of this text to make Jones's narrative and its philanthropic aim less clearly antislavery. It also removes the Golden Rule, a powerful piece of antislavery discourse, all references to the narrative being an antislavery text and the text that identifies readers as reading out of a concern for enslaved people ('to the earnest friends of the Slave'), replacing this with a more general charitable purpose that is less clearly antislavery: 'to the earnest friends of humanity'.[95]

The notice that appears in the *Presbyterian Witness* (Figure 3.6) is far shorter and differs in focus. Rather than positioning Thomas

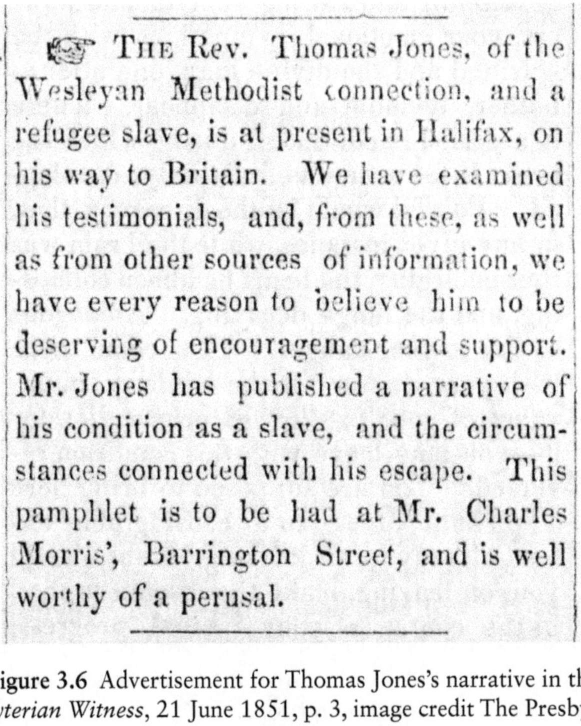

☞ THE Rev. Thomas Jones, of the Wesleyan Methodist connection, and a refugee slave, is at present in Halifax, on his way to Britain. We have examined his testimonials, and, from these, as well as from other sources of information, we have every reason to believe him to be deserving of encouragement and support. Mr. Jones has published a narrative of his condition as a slave, and the circumstances connected with his escape. This pamphlet is to be had at Mr. Charles Morris', Barrington Street, and is well worthy of a perusal.

Figure 3.6 Advertisement for Thomas Jones's narrative in the *Presbyterian Witness*, 21 June 1851, p. 3, image credit The Presbyterian Church in Canada Archives.

118   *Beyond the antislavery haven*

Jones as a charitable subject, it highlights conventional aspects of the slave narrative genre in Jones's text and suggests that these might be of interest to its readers. Unlike the *Wesleyan* notice, it is not suffused with the language of Jones as a needy Christian recipient of the generosity of the benevolent men and women of Halifax. The narrative is about 'his condition as a slave and the circumstances of his escape', showing the reviewer's knowledge of the conventions of the genre.[96] The narrative is described as being of value and interest, rather than demonstrating the Christian piety of the reader. This foreshadows the treatment of the narrative in the United States. A frontispiece was added to the 1862 edition, produced by Boston engravers Taylor and Adams, showing Jones fleeing aboard a raft during his escape to New York. This moment receives only a brief textual treatment in the narrative, consisting of just a few paragraphs, compared to the eight pages charting his process of learning to read, but this choice of image may be an attempt to underscore the excitement and appeal of Jones's narrative. This invites the reader to approach the text along more traditional slave narrative lines. The *Presbyterian Witness* positions Jones's text more as an antislavery narrative than the *Wesleyan*, but its notice also sells it as a thrilling story. This was not the first time the sensational aspect of the narrative of fugitives from slavery was emphasised. In what appears to be an original review for *Life in the South: A Companion to Uncle Tom's Cabin* by C. H. Wiley, the story of Wild Bill's journey for liberation is described as a series of 'startling adventures', including 'wild beasts, attacks by pirates, [and] tragical murders [...] common in the Southern States'.[97]

Approaching Thomas Jones's narrative through the newspapers

This section provides a more contextualised reading of Jones's narrative. It suggests that the evangelical religious reading available in Jones's narrative explains its continued appeal during the nineteenth century and after the abolition of slavery in the United States. By approaching Jones's narrative through the religious newspapers and treating them as paratexts or 'threshold[s]' to his text, this chapter recontextualises his narrative to imagine how contemporary readers in Canada were invited to approach it.[98]

Thomas Jones in Nova Scotia and New Brunswick   119

Religious newspapers provide a way to examine the worldview and beliefs underpinning Jones's narrative. Jane P. Tompkins noted in the 1980s that literary critics were devaluing and misreading American sentimental fiction such as *Uncle Tom's Cabin* as sensational fiction.[99] She argued that its cultural 'power' can only be appreciated by placing it in the context of 'the system of beliefs that undergirds the patterns of sentimental fiction' and evangelical Christianity.[100] Jones presents his loss of faith and Christian despair in terms that readers of the religious newspapers would have understood. Throughout the newspapers, the idea that readers can quickly lose their faith if not committed to its maintenance is reinforced through the need for the repetitive reading of sustaining narratives. For example, the short story 'Martin's Rose' demonstrates the wider view that absence of a mother and a family home can precipitate despair in Christian believers. It tells the story of a young woman who is distracted by worldly pursuits when sent away to school and who loses her faith. The girl rekindles her religious enthusiasm upon her return home because of the Christian teachings of her mother's male servant.[101]

In the closing moments of the text, Jones offers a prayer of gratitude for the 'kindness' of his friends, who have met his suffering with 'sympathy, love and generous aid', saving him and his family from 'pinching want'.[102] Jones calls upon God to witness this kindness and hopes that those who have been generous to him will receive blessings from heaven. This bears a superficial similarity to the language and tone of the notice printed in the *Wesleyan*, which characterised Jones as an individual who would welcome the charity of Christian sympathisers. However, Jones goes beyond the conventions of the grateful slave trope depicted in other, presumably white-authored, newspaper narratives, instead presenting God as the only audience and true recipient of his gratitude, rather than his enslaver.[103] He says, 'God will know, and He alone can know, the deep and fervent gratitude and joy' and suggests that recollecting the kindness of others in his past allows his heart to swell with gratitude, an evangelical sign for strengthening one's faith and relationship with God.[104] Jones refuses to express the imagined gratitude of enslaved people to their enslavers as seen elsewhere in contemporaneous texts such as *Uncle Tom's Cabin* or in the religious newspapers that reinforced ameliorative positions on American slavery and their accompanying racist tropes.

120 *Beyond the antislavery haven*

Today, the dominant and idealised national narrative that persists is that Canada was a place of safety and freedom at the end of the Underground Railroad during chattel slavery in the United States. This chapter has demonstrated that paying attention to the larger political and religious environment created by newspapers and their editorial politics (reprints, notices, and reviews) undercuts this vision. In doing so, it contributes to an expanding field of scholarship that seeks to unsettle and complicate the narrative of Canada as a benevolent haven.[105] The newspapers are a space to encounter the messiness of this history and the religious and economic structures that used anti-Black racism in the service of enslavement. Examining the *Presbyterian Witness* and the *Wesleyan* holistically and looking at their wider handling of slavery has revealed details of the specificity of the circulation context of Jones's narrative in Canada. Reading book-length slave narratives alongside lesser-known newspaper narratives gives a more complex account of Canadian attitudes to slavery. It shows how antislavery narratives could circulate alongside notions about the class and racial inferiority of African Americans, enslaved or free. It might be tempting to assume that Canadian readers consumed antislavery narratives and felt morally outraged by the institution. The way Jones's narrative was framed suggests that, when circulated in Canada, narratives of the experiences of enslaved people could be positioned in ways that supported an abolitionist, an ameilorationist, or even an apologist stance on chattel slavery. Slave narratives circulated across the Canada–US border but so too did racist stories that justified slavery or called for the amelioration of slavery rather than its abolition, and these accounts could circulate in the same textual space within individual newspapers.

One way to extend the map of slave narratives and our sense of their geographical diversity, as Goddu calls for, is through more comprehensive study of narratives of liberation and of how these circulated in locations in what became Canada.[106] Newspapers are an important source for recovering the lives and presence of self-liberated activists like Jones in Canada. Unlike many newspapers in the United States that have been digitised and are text-searchable online, many Canadian newspapers have only recently been made accessible in this way or still need to be consulted and searched by hand on microfilm, and this serves to hamper a fuller account of cross-border Black print culture. Nineteenth-century newspapers like those published in New Brunswick and Nova Scotia examined in this chapter were receptive to texts demonstrating a cross-border and hemispheric mobility, and this is evident in the texts about slavery that they printed, the excerpted slave narratives, and the notices for Jones's slave narrative. The advertisement sections provided a space for Black activists like Jones to write their life stories and to consolidate and grow their networks. However, as his card in the *Weekly Chronicle* demonstrates, Jones had a narrow space in which to write his presence and life story into the newspaper form; he had to conform to the expected genre conventions of the notice or advertisement. Using Roy's argument that slave narratives are 'fugitive texts' that could shift between medias, we can see Jones's card as a supplementary part of his narrative and addition to his life story and as reflecting his agency as he wrote himself into public life in Canada.[107] Through piecing together these fragments that Jones left in the Canadian newspapers, we come to a more detailed understanding of his life as a Wesleyan preacher and his abolitionist activism.

Notes

1 For an early call to explore slave narratives as part of the Canadian literary canon, see George Elliott Clarke, '"This Is No Hearsay": Reading the Canadian Slave Narratives', *Papers of the Bibliographical Society of Canada* 43:1 (2005), 7–32. https://doi.org/10.33137/pbsc.v43i1.18415. Winfried Siemerling, 'Slave Narratives and Hemispheric Studies', in John Ernest (ed.), *The Oxford Handbook of the African American Slave Narrative* (Oxford: Oxford University Press, 2014), pp. 344–61. Nele Sawallisch, 'Radical Legacies in Black Nineteenth-Century Canadian Writing', in Ronald Cummings and Natalee Caple (eds), *Harriet's Legacies: Race, Historical Memory, and Futures in Canada* (Montreal and Kingston: McGill-Queen's University Press, 2022), pp. 104–117; Alyssa MacLean, 'Writing Back to Massa: The Black Open Letter in Transnational Abolitionist Print Culture', in Gillian Roberts (ed.), *Reading between the Borderlines: Cultural Production and Consumption across the 49th Parallel* (Montreal and Kingston: McGill-Queen's University Press, 2018), pp. 42–66.

2 Nele Sawallisch, *Fugitive Borders: Black Canadian Cross-Border Literature at Mid-Nineteenth Century* (Bielefeld: Transcript Verlag, 2019), pp. 9–10.

3 Marcy J. Dinius, *The Textual Effects of David Walker's Appeal: Print Based Activism against Slavery, Racism and Discrimination 1829–1851* (Philadelphia: University of Pennsylvania Press, 2022), chapter 6, especially pp. 198–230, 224 and 230.

4 Winfried Siemerling, *The Black Atlantic Reconsidered: Black Canadian Writing, Cultural History and the Presence of the Past* (Montreal: McGill-Queen's University Press, 2015), pp. 52–66.

5 For a discussion of this in the context of the texts distributed by the American Anti-Slavery Society, particularly in the 1830s, see Teresa A. Goddu, *Selling Antislavery: Abolition and Mass Media in Antebellum America* (Philadelphia: University of Pennsylvania Press, 2020).

6 An example of this approach can be found in several of the essays in Audrey Fisch (ed.), *The Cambridge Companion to the African American Slave Narrative* (Cambridge: Cambridge University Press, 2007).

7 Teresa A. Goddu, 'The Slave Narrative as Material Text', in Ernest (ed.), *Oxford Handbook*, p. 149.

8 *Ibid.*, p. 150.

9 Michaël Roy, 'The Slave Narrative Unbound', in Brigitte Fielder and Jonathan Senchyne (eds), *Against a Sharp White Background: Infrastructures of African American Print* (Madison: University of Wisconsin Press, 2019), p. 270.

10 *Ibid.*, pp. 269–70.

11 Michaël Roy, *Fugitive Texts: Slave Narratives in Antebellum Print Culture* (Madison: University of Wisconsin Press, 2022), p. 10.

12 Eric Gardner, 'Slave Narratives and Archival Research', in Ernest (ed.), *Oxford Handbook*, p. 36.

13 John Ernest, 'Beyond Douglass and Jacobs', in Fisch (ed.), *The African American Slave Narrative*, p. 218.

14 Michaël Roy, 'Cheap Editions, Little Books, and Handsome Duodecimos: A Book History Approach to Antebellum Slave Narratives', *Melus* 40:3 (2015), 69–93, pp. 70 and 86.

15 Bryan Sinche, 'The Walking Book', in Fielder and Senchyne (eds), *Against a Sharp White Background*, pp. 278, 287 and 292.

16 *Ibid.*, p. 279.

17 Roy, *Fugitive Texts*, p. 6.

18 Roy, 'Cheap Editions', 73–74.

19 Lori Leavell, '"Not Intended Exclusively for the Slave States": Antebellum Recirculation of David Walker's Appeal', *Callaloo* 38:3 (2015), 679, 691.

Thomas Jones in Nova Scotia and New Brunswick   123

20 Gérard Genette, *Paratexts: Thresholds of Interpretation*, trans. Jane E. Lewin (Cambridge: Cambridge University Press, 1997), p. 2.

21 John Marrant, 'A Narrative of the Lord's Wonderful Dealings with John Marrant, A Black' (London, 1785), in Vincent Carretta (ed.), *Unchained Voices: An Anthology of Black Authors in the English-Speaking World of the Eighteenth Century, Expanded Edition* (Lexington: University Press of Kentucky, 2004), p. 127.

22 John Marrant, *A Narrative ... The Sixth Edition* (London: printed and sold by Gilbert and Plummer, 1788), p. 40, *ECCO*. Carretta (ed.), *Unchained Voices*, p. 132, n. 60.

23 John Marrant, *A Journal of the Rev. John Marrant, From August the 18th, 1785 to the 16th March, 1790 to Which Are Added: Two Sermons, One Preached on Ragged Island on Sabbath Day, the 27th Day of October, 1787, the Other at Boston, in New England, on Thursday, the 24th of June, 1789* (London: printed for the author, sold by J. Taylor and Mr. Marrant, 1790), pp. 68–71.

24 *Ibid.*, pp. 76, 57 and 73.

25 Carretta (ed.), *Unchained Voices*, p. 367, n. 21.

26 Boston King, 'Memoirs of the Life of Boston King', in Carretta (ed.), *Unchained Voices*, p. 357.

27 *Ibid.*, p. 358.

28 *Ibid.*, p. 360.

29 *Ibid.*, pp. 105–10, 157–61, 209–13, and 261–65. For a thorough discussion of Boston King's time in England, see Ryan Hanley, 'Boston King, Kingswood School and British Methodism, 1794–1798', in Ryan Hanley, *Beyond Slavery and Abolition: Black British Writing c. 1770–1830* (Cambridge: Cambridge University Press, 2019).

30 George, 'An Account', in *Methodist Magazine*, 340.

31 David George, 'An Account of the Life of Mr David George, from Sierra Leone in Africa; Given by Himself in a Conversation with Brother Rippon of London and Brother Pearce of Birmingham', in Carretta (ed.), *Unchained Voices*, pp. 336–40.

32 This mistake is listed in many library catalogues. A recent example incorrectly identifying Marrant's *Narrative* as reprinted in Canada is the otherwise excellent Astrid Haas, 'Native Bondage, Narrative Mobility: African American Accounts of Indian Captivity' *Journal of American Studies* 56:2 (2022), 251 and n. 39. https://doi.org/10.1017/S0021875821000852.

33 On J. Nicholson as based in Halifax, West Yorkshire and not Canada, see James Green, 'The Publishing History of Olaudah Equiano's Interesting Narrative', *Slavery and Abolition* 16:3 (1995), 362–75, 367, 374. https://doi.org/10.1080/01440399508575167. On the office

124 *Beyond the antislavery haven*

of J. Nicholson, see Douglas Taylor, *The Nicholson Family: Printers & Publishers* (Halifax: Halifax Antiquarian Society, 1977). For the Halifax (West Yorkshire) editions, see John Marrant, *A Narrative of the Life of John Marrant* (Halifax: J. Nicholson, 1812) and John Marrant, *A Narrative of the Life of John Marrant* (Halifax: J. Nicholson, 1813). For the Equiano publication dates, see Henry Louis Gates, Jr., *The Signifying Monkey: A Theory of African American Literary Criticism, with a New Preface by the Author* (New York: Oxford University Press, 2014), p. 154.

34 David A. Davis, 'Thomas H. Jones', in William L. Andrews et al. (eds), *North Carolina Slave Narratives: The Lives of Moses Roper, Lunsford Lane, Moses Grandy, and Thomas H. Jones* (Chapel Hill: University of North Carolina Press, 2003), p. 200 and p. 194.

35 Peter Ripley (ed.), *The Black Abolitionist Papers: Volume II: Canada* (Chapel Hill: University of North Carolina Press, 1986), pp. 133–34 and pp. 212–14.

36 Harvey Amani Whitfield, *North to Bondage: Loyalist Slavery in the Maritimes* (Vancouver: University of British Columbia Press, 2016) and *Biographical Dictionary of Enslaved Black People in the Maritimes* (Toronto: University of Toronto Press, 2022).

37 Harvey Amani Whitfield, *Blacks on the Border: The Black Refugees in British North America, 1815–1860* (Lebanon: University of Vermont Press, 2006). See also the history of the Jamaican Maroons who arrived in Halifax in 1796.

38 Davis, 'Thomas H. Jones', p. 190.

39 *Ibid.*

40 Eugene B. McCarthy and Thomas L. Doughton (eds), *From Bondage to Belonging: The Worcester Slave Narratives* (Amherst: University of Massachusetts Press, 2007), pp. 122–23.

41 William L. Andrews, *To Tell a Free Story: The First Century of Afro-American Autobiography, 1760–1865* (Urbana: University of Illinois Press, 1986), p. 290.

42 Andrews et al. (eds), *North Carolina Slave Narratives*, p. 12.

43 Roy, 'The Slave Narrative Unbound', in Fielder and Senchyne (eds), *Against a Sharp White Background*, pp. 261–62.

44 Andrews et al. (eds), *North Carolina Slave Narratives*, p. 12.

45 *The Experience of Rev. Thomas H. Jones, Who Was a Slave for Forty-Three Years* (Boston: A. T. Bliss and Co., Printers, 1880).

46 Andrews, 'Slave Narratives, 1865–1900', in Ernest (ed.), *Oxford Handbook*, p. 224.

47 George L. Parker, *The Beginnings of the Book Trade in Canada* (Toronto: University of Toronto Press, 1985), pp. 119–20.

Thomas Jones in Nova Scotia and New Brunswick   125

48 Library and Archives Canada E444 J793 1853.

49 *From Bondage to Belonging* and *North Carolina Slave Narratives*.

50 'Narrative of a Refugee Slave', *Wesleyan* (21 June 1851), p. 5; 'The Rev. Thomas Jones', *Presbyterian Witness* (21 June 1851), p. 3.

51 Thomas Jones, *The Experience of Thomas Jones, Who Was a Slave for Forty-Three Years, Written by a Friend as Given by Brother Jones* (Saint John, N. B. [New Brunswick]: J. & A. McMillan, 1853).

52 Meredith L. McGill, *American Literature and the Culture of Reprinting, 1834–1853* (Philadelphia: University of Pennsylvania Press, 2003), p. 41.

53 *Ibid.*, p. 270.

54 Eli MacLaren, *Dominion and Agency: Copyright and the Structuring of the Canadian Book Trade, 1867–1918* (Toronto: University of Toronto Press, 2011), p. 5, pp. 103–4.

55 C. L. Innes, *Slave Life in Virginia and Kentucky: A Narrative of Francis Fedric, Escaped Slave* (Baton Rouge: Louisiana State University Press, 2010), pp. ix–xxxviii.

56 'Thomas H. Jones', *Liberator* (30 May 1851), p. 4, *Nineteenth-Century U.S. Newspapers*.

57 Thomas H. Jones, *The Experience of Rev. Thomas H. Jones, Who Was a Slave for Forty-Three Years* (New Bedford: E. Anthony and Sons, 1885), p. 70. *Documenting the American South*.

58 'Rev. Thomas H. Jones', *Liberator* (19 August 1853), p. 3, *Nineteenth-Century U.S. Newspapers*.

59 Thomas H. Jones, Letter to William Lloyd Garrison, 16 February 1854, Boston Public Library, https://archive.org/details/lettertodea rmrga00jone_1/mode/2up (accessed 10 August 2022).

60 This research was made possible by a British Association for American Studies Early Career Postgraduate Research Assistance Award 2020–21 that funded fifty hours of remote research assistance with the New Brunswick newspapers held at the Harriet Irving Library at the University of New Brunswick (UNB). I am grateful to Andy Post, a PhD student at UNB, for his assistance with examining the newspapers published in New Brunswick.

61 'Took Her Freedom', *St. John Chronicle and Colonial Conservative* (5 September 1851), p. 1. For excerpts of *Twelve Years a Slave*, see 'Thrilling Narrative', *Morning News* (27 July 1853), p. 1 (29 July 1853), p. 1, and (1 August 1853), p. 1.

62 'Fugitive Slaves in Canada', *New Brunswick Courier* (3 April 1852), p. 2; 'Mechanics Institute', *St. John Chronicle and Colonial Conservative* (6 February 1852), p. 2.

63 'The News Boy's Address, respectfully presented to the Patrons of the St. John Chronicle', *St. John Chronicle and Colonial Conservative* (7 January 1853), p. 4.

64 Thomas H. Jones, 'Card', *Weekly Chronicle* (13 June 1851), p. 3. Jones's card thanks all the religious figures who have helped and sympathised with him during his first months in Saint John. This includes individuals also known to broadly support the abolitionist cause. The Rev. Mr McLeod is probably Ezekiel McLeod (1812–67), who directed the Free Baptist Church of Saint John and edited the *Religious Intelligencer*, a newspaper that, amongst other things, opposed slavery. The Rev. Mr Irvine is probably Robert Irvine, a Presbyterian minister in Saint John closely associated with the Rev. William Ferrie, a Presbyterian pastor who gave an antislavery lecture at the Mechanic's Institute in February 1852.

65 Genette, *Paratexts*, p. 11.

66 'experience', *Oxford English Dictionary Online*, https://doi.org/10.1093/OED/5485237439 (accessed 2 November 2024).

67 Ted A. Campbell, 'Spiritual Biography and Autobiography', in Jason E. Vickers (ed.), *The Cambridge Companion to American Methodism* (Cambridge: Cambridge University Press, 2013), pp. 257, 243, and 249.

68 Carretta (ed.), *Unchained Voices*, p. 9.

69 Jones, *The Experience of Thomas Jones*, p. 27.

70 *Ibid.*, p. 31.

71 *Ibid.*, p. 33.

72 Gertrude E. N. Tratt, *A Survey and Listing of Nova Scotia Newspapers, 1752–1957: With Particular Reference to the Period Before 1867* (Halifax: Dalhousie University, 1979), pp. 93, 107, and 238.

73 *Ibid.*, p. 93.

74 Quoted in *ibid.*, p. 107.

75 'Commencement of the New Year', *Presbyterian Witness* (1 January 1853), p. 2.

76 Marguerite Van Die, 'Religion and Law in British North America, 1800–1867', in Stephen J. Stein (ed.), *The Cambridge History of Religions in America: Volume II: 1790 to 1945* (Cambridge: Cambridge University Press, 2012), p. 55.

77 *Ibid.*, p. 55.

78 Allen P. Stouffer, *The Light of Nature and the Law of God: Antislavery in Ontario, 1833–1877* (Montreal: McGill-Queen's University Press, 1992), p. 152.

Thomas Jones in Nova Scotia and New Brunswick   127

79 *Ibid.*, p. 219.

80 'Old Moses', *Wesleyan* (20 September 1851), p. 1; 'The Old Oak Tree', *Wesleyan* (24 February 1853), p. 1; 'Old Jeddy, There's Rest at Home', *Wesleyan* (20 October 1853), p. 1.

81 George Boulukos, *The Grateful Slave: The Emergence of Race in Eighteenth-Century British and American Culture* (Cambridge: Cambridge University Press, 2008), p. 14.

82 'A Real Uncle Tom', *Presbyterian Witness* (30 October 1852), p. 5.

83 'Uncle Tom', *Liberator* (27 August 1852), pp. 1–2.

84 Tompkins, *Sensational Designs*, p. 131.

85 'Nova Scotia Historical Newspapers', http://www.novascotia.ca/archives/newspapers/results.asp?nTitle=Acadian+Recorder (accessed 1 January 2023).

86 'Educational Works', *Presbyterian Witness* (11 September 1852), p. 3.

87 It contains scenes of Jones's sister being violently beaten that first appeared in the 1857 edition, but it does not include a line added to a later edition about Jones going to Canada.

88 Jones, *The Experience of Thomas Jones*, p. 8.

89 *Ibid.*, p. 47.

90 'Narrative of a Refugee Slave'.

91 *Ibid.*

92 *Ibid.*

93 *Ibid.*

94 Brycchan Carey, *From Peace to Freedom: Quaker Rhetoric and the Birth of American Antislavery, 1657–1761* (New Haven: Yale University Press, 2012), pp. 30, 50–51, and 74–78.

95 'Narrative of a Refugee Slave'.

96 'The Rev. Thomas Jones'.

97 'Literature: Life in the South – a Companion to Uncle Tom's Cabin', *Presbyterian Witness* (21 August 1852), p. 3.

98 Genette, *Paratexts*, p. 2.

99 Tompkins, *Sensational Designs*, p. 125.

100 *Ibid.*, pp. 126–27.

101 'Martin's Rose', *Presbyterian Witness* (20 November 1852), pp. 1–2.

102 Jones, *The Experience of Thomas Jones*, p. 48.

103 On the earlier tradition, see Boulukos, *Grateful Slave*, chapter 5, especially p. 182.

104 Jones, *The Experience of Thomas Jones*, p. 48.

105 For some recent examples, see Cummings and Caple, *Harriet's Legacies*; Michele A. Johnson and Funké Aladejebi (eds), *Unsettling the Great White North: Black Canadian History* (Toronto: University

of Toronto Press, 2022); Nina Reid-Maroney, Boulou Ebanda de B'béri, and Wanda Thomas Bernard (eds), *Women in the 'Promised Land': Essays in African Canadian History* (Toronto: Women's Press, 2018).
106 Goddu, 'Slave Narrative', p. 150.
107 Roy, *Fugitive Texts*, p. 10.

4

Broken Shackles: a narrative of slavery in the United States and Canada's first major book distributor, 1889

Beyond the antislavery haven ends with the year 1889, when *Broken Shackles* was published, which itself seems to offer the promise of a first: a book-length publication about slavery in the United States published by William Briggs, often seen as the first major Canadian literary book publisher. Focusing only on books published in Canada by a Canadian publisher would overlook the slave narratives and texts that were printed for their authors in Canada.[1] It would neglect the slave narratives examined in the previous two chapters, such as Thomas H. Jones's slave narrative that was circulated in pamphlet form and described in newspapers and reprinted in Canada, and the slave narratives that depict the lives of Black settlers in Canada that were published in the United States and Britain, as examined in Chapter 2; nevertheless, the publication of a narrative about slavery in the United States and Black settlement in Canada bearing the imprint of Briggs marks an important stage in the history of slavery and print in Canada.

Broken Shackles is a narrative about slavery in the United States written in Ontario by John Frost. Frost was a lawyer and mayor of Owen Sound, Ontario. As Peter Meyler notes in his 2001 edition of *Broken Shackles*, 'it is said that the Frosts helped to provide shelter to several African Americans', and that Frost had antislavery sympathies and met Harriet Beecher Stowe. *Broken Shackles* was '[Frost's] only book'.[2] In part, the narrative provides a history of slavery in the United States, giving a basic history of slavery and its abolition. At the core of the text is the story of the self-liberated Jim Henson. The narrator Glenelg, living in Owen Sound, Ontario, in 1888–89, collects and transcribes the oral stories of Henson, who

130   *Beyond the antislavery haven*

has lived for many years in Canada after fleeing from the United States in 1850. This text poses some challenges in its interpretation. On the one hand, *Broken Shackles* is not an abolitionist text as it was published many years after the abolition of slavery in the United States. However, on the other, it *is* an antislavery narrative, which reads in part as a history of slavery and abolition in the United States. It is clear that the narrative takes slavery as a Christian sin and morally reprehensible, and the narrative celebrates the abolition of slavery in the United States. Given that *Broken Shackles* was published many years after the abolition of slavery, its antislavery purpose cannot be explained as part of a political campaign for the abolition of slavery, unlike the texts examined so far in this book.

Broken Shackles has a frame narrative; it opens in Sydenham (now Owen Sound, Ontario) in the year 1888, and it closes in the same location in 1889. In the first chapter, the reader is introduced to Glenelg, who is a constructed author/narrator and amanuensis of the text and a Canadian living in Owen Sound. The narrator Glenelg is separate from the author John Frost, who is mentioned in chapter 36 by John Hall, who tells Henson that Frost ('Mister-ah-Frost, the merchant') informed him that a new Black settler was arriving.[3] Glenelg describes meeting the self-liberated Jim Henson in the streets of Owen Sound, and recounts that he read out a letter to him from his estranged family living in the United States.[4] Glenelg explains that this inspires Henson to begin to recollect his 'former slave life', and describes how he copied this down into the present volume: 'The letter set him thinking and talking of his long-lost home, and of stirring incidents of former slave life, as given in the following pages.'[5] Glenelg describes writing Henson's recollections of slavery in the United States into a publishable narrative as a seamless process, imagining his pen as a conduit for Henson's stories. From the second chapter, the narrative is largely composed of Glenelg's third-person narration of Henson's stories of plantation life. In the final chapter the narrative focus returns to Glenelg in Owen Sound in 1889. A year has passed from when Glenelg started writing down Henson's experiences of slavery, and Glenelg describes completing the book *Broken Shackles*.

Jim Henson was born in Maryland with 'slave' status. Chapters 2–25 focus on Henson's experiences as an enslaved man, including his conversion to Christianity. Chapter 26 relates his decision to

Broken Shackles 131

escape from slavery, and in chapter 27, entitled 'The Escape', Henson travels to Pennsylvania. After becoming a free man in Columbia, Pennsylvania, he subsequently flees to New Jersey to evade recapture. Henson later returns to Philadelphia, where he marries and becomes 'comfortable and contented'.[6] After the passage of the second Fugitive Slave Law in 1850, Henson, his wife Catherine, and their three daughters move to Canada, where they initially remain with him. His wife and two surviving daughters return to the United States, and in 1854, Henson moves to Owen Sound in Grey County in what is now known as Ontario, and he is still living there when the narrative opens in 1888. The final chapter of *Broken Shackles* describes Henson's life in Canada and brings the narrative back to the present day in 1889. Throughout the text Glenelg goes on narrative diversions, sketching out the history of slavery and abolition in the United States. For example, in chapter 3, 'Scars and Stripes', Glenelg describes of the origins of slavery in the United States and shows that this was enshrined in the Declaration of Independence. Glenelg takes an antislavery stance in depicting the failure of the United States to abolish slavery in the Declaration of Independence and the fact that the nation was founded on slavery. He informs his reader that 'the new flag of stars and stripes was flung to the breeze as an emblem of national freedom, and yet it floated over hundreds of thousands of slaves, and was destined yet to float over them until increased to some millions in number'.[7]

Broken Shackles has been little explored by literary critics. As George Elliott Clarke notes, like other Canadian slave narratives, it has been 'absent from most anthologies and guides of Canadian literature'.[8] Clarke includes *Broken Shackles* in his bibliography of nineteenth-century Canadian slave narratives.[9] However, scholars have yet to offer a sustained textual analysis of this narrative or to successfully read it within a context of the literary tradition that preceded it. In 2001 a new edition was published, edited by Peter Meyler. The blurb argues that *Broken Shackles* is a 'very unique book'. It describes Henson's narrative as 'one of the very few books that documented the journey to Canada from the perspective of a person of African descent'. Chapter 2 of this book explored a tradition of portraying in literature the experience of self-liberated African Americans and their experiences after arriving in Canada, which *Broken Shackles* came out of. Afua Cooper briefly mentions

132 *Beyond the antislavery haven*

Broken Shackles in her examination of the life and trial of the Canadian enslaved woman Marie-Joseph Angelique, situating it in the Canadian slave narrative tradition that she argues stretches back to the unpublished trial transcripts of Angelique.[10] Cooper does not mention the character of the amanuensis Glenelg or his role and presence in the narrative. She positions Jim Henson rather than John Frost as the author who penned and initiated the publication of his memoir. Similarly, in his bibliography of Canadian slave narratives, Clarke lists Henson as the author of *Broken Shackles* and describes John Frost as its editor.[11]

Clarke and Cooper read *Broken Shackles* as a Black Canadian autobiography, and this approach finds some parallels within the critical treatment of slave narratives. Sara Salih explores the slave narrative of Mary Prince, *The History of Mary Prince*, and argues that a narrow focus that looks for a stable Black subject misreads the genre. Salih argues scholars should look at the interplay of voices in the slave narrative such as the presence of editors and even look at how newspapers can challenge the 'textual integrity' of the slave narrative.[12] Salih's reading of *The History of Mary Prince* reflects a general shift in the critical treatment of the slave narrative, away from earlier readings that tried to recover Prince's West Indian female voice; more recently, scholars have explored the narrative as a 'composite text', examining the role of the amanuensis Susanna Moodie and the editor Thomas Pringle as well as Prince in shaping the narrative, and seeing it as impossible to disentangle these voices from each other.[13]

Cooper's, Clarke's, and to an extent Meyler's, readings of *Broken Shackles* find parallels in recent approaches that seek to recover Black voices and histories by lifting them out of the container texts that frame them.[14] Such work rereads rather than misreads what Nicole N. Aljoe describes as 'embedded narratives' and reimagines them for current-day audiences by focusing on the agency of self-liberated people.[15] For Meyler, this is important for the recovery of Henson as a historical individual and of his lived experience.[16] This chapter takes a complementary approach that seeks to explore the construction of 'Henson' within the 1889 edition of the text as readers approached it, to examine the construction of Canada's antislavery identity. The broader approach to reading slave narratives that

Salih advocates seems particularly pertinent in relation to *Broken Shackles*, given that the presence of the amanuensis in the text is so dominant.

This chapter argues that Glenelg is a strong presence in the narrative and indivisible from Henson's voice and Frost's artistic project. *Broken Shackles* is understood in the context of a book publishing trade in Canada in the nineteenth century in which Canadian book publishers were largely distributors of books published in the United States and Britain. *Broken Shackles* sits at the end of a textual tradition for representing slavery and Canada in print stretching across a century, as explored in the previous three chapters. Frost carefully developed his narrative out of previous literary forms, revising them. Frost blends three literary traditions: the slave narrative, Methodist autobiography, and American local colour writing, which was in vogue when Frost penned this narrative. By comparing the 2001 and 1889 editions of *Broken Shackles*, the effect of removing Henson's dialect speech from the recent edition will be examined. While there are understandable reasons for Meyler wanting to remove historically inaccurate and racist colour dialect from the 2001 edition, it will be argued that removing the dialect changes how Canadian antislavery attitudes in the narrative read and takes Henson's voice out the doublethink of Canadian antislavery sentiment and racism in which it was originally presented. Moreover, published post-abolition, *Broken Shackles* reproduces the antislavery haven image of Canada that persists to this day and does not address contemporary issues such as racism post-emancipation in Canada or the United States.

Broken Shackles and the Canadian publishing trade

Placing *Broken Shackles* in a nineteenth-century Canadian book history publication context shows that what has been explored in the past three chapters is partly a story of Canadian publishing. This situates *Broken Shackles* at the end of a tradition that looks back on the newspapers and slave narratives in the previous chapters, and explains the earlier representations of slavery and Canada in print. *Broken Shackles* carries the imprint of the Methodist Book

134 *Beyond the antislavery haven*

and Publishing House based in Toronto, where William Briggs was the book steward between 1879 and 1919. In the front of the 1889 edition, it is listed as entered for copyright protection by William Briggs.[17] The imprint on the title page shows that the narrative was also distributed by a Methodist reading room in Montreal and a Methodist publishing house in Halifax, Nova Scotia, and that these were both linked to the Methodist Book and Publishing House in Toronto.

Briggs is often celebrated as Canada's first major book publisher of original book titles. However, Eli MacLaren's work on the Canadian book publishing trade demonstrates that there was little original literary book publishing in nineteenth-century Canada. MacLaren argues Briggs was not a publisher but a distributor of books that were published in Britain and the United States; when Briggs's imprint appeared on title pages, this usually reflected that Briggs was producing a Canadian issue of a foreign edition of a book with the permission of the foreign publisher.[18] MacLaren defines a publisher as someone who 'cultivat[es] a relationship with the author and initiates, organises, and finances the transformation of a manuscript into an edition' as well as 'wholesaling it in one or more markets', whereas a distributor or wholesaler 'does not create an edition' but sells a book published elsewhere by a foreign publisher. MacLaren highlights how nineteenth-century Canadian book publishing was shaped by Canada's proximity to the United States and its relationship with Britain in the form of imperial copyright law.[19] The North American copyright divide ensured that the United States could reprint British texts and import them into Canada, but firms in Canada were not legally able to reprint unauthorised Canadian editions of British copyright texts. MacLaren has characterised nineteenth-century North America as single space that cannot be divided in the context of book publishing, explaining that 'when it came to general literature, anglophone North America was essentially one book market'.[20] MacLaren describes how this led to the proliferation of editions of books from the United States in nineteenth-century Canada and created a context that was 'more or less incompatible with original literary publishing'.[21] MacLaren notes that this led to the 'exodus' of authors to the United States, where they were protected by copyright laws.[22] *Broken Shackles* may have been the first book-length narrative about slavery published by a literary publishing house in Canada. However, it is more likely that its Canadian imprint reflects the fact that it was distributed rather than published in Canada, and that the newspapers and slave narratives examined in the previous chapters were produced at a time when Canadian printing was restricted to newspapers, religious periodicals, and government and local printing.[23] Canadians largely consumed books published elsewhere and imported and 'reanimated' them within a Canadian context.

The publishing context of *Broken Shackles* reflects a model of Canada and the United States as part of an indivisible publishing space. An illustration of how contemporaries could think about Canada and the United States as a single publishing space is found in the slave narrative of the former slave and Canadian resident Samuel Ringgold Ward. Ward characterises the United States and Canada as having a porous border that allowed the traffic of bodies, goods, and ideas to freely circulate. Ward's depiction of Canada as vulnerable to the proliferation of pro-slavery ideas from the United States because of Canada's porous border could be taken as an analogy of Canada as part of a wider North American land mass when it came to nineteenth-century publishing:

> there is a vast amount of intercourse with the adjoining States, and a great deal of traffic, and Canadians travel extensively in the States, as do the people of the States in Canada. Thus the spread of slaveholding predilections is both favoured and facilitated; and, what is more, there is abundant evidence that some Americans industriously use these opportunities for the purpose of giving currency to their own notions. Moreover, in various parts of Canada Yankees have settled, and for miles around them the poison of their pro-slavery influence is felt.[24]

The 'traffic' Ward describes could easily be the huge number of American reprints dominating the Canadian book market, as well as people and goods that were freely traded between Canada and the United States following the passage of the free trade agreement, the Reciprocity Treaty, which lifted import duties between Canada and the United States (1854–66).[25] Of course, Britain was also a part of this flow and cross-border relationship, in enshrining the imperial laws that encoded it and in the sense that many of these books were imperial works reprinted in the United States, with the

136   *Beyond the antislavery haven*

royalties upon importation of these reprints of British copyright works sent back to Britain.

The recirculation of foreign books and the 'exodus' of authors to the United States where they were protected by copyright laws has obscured the Canadian dimension of slave narratives.[26] It has shaped the fact that we have been looking at Canada as a place of re-circulation for slave narratives published in the United States, and the way Canada is imagined in African American slave narratives. To some extent, this is one answer to Clarke's observation that Canadian slave narratives have been exiled from the Canadian literary canon. It indicates that the publishing context may have disguised Canada's impact on slave narratives, especially as scholars tend to focus on place of publication and book-length narratives when assigning national labels to texts. Rhondda Robinson Thomas discusses the multiple locations in slave narratives and questions the validity of seeing slave narratives within a Canadian literary tradition. Thomas argues that the lack of slave narratives published in Canada is compelling evidence that challenges a call to see them as Canadian texts: 'Clarke's claim for a distinct Afro-Canadian tradition becomes more problematic through his choice of slave narratives by authors who lived in Canada temporarily but resettled and published their narratives in America.'[27] Thomas's argument does not take into account the 'exodus' of huge numbers of Canadian authors to the United States in the mid-nineteenth century because of the uncertain publishing climate. Thomas's interpretation does not acknowledge that Canada was part of a wider North American publishing space and that this may have obscured some of Canada's literary history, given that places of original publication are more readily taken as reflecting the national identity of texts. An implicitly United States-centric view of the publication history of slave narratives does not work when we are looking to examine Canada's part in this transatlantic print history.

Frost crafts a frame narrative situating the production of *Broken Shackles* by the fictional character Glenelg in Owen Sound, Ontario between 1888 and 1889, perhaps as a response to this uncertain climate for original Canadian book publishing. To some extent the frame narrative inscribes the Canadian production of the narrative into the fabric of his text, regardless of its place of publication. This had a precedent too in narratives from the 1850s, such as Drew's

Broken Shackles 137

The Refugee. Frost also complicates this by not mentioning that the location of Glenelg is Owen Sound in chapter 1 (the reader is left to find this out in the final chapter) and by naming his character Glenelg, as his name speaks to a United States–Canadian hybridity: 'Glenelg is the name of a nearby township (in Ontario); it is also a town near Baltimore, Maryland', as Meyler notes.[28]

Broken Shackles and genre: colourism and the slave narrative

Broken Shackles is an antislavery narrative about slavery in the United States published many years after the abolition of slavery there. This indicates that the value of this antislavery stance is something other than political liberation for enslaved people. The previous chapter explored Thomas Jones's slave narrative, which had a life beyond the end of the American abolition movement, and showed that the evangelical and missionary aspect of the narrative may have contributed to its lasting success during and after the abolition movement. This section explores the perceived value of *Broken Shackles*, and looks at some explanations that account for why such a narrative was produced in the late nineteenth century and circulated in Canada.

Broken Shackles makes most sense when we read it within the slave narrative and local colour tradition, popular in the postbellum era. It contains two key devices found in colourism: the frame narrative and 'dialect speech'.[29] Examples of early local colour writing seen as important antecedents of the genre are the short stories of Bret Harte, for example 'The Luck of the Roaring Camp' (1868); and Harriet Beecher Stowe's novel *The Pearl of Orr's Island* (1862). Notable regional authors and texts include Mark Twain, *Huckleberry Finn* (1885); Sarah Orne Jewett, *The Country of the Pointed Firs* (1896); and George Washington Cable, *Old Creole Days* (1879). However, to this we could also add Southern regional writers, for example Joel Chandler Harris, *Uncle Remus*; Kate Chopin, *Bayou Folk*; and Charles W. Chesnutt, *The Conjure Woman*.[30]

The opening of chapter 2 represents a blend of the slave narrative and local colour writing, and signals this generic choice to the reader. It opens with the amanuensis reporting that Henson relates

138 *Beyond the antislavery haven*

where he was born with 'slave' status: "'I wuz bo'n'", he continued, "on ole Dick Crocksell's plantation, Garrison Forest, neah de City of Baltimo', in de wery midst of slavery"'.[31] This evokes the classic conventional opening of the slave narrative genre that begins with 'I was born a slave'.[32] The way Henson's speech is presented anticipates a reader who knows the tradition of the slave narrative genre. Glenelg interrupts Henson's speech and signals his own presence with 'he continued'. This breaks up the flow of Henson's speech and the classic opening line of the slave narrative, and signals Glenelg's role in the text as the amanuensis who records Henson's dialect speech. Glenelg's interruption functions as a shared joke between Glenelg and the reader. By disrupting the conventional opening of the slave narrative, this operates as a moment of generic awareness, in which the reader and Glenelg are able to share a recognition that the text revises an already existing genre that the reader has encountered many times before. Glenelg's presence reads as unexpected and alien within the conventional opening line of the slave narrative. The interruption of an amanuensis into the first-person voice of the self-liberated person does not find narrative precedent in slave narratives from the 1850s, although these texts were often heavily edited and shaped by amanuenses and editors. For example, Henry Bibb's slave narrative opens 'I was born May 1815, of a slave mother, in Shelby County, Kentucky, and was claimed as the property of David White Esq.'[33] Similarly, the opening line of James W. C. Pennington's slave narrative reads 'I was born in the state of Maryland, which is one of the smallest and most northern of the slave-holding states; the products of this state are wheat, rye, Indian corn, tobacco and some hemp, flax, &c.'[34] *Broken Shackles* has a different tone from the slave narratives published in the 1850s and can be understood as part of the slave narrative genre that shifted after the Civil War. This conforms to some extent to what we might expect, since slave narratives after 1865 differed in tone and thematic focus to pre-Civil War slave narratives, as William L. Andrews has noted.[35] Andrews highlights a range of differences in the later slave narratives. He notes they tend to focus less on the acts of assertion or individualisation by self-liberated people, such as running away or violent resistance, and they more typically focus instead on presenting the importance of individuals serving the Black community, engaging in collective uplift, and showing 'manliness achieved through the gospel'.[36] These post-slavery narratives could portray slavery less negatively than their predecessors and present it as a 'training ground' for pride, endurance, and a spiritual life.[37]

The handling of Henson's voice and the narratorial attempts to present it as something that has been authentically collected corresponds to how the dialect voice is depicted within American local colour writing. The local colour tradition took a group of people or a location that was anticipated to be unfamiliar to readers and presented it to them. Richard H. Brodhead notes that the local voices presented in colourism had to be 'unfamiliar' in order to fulfil the promise of presenting 'knowledge of some yet-unrecorded indigenous culture'.[38] Brodhead argues that in local colour writing, a key skill of the author is to 'produce authoritative transcriptions of vernacular speech', and he then qualifies this with '[a]uthoritative sounding ones, at least: since the whole point is that this speech is not known to its readers otherwise than through the regionalist's transcription'. He argues that the dialect voice has to pass for authentic rather than *be* authentic.[39] The asides of the narrator Glenelg in *Broken Shackles* present the voice of Henson as 'authentic'. Throughout the narrative, Glenelg comments on how Henson's voice sounds and its tone, and draws attention to its orality. He describes Henson as speaking as if to himself ('information contributed in a half-soliloquising manner by [Henson]').[40] The asides of the narrator function as reminders that the reader is invited to see the narrative as based on the oral outpouring of Henson's stories that have been collected by Glenelg. This is given emphasis in chapter 2, when Glenelg relates, 'The question, "Do you know anything about your ancestry?" elicited the reply, "Suteny, I know suthin' 'bout my ancestry", and brought out the following feature of African life. His mother's mother [...]'.[41] This tells the reader that the third-person narration, told from the point of view of Henson, is based upon a conversation that is taking place in the present between Henson and Glenelg and which Glenelg is conducting like an oral interview. Later in the narrative, occasional asides describe the narrative as coming out of the mouth of Henson: '"I wuz soon seated at de table", Charley relates.'[42] The phrase 'Charley relates' draws the reader's attention back to the sense that the narrative is based on an ongoing conversation taking place in the present

140 *Beyond the antislavery haven*

between Glenelg and Henson, and that his authentic voice is being recorded in print.

The narrator-amanuensis, Glenelg, reveals a fascination with fixing history in objects. This is reflected in the images of a stuffed horse on the top floor of Girard College in Philadelphia and a bronze statue of an enslaved person exhibited in an art gallery. In chapter 29, Glenelg relates Henson's experience of labouring on the farm of Stephen Girard while hired out by his enslaver. Girard is depicted as riding his horse and commanding him through a gate held open by Jim Henson: '"Get up, Dick", Mr. Girard would say as he touched his favourite horse with the whip, and off they started toward the dairy' while Henson held 'open [...] the gate wide to let Dick and his gig [...] pass through.'[43] In the next paragraph, there is an abrupt movement forward in time as Glenelg describes Girard's horse and gig in the present day as now in an upper room of Girard college, describing it as 'the selfsame for which Henson used to open the farm gate wide', and where it is now a visitor attraction for thousands of people each year. Glenelg enjoys the swift transformation of Girard's horse into a stuffed creature. Glenelg transforms Girard, commanding his horse Dick by touching him with his whip, 'Get up Dick', and him obeying into a piece of history through jumping forward in the next paragraph to describe how 'there stands a stuffed grey horse, clad in an old harness and hitched to a gig, which has been shown to thousands of visitors as a curiosity'. Glenelg creates a sense of the passage of time by describing it as the same horse and gig that Henson used to 'open the farm gate wide' for. The past is presented as something that can be perfectly preserved. The messiness and energy of the American Civil War is conveyed through the description of its 'rattle of rifles, boom of cannon, bursting of bombs'. A contrast is developed between the sensory overload of this description and the collection of this history into an exhibit for the public to view at an art gallery in the present day. This is presented when the narrator abruptly shifts forward in time in the middle of a short history of Lincoln's Emancipation Proclamation ('Noble Lincoln! Grand proclamation, and wonderful deliverance of downtrodden people') and describes how this historical moment has been fixed into an object at an art gallery in Philadelphia:

Broken Shackles 141

> There stood in the Art Gallery, at the Centennial Exhibition in Philadelphia in 1876, a bronze slave, with a broken shackle in one hand, and in the other hand a scroll, on which was inscribed this celebrated proclamation of freedom by President Lincoln. Visitors, as they looked upon that bronze statue with its inscribed proclamation and broken shackles, wondered that so gigantic a traffic in human flesh could have flourished at so recent a period in a civilised, great and prosperous country.[44]

The fascination with preserving and showcasing historical artefacts of slavery hints at the temporariness of the power of the abuser Girard and reduces him to a ridiculous object, with his technologies of power and control no longer vital. More significantly, it conveys an idea of time and history as collectable and fixable, and it presents an argument for the importance of preserving history.

Glenelg treats Henson as a historical relic, and through his descriptions, expresses a desire to preserve Henson by writing his story. In the opening and closing chapters, Glenelg focuses on Henson's physicality, describing his aged, wizened, and slow-moving body; for example, in the final chapter, Glenelg describes watching Henson from his window:

> The writer on looking out of an office window today – the hottest so far this summer – saw […] the same bent, broad figure […] old man Henson, with his axe in one hand and his bucksaw in the other – using both to aid him in his locomotion – stopped and leaned his axe against one leg and his saw against the other, took off his hat, pulled out of his pocket a large red handkerchief and wiped the great drops of perspiration from his forehead, and then passed on with the crowd out of sight.[45]

The slowness of Henson's movements and the effort it takes him to walk a short distance is conveyed in this extract through the use of several verbs crammed together that convey his laboured movement and depict him as frequently stopping and using his axe and bucksaw to help him walk. Glenelg's observations of Henson's physical body, represented in this example, and his role in recording his speech throughout the text reflect that Glenelg is performing the role of a curator or collector of history in the text. Henson is figured as a symbolic last fugitive from slavery in the world of the text, presented through the heavy emphasis on Henson's age throughout the

142   *Beyond the antislavery haven*

text. He is referred to as 'one of the oldest men in town', as almost impossibly old and perhaps near to death: 'This man, now linked to two centuries and rapidly nearing a third.'[46] In the final chapter, the narrator/author Glenelg addresses the reader to give them their last 'glimpse' of Henson in the text, a moment which prepares the reader for the final moment of Henson's first-person speech:

> This too is the last glimpse of him save one for the reader. It would be unfair to the man if, in conclusion, a peep were not given into the little brick church on the bank of the Sydenham River, in which he worships from Sabbath to Sabbath. Here in a recent fellowship meeting, he spoke as follows 'Brethren, the lord has spared me many years. I've for a long time past put my trust in Him.'[47]

The final 'glimpse' we get is aural, not visual, and it implies that hearing the 'unmediated' voice of Henson is the best way to see him and for the reader to secure a final image of the self-liberated Henson in their mind. The power and control Glenelg exhibits in allowing this moment of connection between the reader and Henson depicts Glenelg as a museum curator carefully unveiling and displaying his object for the imagined rapt attention and delight of his viewer/reader.

Broken Shackles and genre: Methodist autobiography

One explanation for the perceived value of *Broken Shackles* as an antislavery narrative published many years after the abolition of slavery in the United States is its religious imperative. *Broken Shackles* was published by a Methodist publishing house when a key part of its remit was to circulate religious texts, during a period when the publishing house was still predominately publishing religious tracts and narratives and before it began to publish secular titles.[48] This is reflected in the structure of the Methodist autobiography, which underpins aspects of the narrative. There are Methodist underpinnings to three occasions in the narrative where Henson speaks at length in the first person: Henson's conversion to Christianity, marriage, and speech at a fellowship meeting.[49] Here, the narrator steps back and lets Henson speak 'in his own words', in the first person.[50] For example, before Henson's account of his wedding ceremony, Glenelg states 'as to the rest, Charley must give the account in his own words'.[51] This presents Henson's account of his wedding ceremony as his own and implies Glenelg as the gate-keeper to Henson's authentic voice. With the slippage to Charley (the name Henson used while held in slavery), Glenelg invites the reader to see the first-person account of the wedding as in the voice of Charley, rather than the voice of the older Henson looking back. In *Broken Shackles*, Glenelg's asides are narratorial energies that attempt to make Henson's voice pass for an authentic one.

Broken Shackles uses the conventions of Methodist autobiography to present 'exciting' and entertaining 'accounts of pre-conversion life', presenting the religious conversion of Jim Henson.[52] The religious imperatives of *Broken Shackles* and the Methodist publication context suggest why this narrative was circulated and perhaps published in Canada when original book publishing was rare. The narrative was possibly used as a fundraiser to support Henson's trip home, perhaps published by Frost with subscriptions from others involved with abolitionism; Henson was selling post-cards bearing his photograph for this purpose.[53] His narrative contains a letter from his niece dated 1888 informing him that his wife Catherine was still alive and that 'we want you to come here and live with us'. Meyler presents convincing evidence that Henson was reunited with his wife and family for a short time and perhaps was the James Hensen (sic) whose death was recorded in Cinnaminson, New Jersey, in November 1891.[54]

Broken Shackles celebrates the end of slavery in the United States, countering stereotypes about Black people not wanting freedom. However, it also contains minstrel humour and frolics, including casual violence against animals, drinking and gambling on the Sabbath, and romanticised scenes of corn-shucking and feasting. Henson's nostalgia for life on the plantation poses a problem of interpretation for a modern reader. Other post-abolition 'minstrel humour' narratives, including William Wells Brown's *My Southern Home*, first published in 1880, also contain what we might today see as offensive, racist humour. For example, William Wells Brown's narrator spouts racist views of African Americans as natural 'hewers of wood, and drawers of water' and presents scenes of minstrel humour.[55] *My Southern Home* carries an active political message to call for continued change and improvement to African Americans'

144 *Beyond the antislavery haven*

lives and rights. By contrast, Jim Henson has a comparative lack of agency over his own voice, and in the world of the text, there is some ambiguity about who gained the moral high ground from these depictions, which are problematically recouped by Glenelg, rather than Henson. William Andrews points out that Brown's text also critiques and exposes the narratives of white southern power as constructed fictions.[56] In part, this reading of *My Southern Home* is reinforced by knowledge of Brown's literary competence, as the author of an earlier slave narrative and other texts, including the novel *Clotel*, and his role as a Black abolitionist, and thus he is able to represent, construct, and control his own text. Brown's depiction of plantation life as socially corrupting may have intended to highlight the challenges for racial equality and justice in the Reconstruction period. His temporal frame reaches beyond the antebellum period into the Reconstruction era (1865–77) and its aftermath, and his attempt to bring these periods into conversation with one another underscores his aim of addressing the new challenges African Americans faced after the Reconstruction era. Hence, Brown's text uses fictionalised nostalgia to look forward. Bringing this text into conversation with *Broken Shackles* elucidates a number of differences, which opens up what is troubling about this text: the voice of Jim Henson is edited, cropped, and represented for him, and he does not have authorial control over his own representation. The dominance of the white amanuensis and narrator intrudes into the text and shapes the way the reader relates to Henson.

Broken Shackles invites its religious readers to disapprove of the plantation frolics it displays. It shows enslaved characters engaging in non-Christian activities: they attend public houses and drink alcohol, harm small animals, play cards, and ignore the Sabbath. This contrasts with antebellum slave narratives, which tend to associate non-Christian activities with enslavers. Glenelg adopts the carefree tone of the non-Christian enslaved person who does not know better than to enjoy these 'amusements'. The uncritical way Charley decides to spend his earnings on amusements and alcohol that are already linked with Sabbath-breaking presents his lack of religious awareness:

> Charley, for his first ten days' work, carried home ten dollars to his master, who said 'Good boy, Charley.' This was his only reward on

Broken Shackles 145

that or any other occasion when he brought home his earnings. Mr Raven was more generous, and paid him for his leadership, and for his own use a shilling a day. This he was glad to get to spend in the Bull's Head.[57]

This reads as a list of vices, and the focus on the Bull's Head as a place enslaved people visit on the Sabbath reinforces the non-Christian nature of what they term harmless 'amusements'. The reader is invited to look down on Henson for his ignorance and lack of awareness of his own sin and his behaviour that does not conform to Christian belief.

In Thomas Jones's slave narrative, he uses 'two distinct voices'; he relates his experience as a non-Christian enslaved person from the point of view of the redeemed Christian. Henry Louis Gates Jr. argues that using 'two distinct voices' in 'dialogue' is a Black trope in the slave narrative, dating back to Equiano's *The Interesting Narrative* (1789).[58] According to Gates, the trope combines the voices of the enslaved child with limited knowledge and experience and the voice of the self-liberated person looking back from a position of knowledge.[59] The reformed person looking backwards in fiction at the experiences of their unconverted self is a tradition going back to *Moll Flanders* and even further, into the classical period. Critics have noted, for example, that there are 'two Molls' in *Moll Flanders*: 'the young sinner and the old penitent'.[60] When Thomas Jones relates his experience of his former enslaved self on the brink of despair, he does so from the position of one who has reaffirmed his faith in God and Christian identity. Jones describes experiencing a crisis of faith after his religious conversion. His experiences as an enslaved person made him question his Christian beliefs and shook his faith in God: 'In an agony of despair, I have at times given up prayer and hope together, believing that my master's words were true, that "religion is a cursed mockery, and the Bible a lie".'[61] In the next sentence, Jones reflects on the despair that he used to feel and asks for forgiveness from God: 'May God forgive me for doubting, at such times His justice and love', and in doing so he reaffirms his enduring faith. However, in *Broken Shackles*, although Henson is a reformed Christian at the time his narrative was penned by Glenelg, it is Glenelg who provides the second voice of the reformed Christian; Henson does not have 'two distinct voices' and does not

146   *Beyond the antislavery haven*

present his experiences and behaviour before becoming a Christian (such as brawling and drinking) in the voice of a reformed Christian man looking back on this with abhorrence.

In the world of the text, there is some ambiguity about who gains the moral high ground from these depictions of non-Christian behaviour on the plantation, which appears to be problematically recouped by Glenelg, rather than Henson. Brodhead notes that, in local colour writing, the reader accesses a regional culture and what passes for an authentic voice 'through another outlook that makes it appear barbaric and grotesque'. He argues that the genre appears to contest the cultural hegemonic 'centre' but in reality it does its bidding and serves the cultural needs of an urban elite in the United States.[62] Viewing Henson through the implicit lens of a Methodist Christian worldview of 'the [cultural] centre' and through the eyes of Glenelg produces an image of Henson that contains a racial and class-based disgust. It is Glenelg who contains the voice of the wayward unreformed Christian Jim Henson, or Charley. The effect of this is for Henson to lose the second voice, which could enable him to recoup his moral status. He is unable to frame his past experiences from the position of abhorrence, and this is essential in the world of the text if he is to secure his position as penitent in the eyes of the reader. The reformed Moll, or more specifically Moll when she performs her identity as a reformed penitent, sees her old life through a lens of 'abhorrence' in *Moll Flanders*, and identifies this as a key mark of her repentance in the text: 'I now began to look back upon my past life with abhorrence.'[63] Similarly, Defoe's preface sees Moll's attitude of 'abhorrence' towards her former life as proof of her penitent identity.[64] Thomas Jones takes a tone of abhorrence when reflecting on his experience while held in slavery in his narrative. In this context, Henson's non-Christian behaviour on the plantation bolsters and reaffirms Glenelg's moral and social status despite Henson's Christian status at the time the narrative was compiled. When the narrator-amanuensis Glenelg gives the reader an image of Henson's reaction to his former days in slavery, he presents us with Henson's nostalgia for the richness of the food he used to enjoy, not the voice of a redeemed penitent looking back on his life before his conversion with abhorrence. Glenelg describes Henson's manner when describing the food he ate whilst enslaved as wistful and nostalgic. He states that Henson 'contributed' this

Broken Shackles 147

'information' 'in a half-soliloquising manner [...] as if he were again in imagination feasting on thick milk, brown bread, "a pone o' co'n cake", and salt herrings'.[65] This interpretation by Glenelg of Henson's feelings towards his life on the plantation does not present regret for his non-Christian behaviour while an enslaved person and it does not show that Henson has become more enlightened and able to reflect from a distanced Christian position of knowledge when relating events that he experienced as a child. Glenelg invites the reader to see a continuity in Henson's attitudes towards the decadent luxuries of plantation life, at the time and years later when the narrative is compiled.

Slavery and antislavery in Canada in *Broken Shackles*

Broken Shackles makes most sense when we place it at the end of the textual tradition explored in previous chapters and consider how it develops out of and revises the textual traditions that came before it. *Broken Shackles* is, in part, a history of slavery and abolition in the United States. In chapter 3, Glenelg explains how slavery became enshrined in the Declaration of Independence, and acknowledges in passing the existence of slavery (and its abolition) in Upper Canada: 'early in the present century, "Negro sale advertisements" were not uncommon in this Province. Among these is one by Governor Russell, in 1806, for the sale of Peggy, aged forty, a cook, for $150, and her son Jupiter, aged fifteen, for $200, which promised a discount for cash.'[66]

Slavery in Canada is not denied absolutely, but it is placed within a context of the United States and its supposedly 'worse' historical record when it comes to slavery. The narrative focus of *Broken Shackles* is slavery in the United States, reflected in the inclusion of Jim Henson's experiences of slavery there; it is the history of slavery in the United States that is shown as worthy and needing to be collected and preserved in the memory. Scholars today characterise slavery in Canada as subject to a national amnesia, as discussed in Chapter 1 and the Introduction, but this does not reflect what is going on in this extract. Canadian slavery is part of the national memory for Canadians, but it is remembered within a context in which the Canadian antislavery narrative is prioritised. This

148   *Beyond the antislavery haven*

reflects a continuity with what took place in the Canadian newspapers examined in Chapter 1, where slavery in Canada is present,
but within a context of Canadian antislavery that is given a greater
focus and textual space.

Glenelg turns in this extract to newspaper advertisements for
the evidence of slavery in colonial Canada. Chapter 1 of the cur-
rent book explored how enslaved people in Canada are most
textually present in the colonial Canadian newspaper. Glenelg prioritises printed materials rather than manuscripts and this reflects
the particular prominence he gives to printed texts in finding this
history. Glenelg's description of slavery in Canada takes the structural form of the colonial advertisement, as examined in Chapter
1. This advertisement, reproduced by Glenelg, outlines the gender,
age, and occupation of the person being sold, in the third-person
voice of the printer who acts as an 'intermediary' to the sale on
behalf of the enslaver.[67] For example, an advertisement printed in
the *Montreal Gazette* in April 1789 reads: 'TO BE SOLD A stout
healthy NEGRO MAN, about 28 years of age, is an excellent cook.
Enquire of the printer. L.'[68] Glenelg echoes the structure of earlier colonial advertisements in his description of Canadian slavery. He squashes into a single sentence information concerning the
gender, age, and skills of Peggy and Jupiter. Glenelg's description
of Peggy and Jupiter has two differences to the late eighteenth-
century advertisements: he does not describe the physical robust-
ness and health of the two enslaved people, dropping some of the
language of the colonial advertisement; and he describes Peggy as
a cook rather than listing cooking as one of her skills. Glenelg borrows from the form of the colonial advertisement, but in his hands
it provides biographical information about the enslaved people,
presenting historical evidence of slavery in Canada, rather than
advertising.

Broken Shackles does not exhibit amnesia about slavery in colonial Canada. The reference to slavery in Canada in *Broken Shackles*,
a narrative that depicts Canada as an antislavery haven for Henson,
reflects the fact that Frost feels that contradictory positions can go
together side by side without damaging the view of Canada as a
haven for fugitives from slavery. This functions as a form of doublethink, reflecting that Canadians could be aware of their own
legacy of slavery and see themselves as antislavery at the same time,

Broken Shackles 149

representing a continuity with the doublethink found in colonial newspapers in Chapter 1.

The 2001 edition of *Broken Shackles*

The modern edition of *Broken Shackles* changes how the antislavery element of the narrative reads by removing the dialect and 'racism' that surrounds its antislavery stance. This reflects a remaking of the narrative as a more straightforwardly antislavery text, removing the seeming contradiction of Canadian racism that contemporaries consumed together. The term 'racism' is used in this section to refer to how Jim Henson is represented at various moments in the narrative in ways that perpetuate notions about the 'natural' stereotypical characteristics of Black people and in the context of an assumption of Black inferiority. Two examples of the racist elements in the text are the way that the text displays Jim Henson's black skin as part of a joke for the reader and the racialised presentation of enslaved people enjoying plantation life in the manner of blackface minstrel shows. In a broad sense, the term 'racism' relates to the shift by the mid-nineteenth century to a fixed racial essentialism and a scientific racism, whereby Black physical features and characteristics were seen as biologically determined and 'natural' reflections of the innate difference between races. This reflected a departure from the more mutable conception of racial difference in the eighteenth century, which recognised a wider variety of markers of human difference than skin colour, and when the view of monogenesis, explaining human creation as coming from the same shared origins, dominated.[69] In the text's specific historical and geographical moment, racial segregation and racial exclusion were part of the context in which the antislavery movement operated in the United States in the nineteenth century.[70] The use of the term 'racism' to describe the narrative is contextual. It relates too to a bigger picture than the examples of isolated racist imagery and scenes. Scholars have shown that Black dialect, for example, could be racist and support a pro-slavery agenda, but it could also be used in subversive ways, and hence it is important to explore whether *Broken Shackles* presents ostensibly racist elements in ways that speak of Henson's agency and his subversion of racist tropes.[71] A

150   *Beyond the antislavery haven*

wider reading of the narrative highlights that this is not the case. In addition to the scenes that ridicule Henson or draw out stereotypes about Black people, there is a broader power dynamic at play in the text that makes Henson into a curiosity and an object, rather than the craftsmen of his own story. This power dynamic relates to the way that the literary mode of colourism positions Henson and how this impacts the relationship between narrator and reader, as well as Henson's relationship with narrator and reader. This combines with the other more obvious moments in the text where racist ideas, images, or stereotypes are voiced (and not challenged) in the world-view of the narrative. The use of term 'racism' relates to the overall power structures of the text and how Henson is represented and how the racist elements (which will be more fully explored below) sit within this wider context.

In the original edition of *Broken Shackles*, antislavery arguments and racist attitudes sit together. The modern edition removes racist Canadian assumptions, and this crafts a more palatable version of the Canadian antislavery narrative for modern readers. The modern edition of the text, published in 2001 and edited by Peter Meyler, takes out Canadian racist attitudes. In the 1889 edition, Henson's speech is presented in the 'dialect tradition'. John Edgar Wideman notes:

> from the drama of the colonial period through the late nineteenth century [...] [Black] dialect in drama, fiction and poetry was a way of pointing to the difference between blacks and whites; the form and function Black speech as it was represented was to indicate black inferiority [...] Black speech in the form of negro dialect entered American literature as a curiosity, a comic interlude, a short hand for perpetuating myths and prejudices about black people.[72]

The modern edition of the text standardises Henson's dialect throughout, excising racist Canadian attitudes present in the original text, which was part of the antislavery narrative in its original form. This makes the Canadian antislavery in the narrative more acceptable, presumably for its modern-day Canadian readers. Meyler removes a narratorial comment from the 1889 edition of the text that expresses a derogatory view of Henson's dialect: '[he] us[es] language much in advance of the ordinary negro patois of the South, pronouncing "this" and "that" – now as plainly as

Broken Shackles   151

any one'.[73] Glenelg's assumption that Henson's dialect is deficient and that it has been improved by his adoption of some standardised English whilst living in Canada reflects the view that Henson's dialect is taken as a badge of his racial 'inferiority'. The matter-of-fact tone the amanuensis takes in commenting on Henson's speech assumes that the readers will share his opinions. Henson's voice is represented in dialect form by his amanuensis throughout the 1889 edition of the text. An example of this is a moment when Henson replies to the grocer, who will only sell him a whole watermelon:

> 'Wal, I'se got my 'spectashun up fer a watahmillion', said Henson, 'an' as it peahs to be 'hul hog or nun, I s'pose I must buy a 'hul million'.

> 'Well, I've got my expectations up for a watermelon', said Henson, 'and [as] it appears to [be a] whole hog or none, I suppose I must buy a whole melon'.[74]

It is clear reading these passages side by side that in the 1889 edition, it is less what is being said here than the messy representation of Henson's speech in dialect form, given by the amanuensis, that is the feature of this text. His Black speech is represented as comedic. The text in the 1889 edition creates a very different set of sounds. A joke is being made with the cramming together of so many 'h' and 's' sounds, and this makes Henson's speech into a sort of verbal tongue twister; this textual moment provides a space for the reader to enjoy his speech as a 'curiosity [and] a comic interlude [...] perpetuating myths and prejudices about black people'.[75]

The standardisation of Henson's speech also alters how other parts of the narrative read, downplaying their racism. An example is the description of Henson eating a watermelon, which directly follows his conversation with the grocer just examined. In both editions, this reads: '[he] commenced to partake of his highly prized refreshment'. However, while it is just possible to read this in the modern edition as reflecting Henson's own voice (and view of the melon) as delicious and welcome refreshment, in the 1889 edition, because of the context of the non-standardised speech that comes before it, this reads differently. This adjective chimes with two voices: Henson and Glenelg. In the 1889 edition, it is more meant as a joke, as the amanuensis comments on the prized nature

152   *Beyond the antislavery haven*

of the melon in Henson's eyes, which he (Glenelg) sees as faintly ridiculous.

Dialect speech is not the only racist element removed from the 1889 edition of *Broken Shackles* in Meyler's modern edition. Meyler removes racist epithets and makes minor editorial changes to punctuation that places Glenelg in a position where he seems to disagree with the racist attitudes of some of the characters in the text. In the 1889 edition, Glenelg is less clearly separate from the racist attitudes voiced by these characters. For example, in chapter 6, which relates Henson's experiences as a boy, when he was called Charley and was being trained by the miller Jack Owens in a mill that produces flour, the modern edition makes two adjustments that alter how the reader is invited to read this moment. Meyler handles the racist views of the miller differently in the modern edition of *Broken Shackles*. Owens is reluctant to teach Charley his trade as a miller because he harbours racist views:

> At this, the miller Jack Owens, rebelled, and declared, 'He would never teach a [...] [black person] a trade, and take the bread out of a white man's mouth;' as if a black man had not as much right to earn a living and eat the fruit of his labour as a white man.

> At this the miller, Jack Owens, rebelled and declared, 'He would never teach a [...] [black person] a trade, and take bread out of a white man's mouth.' As if a black man had not as much right to earn a living and eat the fruit of his labor as a white man.[76]

In this example Meyler does not change any of the words from the 1889 edition, but he changes the punctuation, and this means it reads differently. The effect of making this into one long sentence in the modern edition with a semicolon joining Owens's racist point of view, reported as direct speech, with what reads as an editorial voice ironically debunking Owens's racist stance, 'as if a black man ...', is that it seems to challenge Owens's view in the same breath as voicing it. In the 1889 original edition, where it is presented as two sentences, the text reads differently. The sentence starting 'As if a black man' reads as a gentle criticism of Owens's racist sentiment, but it is also possible to read it as a statement paraphrasing his point of view. There seems to be less criticism of Owens's racist perspective. The second sentence reads less as an editorial comment containing two voices and attitudes than it does in the modern edition.

Meyler makes a second alteration to this moment: the description of Henson getting covered in flour is more clearly a racist joke in the 1889 edition of the text. Meyler's reprints this as: 'With his head and face all powdered white with flour, the young miller was quite a sight at times.' In the 1889 edition, this reads: 'With his black wooly head and face all powdered white with flour the young miller was quite a sight at times.' In the 1889 edition, the description of Henson as 'quite a sight' more clearly holds up his black skin and the contrast to the white flour for ridicule by the addition of racist epithets describing his 'black wooly hair'. The way this racist joke is presented alters how we read the passage. In the 1889 edition, it is clear that Glenelg is participating in mocking Henson as 'the young miller' and taking pleasure in a racist image of him covered in flour. In the 1889 edition, it is *just* possible to read the sentence describing Owens's racist perspective 'As if a black man ...' as also containing the voice of the narrator who criticises this viewpoint. However, it could also read simply as Owens's point of view and especially so in the context of the racist image of Henson covered in flour, which the narrator describes a few lines afterwards when he participates in a racist belittling of Henson. Taken together, the two changes made by Meyler remove some of the racist elements from the 1889 edition of the text and distance the Canadian narrator from these views, even placing him in a position where the narrator seems to disagree with the racist attitudes of some of the characters in his text.

Although Meyler removes some Canadian attitudes, he does not take the advertisements for enslaved people out of *Broken Shackles* when he reprints it. Meyler removes some of the Canadian racist attitudes from *Broken Shackles* that sat together with its antislavery polemic and the image of Canada as a refuge at the end of the Underground Railroad. The modern edition removes the racist, class-based superiority assumed in the text, editing out these Canadian attitudes, but this is problematic because it removes Canadian anti-slavery from its context and reflects how we want to re-package this narrative today. Today, the modern edition of *Broken Shackles* is reaching new audiences and copies of this now outnumber the 1889 edition. There are just five known surviving copies of the 1889 edition in Canadian and UK rare book and archive collections.[77] *Broken Shackles* is treasured by members of the local community

154   *Beyond the antislavery haven*

in Owen Sound as a rare narrative that records a Black presence and perspective in nineteenth-century Canada.[78] Meyler's editorial decision to remove the dialect speech from the narrative was an attempt to remove some of the racism in this narrative and make it more palatable for a modern audience. In private correspondence since publishing the book, Meyler states, '[m]y purpose in the new edition was to better reflect the actual Black individuals and take their voice out of the bigoted Victorian "colourism" writing style'.[79] However, the anti-Black racism in the first edition of the narrative shows that Canadian antislavery sentiment was mixed with racism and class superiority, and provides a more complex account of a narrative that cannot be categorised as containing a stable Black unmediated voice. It also shows us that Canadians were committed to repeating an abolitionist narrative about Canada long after abolition had become an active political issue. This historical racism is important to study alongside the post-abolitionist messages in the text, to come to a more balanced understanding of Canada's past and self-construction.

Broken Shackles, published in 1889, represents the culmination of more than a century of textual engagement with slavery in Canada. This narrative engages with the then familiar figure of the fugitive from slavery in the United States finding refuge on Canadian soil. The narrative was written by a Canadian, John Frost, and set within its frame narrative in Canada, and it collects (what has to pass for) an authentic voice of a self-liberated person living in Canada. This reflects the fact that American slavery was in the cultural zeitgeist for Canadians. It also reflects, of course, the historical fact that Canada was a home for many thousands of self-liberated people from the United States in the nineteenth century, but it speaks more importantly for my concerns in this book to the literary tradition for recording the arrival of self-liberated people in Canada. The fact that this narrative is repeated again in the late nineteenth century and the revisions that Frost makes in his depiction of the life of a self-liberated person Canada reflect that the literary figure of the fugitive from slavery on Canadian soil had become ingrained textually by the late nineteenth century. As this chapter has shown, *Broken Shackles* can be understood as a hybrid of three literary genres: American local colour writing, the slave narrative, and Methodist autobiography. *Broken Shackles* reads very differently

Broken Shackles

from the slave narratives of the 1850s in its handling of the voice of a formerly enslaved person, and this reflects the influence of the mode of collecting the dialect voice popular in the colourism genre. The effect of Henson having a single voice, that of the unconverted enslaved person, rather than two voices, and occupying the role of the reformed Christian looking back on his pre-conversion sins, like his literary predecessor Thomas Jones, is that some of the racist imagery of the Southern plantation remains associated with him. It is the white, male, 'genteel' Canadian narrator Glenelg who accrues moral capital by assuming the position of an enlightened antislavery Christian man and performing the role of the second reformed voice in the narrative. This effect is lost partly in Meyler's modern edition of the text. The 2001 edition presents the Canadian amanuensis Glenelg more favourably than the original, and distances him from the racist sentiments in the text. It removes the racist dialect to produce an image of Canadian antislavery and of Black agency, and not of Canadian antislavery and racism, which in the original edition circulated together.

Notes

1 George Elliott Clarke notes several Canadian slave narratives were published in Canada in '"This Is No Hearsay"', p. 14. For examples of Black texts printed for their authors in Canada, see Paola Brown's *Address Intended to be Delivered in the City Hall, Hamilton*, printed for the author in Hamilton, Ontario, in 1851; and Thomas Smallwood's autobiography *A Narrative of Thomas Smallwood (Colored Man)*, printed for the author in Toronto in 1851. Nele Sawallisch, 'Radical Legacies in Black Nineteenth-Century Canadian Writing', in Ronald Cummings and Natalee Caple (eds), *Harriet's Legacies: Race, Historical Memory, and Futures in Canada* (Montreal and Kingston: McGill-Queen's University Press, 2022), pp. 104–17. Richard Almonte (ed.) and Thomas Smallwood, *A Narrative of Thomas Smallwood (Colored Man)* (Toronto: Mercury Press, 2000). On the Canadian context of the *Address* as an altered version of Walker's *Appeal*, see Marcy J. Dinius, *The Textual Effects of David Walker's Appeal: Print Based Activism Against Slavery, Racism and Discrimination 1829–1851* (Philadelphia: University of Pennsylvania Press, 2022), chapter 6 especially, pp. 198–230, 224, 230.

156 *Beyond the antislavery haven*

2 Peter Meyler, 'Introduction', in Jim Henson, *Broken Shackles: Old Man Henson, From Slavery to Freedom*, Peter Meyler (ed.) (Toronto: Natural Heritage Books, 2001), pp. xiii–xviii, p. xvi.

3 Henson, *Broken Shackles*, ed. Meyler, p. 193.

4 *Ibid.*, pp. 5–6.

5 *Ibid.*, p. 7.

6 *Ibid.*, p. 169.

7 *Ibid.*, p. 14.

8 Clarke, '"This Is No Hearsay"', p. 12.

9 *Ibid.*, p. 16.

10 Afua Cooper, *The Hanging of Angelique: The Untold Story of Canadian Slavery and the Burning of Old Montreal* (Athens: University of Georgia Press, 2007), p. 302.

11 Clarke, '"This Is No Hearsay"', p. 16.

12 Sara Salih, '*The History of Mary Prince*, the Black Subject, and the Black Canon', in Brycchan Carey, Markman Ellis, and Sara Salih (eds), *Discourses of Slavery and Abolition: Britain and Its Colonies, 1760–1838* (Basingstoke: Palgrave Macmillan, 2004), pp. 125, 130, 134.

13 For key examples of the earlier critical treatment of *The History*, see Moira Ferguson, *Subject to Others: British Women Writers and Colonial Slavery, 1670–1834* (London: Routledge, 1992), especially pp. 281–98, 305–7; and Sandra Pouchet Paquet, 'The Heartbeat of the West Indian Slave: *The History of Mary Prince*', *African American Review* 26:1 (1992), 131–46. Examples of the recent critical approach to *The History* are Gillian Whitlock, *The Intimate Empire: Reading Women's Autobiography* (London: Cassell, 2000); K. Merinda Simmons, 'Beyond "Authenticity": Migration and the Epistemology of "Voice" in Mary Prince's "History of Mary Prince" and Maryse Conde's "I Tituba"', *College Literature* 36:4 (2009), 75–9. On the narrative as a 'composite text', see Sara Salih, 'Introduction', in Sara Salih (ed.), *The History of Mary Prince, A West Indian Slave* (London: Penguin, 2004), pp. vii–xxxiv, p. xiii.

14 On this approach to fragmented 'embedded narratives', see Nicole N. Aljoe, *Creole Testimonies: Slave Narratives From the British West Indies, 1709–1838* (New York: Palgrave Macmillan, 2012), p. 13, p. 33.

15 *Ibid.*, p. 13.

16 Meyler, 'Introduction', p. xiii.

17 John Frost and Jim Henson, *Broken Shackles* (Toronto: William Briggs, 1889), p. 5.

18 Eli MacLaren, *Dominion and Agency: Copyright and the Structure of the Canadian Book Trade 1867–1918* (Toronto: University of Toronto Press, 2011), chapter 4, and especially pp. 103–4.

Broken Shackles 157

19 *Ibid.*, p. 16.

20 *Ibid.*, p. 21.

21 *Ibid.*, p. 5.

22 *Ibid.*, p. 3.

23 James N. Green, 'The British Book in North America', in Michael F. Suarez, S. J., and Michael L. Turner (eds), *The Cambridge History of the Book in Britain: Volume V: 1695–1830* (Cambridge: Cambridge University Press, 2009), p. 557.

24 Samuel Ringgold Ward, *Autobiography of a Fugitive Negro: His Anti-Slavery Labours in the United States, Canada, & England* (London: John Snow, 1855), p. 138.

25 *Ibid.*, p. 208.

26 *Ibid.*, p. 3.

27 Rhondda Robinson Thomas, 'Locating Slave Narratives', in John Ernest (ed.), *The Oxford Handbook of the African American Slave Narrative* (Oxford: Oxford University Press, 2014), pp. 337–38.

28 Henson, *Broken Shackles*, ed. Meyler, p. xiv.

29 Richard H. Brodhead, 'The American Literary Field, 1860–1890', in Sacvan Bercovitch (ed.), *The Cambridge History of American Literature, Volume 3, Prose Writing* (Cambridge: Cambridge University Press, 2005), p. 56. Kathryn B. Mckee, 'Region, Genre and the Nineteenth-Century South', in Sharon Monteith (ed.), *The Cambridge Companion to the Literature of the American South* (Cambridge: Cambridge University Press, 2013), pp. 11–25, 23.

30 Anne E. Rowe, 'Regionalism and Local Color', in Charles Reagan Wilson and others (eds), *Encyclopedia for Southern Culture* (Chapel Hill: UNC Press, 1989), pp. 867–68; Brodhead, 'The American Literary Field', p. 47.

31 Frost and Henson, *Broken Shackles*, p. 16.

32 James Olney, 'Slave Narratives, Their Status as Autobiography and as Literature', in Charles T. Davis and Henry Louis Gates, Jr. (eds), *The Slave's Narrative* (Oxford: Oxford University Press, 1985), p. 153.

33 Henry Bibb, 'Narrative of the Life of Henry Bibb', in Yuval Taylor (ed.), *I Was Born: An Anthology of Classic Slave Narratives: Volume Two: 1849–1866*, pp. 5–101, p. 13.

34 James W. C. Pennington, 'The Fugitive Blacksmith; Or Events in the History of James W. C. Pennington', in Taylor (ed.), *I Was Born*, pp. 107–56, 114.

35 William L. Andrews, 'Introduction', in William Andrews (ed.), *Slave Narratives After Slavery* (Oxford: Oxford University Press, 2011), pp. vii–xxxii.

36 *Ibid.*, p. xv.

37 *Ibid.*, p. xvi.

38 Brodhead, 'The American Literary Field', p. 47.

39 *Ibid.*, p. 56.

40 Frost and Henson, *Broken Shackles*, p. 89.

41 *Ibid.*, p. 16.

42 *Ibid.*, p. 232.

43 Henson, *Broken Shackles*, ed. Meyler p. 163.

44 *Ibid.*, p. 187.

45 *Ibid.*

46 *Ibid.*, p. 196.

47 *Ibid.*, p. 197.

48 Janet Friskney, 'Beyond the Shadow of William Briggs Part II: Canadian-Authored Titles and the Commitment to Canadian Writing', *Papers of the Bibliographical Society of Canada* 35:2 (1997), pp. 161–207, 163, 169.

49 Meyler, *Broken Shackles*, pp. 126, 137, 197; examples of shorter portions of reported first-person speech are on p. 8 and p. 149.

50 Frost and Henson, *Broken Shackles*, p. 214.

51 *Ibid.*

52 Ted A. Campbell, 'Spiritual Biography and Autobiography', in Jason E. Vickers (ed.), *The Cambridge Companion to American Methodism* (Cambridge: Cambridge University Press, 2013), p. 249, p. 252.

53 Photographic postcard of James (Jim) Henson, Grey Roots Archival Collection 968.61.15. I am grateful to Peter Meyler for drawing my attention to this postcard and its significance, and noting that one reason for the publication of the narrative may have been Henson's fundraising efforts.

54 On Henson's life after the narrative ends, see Peter Meyler, 'A Watermelon, a Post Card and the Fate of Old Man Henson', *Northern Terminus: The African Canadian History Journal* 11 (2014), 3.

55 William Wells Brown, *My Southern Home, or the South and Its People*, John Ernest (ed.) (Chapel Hill: UNC Press, 2011), p. 71. For an example of minstrel humour, see the teeth-pulling anecdote in chapter 3.

56 For example, see William L. Andrews, 'Mark Twain, William Wells Brown and the Problem of Authority in New South Writing', in Jefferson Humphries (ed.), *Southern Literature and Literary Theory* (Athens: University of Georgia Press, 1990), pp. 1–21, p. 11.

57 Henson, *Broken Shackles*, ed. Meyler, p. 68.

58 Henry Louis Gates Jr., *The Signifying Monkey: A Theory of African American Literary Criticism, with a New Preface by the Author* (New York: Oxford University Press, 2014), p. 166.

59 *Ibid.*

60 David Blewett, 'Introduction', in Daniel Defoe, *Moll Flanders*, David Blewett (ed.) (London: Penguin Classics, 1989), pp. 1–24, p. 19.

61 Thomas Jones, *The Experience of Thomas Jones, Who Was a Slave for Forty-Three Years, Written by a Friend as Given by Brother Jones* (Saint John: N. B., J. & A. McMillan, 1853), p. 28.

62 Brodhead, 'The American Literary Field, 1860–1890', p. 55, p. 57.

63 Daniel Defoe, *Moll Flanders*, David Blewett (ed.) (London: Penguin Classics, 1989), p. 42.

64 *Ibid.*

65 Frost and Henson, *Broken Shackles*, p. 89.

66 *Ibid.*, p. 27.

67 Frank Mackey, *Done with Slavery: The Black Fact in Montreal, 1760– 1840* (Montreal and Kingston: McGill-Queen's University Press, 2010), p. 308.

68 'To Be Sold', *MG* (2 April 1789), p. 4.

69 For a discussion of the fluidity of notions of racial difference in eighteenth-century British literature and on monogenesis as a widely held belief, see Roxann Wheeler, *The Complexion of Race: Categories of Difference in Eighteenth-Century British Culture* (Philadelphia: University of Pennsylvania Press, 2000), especially p. 7.

70 Seymour Drescher, *Abolition: A History of Slavery and Antislavery* (Cambridge: Cambridge University Press, 2009), p. 300.

71 For example, see Sarah Meer, *Uncle Tom Mania, Minstrelsy and Transatlantic Culture in the 1850s* (Athens: University of Georgia Press, 2005), p. 11.

72 John Edgar Wideman, 'Charles Chesnutt and the WPA Narratives: The Oral and Literate Roots of Afro-American Literature', in Davis and Gates (eds), *The Slave's Narrative*, pp. 59–78, p. 60.

73 Frost and Henson, *Broken Shackles*, p. 10.

74 *Ibid.*, p. 11; Henson, *Broken Shackles*, ed. Meyler, p. 4.

75 Wideman, 'Charles Chesnutt and the WPA Narratives', p. 60.

76 Henson, *Broken Shackles*, ed. Meyler, p. 28; Frost and Henson, *Broken Shackles*, p. 45.

77 A search of Library and Archive Canada's online catalogue AMICUS and WorldCat shows that at least four copies of the 1889 edition survive in rare book form in Canadian Libraries; there is also an 1889 edition in the British Library.

78 Meyler, 'Introduction', p. xiii.

79 From personal email correspondence with Meyler in March 2021. I am very grateful to Meyler for his helpful comments and feedback on an earlier version of this chapter.

Conclusion

As discussed above, Canada's relationship with slavery is more complicated than seeing it as a slaveholding space, or as an antislavery haven. Canada was connected to all of these other places in its print culture, and this has been key to how Canadians and Canadian readers have fashioned their self-image in relation to slavery. This book has explored the contradiction that Canadian readers and enslavers may not have recognised their own complicity in slavery, even as they may have known that slavery was practiced in Canada. It has taken scholars in Canadian studies so long to recognise this contradiction partly because scholars have not read newspapers as literature, so they are not explored holistically, and the framing content of texts, which provides meaning, is missed. Another explanation is that, within studies of Atlantic slaveries, there is still a prioritisation of book-length slave narratives, rather than newspaper narratives about slavery. Two important areas of exception are the African American print studies that go beyond the book to explore the various cultural manifestations of first-person testimonies about experiences of slavery, but as explored in Chapter 3, these studies have too often stopped at the Canada–US border rather than seeing Canada as part of this circulation space. Newspapers are also gaining more attention in the study of the slave narrative in the United States. In *Before Equiano*, Zachary McLeod Hutchins shows that newspapers are key to recovering the eighteenth-century prehistory of the slave narrative in the United States and alerts us to the fact that scholars have long undervalued the role of this genre as a space for narratives of slavery.[1]

This book has focused on newspapers and shown that they are central to recovering Canadian attitudes to slavery, and the circulation of printed texts about slavery in Canada and their meanings.

Conclusion   161

Furthermore, the contradiction in Canadian attitudes has been overlooked because there has been a tendency within studies of slavery (including in the United States) to devalue reprinted materials. In the Canadian context, the search for Canadian voices and Canada's uniqueness has created a bias away from Black Atlantic texts recirculated within Canada. It may be that the dichotomisation of the debate – slavery did not exist in Canada – and the important recovery work that shows that slavery *did* exist in Canada has meant that these shades of complexity have not been attended to.

Afua Cooper recollects meeting members of the government and media in 2007, during the commemorations in Canada of the 1807 Act to abolish the British transatlantic slave trade. She identifies that the narrative that needs to be challenged now is not the denial that slavery existed in Canada, which is far better known (if reluctantly admitted to), but a persistent narrative that slavery in Canada was somehow 'not as bad as American slavery' and a view that it was 'mild'.[2] *Beyond the antislavery haven* has shown that this attitude was not new: from the eighteenth century onwards, Canadians situated their stance on slavery in relation to the slave trade and slavery elsewhere, and often used this broader context to claim a higher moral ground when it came to slavery, even while acknowledging its existence in Canada. Cooper's observation reflects the long legacy of the idea explored in this book. It is through appreciating the longevity of this contradiction for Canadian readers and enslavers that we can continue to dismantle and fracture this false belief that slavery in Canada was less violent, or more benevolent, than slavery elsewhere.

This book has contributed to the further unsettling of the Canada-as-antislavery-haven trope enervating other scholarly works, while recognising that the construction of this idealised image often took place in the same texts that also demonstrate Canadian anti-Black racism and the exploitation of Black free and enslaved people. It has recovered these ideas together within a single slave narrative or newspaper and shown that textual models for a more nuanced understanding of Canada existed in the eighteenth and nineteenth centuries. What has been explored in this book is important for our understanding of Canada and the legacies of slavery and racism in Canada today. Understanding Canada's role in Atlantic slavery and abolition cultures is also key to fuller studies of the cultures

162 *Beyond the antislavery haven*

of slavery and abolition in the Black Atlantic world. For too long, scholars of Atlantic slaveries have overlooked Canada's participation in international slavery and abolition cultures and the print highway that connected myriad places in Canada, the Caribbean, the United States, Britain, and France.

There is more recovery work to be done to explore Canada's history of slavery and participation in the transatlantic slave trade and in tracing the role that money from the profits of imported slave-produced sugar, rum, and coffee played in financing public institutions in Canada, including Dalhousie University.[3] As mentioned in the Introduction, Canada's participation in international forums such as the Universities Studying Slavery network and the establishment of new research projects to examine Black history in Canada and embed these histories within education, such as the 'A Black People's History of Canada' project led by Afua Cooper, are promising signs that studies of slavery and free Black life in Canada are becoming more embedded within discussions of slavery and abolition in the Atlantic world and their legacies today. However, there are still barriers to the research undertaken for this book, which reinforce the biases, for example, towards Black print culture in the United States rather than its fuller North American context including Canada, in the disparity between the availability of newspaper sources. Since the research for this book began, some of the newspapers used within it have been digitised and are now fully available and searchable online, notably the Quebec newspapers examined in Chapter 1 (the *Quebec Gazette* and *Montreal Gazette*), although others such as the religious newspapers in Nova Scotia and New Brunswick explored in Chapter 3 are still only available on microfilm, meaning that tracing Black Atlantic journeys and print culture within Canada becomes harder once you cross the border; there is still not a comparable resource for the Canadian context to the Readex database of American newspapers, which provides full text-searchable access to hundreds of regional newspapers in the United States. Until we have easier access to these resources and greater visibility is given to the ephemeral fragmented narratives about slavery in newspapers, the narrative will always be skewed towards more dominant cultural centres such as the United States. As the example of Canada has indicated, there could be a much stronger focus on the importance of reprinting and recontextualisation of texts

Conclusion 163

within studies of Atlantic slaveries and abolition in general and this would need to take a greater account of newspapers. As this study has focused on printed texts that circulated widely to explore how Canadians constructed and responded to slavery textually within Canada, it highlights the work that remains to be done with manuscript source material and across both media (the separation of which is itself a false dichotomy), to get beyond the 'antislavery haven' trope and explore Canada's complicated and nuanced relationship with the cultures of slavery and abolition and its Black Atlantic stories and histories.

Notes

1 Zachary McLeod Hutchins, *Before Equiano: A Prehistory of the North American Slave Narrative* (Chapel Hill: University of North Carolina Press, 2022).
2 Afua Cooper, 'Epilogue: Reflections: The Challenges and Accomplishments of the Promised Land', in Boulou Ebanda de B'béri, Nina Reid-Maroney, and Handel K. Wright (eds), *The Promised Land: History and Historiography of the Black Experience in Chatham-Kent's Settlements and Beyond* (Toronto: University of Toronto Press, 2014), p. 196.
3 Afua Cooper et al., *Report on Lord Dalhousie's History on Slavery and Race* (Halifax: Dalhousie University, 2019). Shirley Tillotson, 'Importing the Plantation: The Greater Caribbean Trade and Loyalist Nova Scotia's Public Revenue, 1789–1835', *Journal of the Royal Nova Scotia Historical Society* 25 (2022), 1–26.

Bibliography

Books and articles

Ahern, Stephen (ed.), *Affect and Abolition in the Anglo-Atlantic, 1770–1830* (Farnham: Ashgate, 2015).

Aljoe, Nicole N., *Creole Testimonies: Slave Narratives from the British West Indies, 1709–1838* (Palgrave Macmillan: New York, 2012).

Anderson, Benedict, *Imagined Communities: Reflections on the Origin and Spread of Nationalism* (London: Verso, 1991).

Andrews, William L., *To Tell a Free Story: The First Century of Afro-American Autobiography* (Urbana and Chicago: University of Illinois Press, 1986).

Andrews, William L., 'Mark Twain, William Wells Brown and the Problem of Authority in New South Writing', in Jefferson Humphries (ed.), *Southern Literature and Literary Theory* (Athens: University of Georgia Press, 1990), pp. 1–21.

Andrews, William L., 'Introduction', in William Andrews (ed.), *Slave Narratives After Slavery* (Oxford: Oxford University Press, 2011), pp. vii–xxxii.

Andrews, William L., 'Slave Narratives, 1865–1900', in John Ernest (ed.), *The Oxford Handbook of the African American Slave Narrative* (Oxford: Oxford University Press, 2014), pp. 219–32.

Andrews, William L., David A. Davis, Tampathia Evans, et al. (eds), *North Carolina Slave Narratives: The Lives of Moses Roper, Lunsford Lane, Moses Grandy & Thomas H. Jones* (Chapel Hill: University of North Carolina Press, 2003).

Armitage, David, 'Three Concepts of Atlantic History', in David Armitage and Michael J. Braddick (eds), *The British Atlantic World, 1500–1800* (New York: Palgrave, 2002), pp. 11–27.

166 *Bibliography*

Barker, Hannah, *Newspapers, Politics and Public Opinion in Late Eighteenth-Century England* (Oxford: Clarendon Press, 1998).

Basker, James G. (ed.), *Amazing Grace: An Anthology of Poems about Slavery, 1660–1810* (New Haven: Yale University Press, 2002).

Belich, James, *Paradise Reforged: A History of the New Zealanders from the 1880s to the Year 2000* (Albany: Penguin Books, 2001).

Bentley, D. M. R., 'Breaking the "Cake of Custom": The Atlantic Crossing as a Rubicon for Female Emigrants to Canada?', in Susanna Moodie, *Roughing It in the Bush*, Michael A. Peterman (ed.) (New York: W. W. Norton & Company, 2007), pp. 442–72.

Berlin, Ira, *Many Thousands Gone: The First Two Centuries of Slavery in North America* (Cambridge MA: The Belknap Press of University of Harvard Press, 1998).

Bibb, Henry, 'Narrative of the Life of Henry Bibb', in Yuval Taylor (ed.), *I Was Born: An Anthology of Classic Slave Narratives: Volume Two: 1849–1866* (Edinburgh: Payback Press, 1999), pp. 5–101.

Boulukos, George, *The Grateful Slave: The Emergence of Race in Eighteenth-Century British and American Culture* (Cambridge: Cambridge University Press, 2008).

Brock, Jared A., *The Road to Dawn: Josiah Henson and the Story That Sparked the Civil War* (New York: PublicAffairs, 2018).

Brodhead, Richard H., 'The American Literary Field, 1860–1890', in Sacvan Bercovitch (ed.), *The Cambridge History of American Literature, Volume 3, Prose Writing* (Cambridge: Cambridge University Press, 2005), pp. 9–62.

Brown, Christopher Leslie, *Moral Capital: Foundations of British Abolitionism* (Chapel Hill: University of North Carolina Press, 2006).

Brown, Paola, *Address Intended to Be Delivered in the City Hall, Hamilton* (Hamilton: printed for the author, 1851).

Brown, William Wells, *My Southern Home, or the South and Its People*, John Ernest (ed.) (Chapel Hill: University North Carolina Press, 2011).

Campbell, Ted A., 'Spiritual Biography and Autobiography', in Jason E. Vickers (ed.), *The Cambridge Companion to American Methodism* (Cambridge: Cambridge University Press, 2013), pp. 243–60.

Carey, Brycchan, *British Abolitionism and the Rhetoric of Sensibility: Writing, Sentiment and Slavery, 1760–1807* (Basingstoke: Palgrave Macmillan, 2005).

Carey, Brycchan, *From Peace to Freedom: Quaker Rhetoric and the Birth of American Antislavery, 1657–1761* (New Haven: Yale University Press, 2012).

Bibliography

167

Carey, Brycchan, 'To Force a Tear: British Abolitionism and the Eighteenth-Century London Stage', in Stephen Ahern (ed.), *Affect and Abolition in the Anglo-Atlantic: 1770–1830* (Farnham: Ashgate, 2013), pp. 109–28.

Clarke, George Elliott, '"This Is No Hearsay": Reading the Canadian Slave Narratives', *Papers of the Bibliographical Society of Canada* 43:1 (2005), 7–32. https://doi.org/10.33137/pbsc.v43i1.18415.

Clarke, George Elliott, 'Must All Blackness Be American?: Locating Canada in Borden's "Tightrope Time", or Nationalizing Gilroy's *The Black Atlantic*', *Canadian Ethnic Studies Association* 28:3 (2007), 56–71.

Clarke, George Elliott, 'Introduction: Let Us Now Consider "African-American" Narratives as (African-)Canadian Literature', in Benjamin Drew, *The Refugee: Narratives of Fugitive Slaves in Canada* (Toronto: Dundurn Press, 2008), pp. 10–22.

Compton, Wayde, *After Canaan: Essays on Race, Writing, and Region* (Vancouver: Arsenal Pulp Press, 2010).

Cooper, Afua, 'Doing Battle in Freedom's Cause, Henry Bibb, Abolitionism, Race Uplift, and Black Manhood, 1842–1854' (unpublished PhD thesis, University of Toronto, 2000).

Cooper, Afua, 'The Fluid Frontier: Blacks and the Detroit River Region: A Focus on Henry Bibb', *Canadian Review of American Studies* 30:2 (2000), 129–49. https://doi.org/10.3138/CRAS-s030-02-02.

Cooper, Afua, *The Hanging of Angelique: The Untold Story of Canadian Slavery and the Burning of Old Montreal* (Athens: University of Georgia Press, 2007).

Cooper, Afua, 'Epilogue: Reflections: The Challenges and Accomplishments of the Promised Land', in Boulou Ebanda de B'béri, Nina Reid-Maroney, and Handel Kashope Wright (eds), *The Promised Land: History and Historiography of the Black Experience in Chatham-Kent's Settlements and Beyond* (Toronto: University of Toronto Press, 2014), pp. 193–209.

Copeland, David, 'America, 1750–1820', in Hannah Barker and Simon Burrows (eds), *Press, Politics and the Public Sphere in Europe and North America 1760–1820* (Cambridge: Cambridge University Press, 2002), pp. 140–58.

Cottreau-Robins, Catherine M. A., 'Searching for the Enslaved in Nova Scotia's Loyalist Landscape', *Acadiensis* 43:1 (2014), 125–36.

Couchman, Dorothy, '"Mungo Everywhere": How Anglophones Heard Chattel Slavery', *Slavery & Abolition* 36:4 (2015), 704–20. https://doi.org/10.1080/0144039X.2014.969581.

Crevecoeur, J. Hector St John, *Letters from an American Farmer* (London: Thomas Davis, 1782).

168 *Bibliography*

Cummings, Ronald, and Natalee Caple (eds), *Harriet's Legacies: Race, Historical Memory, and Futures in Canada* (Montreal and Kingston: McGill-Queen's University Press, 2022).

Davis, David A., 'The Experience of Rev. Thomas H Jones, Introduction by David A. Davis', in William L. Andrews, David A. Davis, Tampathia Evans, et al. (eds), *North Carolina Slave Narratives: The Lives of Moses Roper, Lunsford Lane, Moses Grandy, and Thomas H. Jones* (Chapel Hill: University of North Carolina Press, 2003), pp. 188–202.

Defoe, Daniel, *Moll Flanders*, David Blewett (ed.) (London: Penguin Classics, 1989).

Dickinson, John, and Brian Young, *A Short History of Quebec*, 4th edn (Montreal: McGill-Queen's University Press, 2008).

Dinius, Marcy J., *The Textual Effects of David Walker's Appeal: Print Based Activism Against Slavery, Racism and Discrimination 1829–1851* (Philadelphia: University of Pennsylvania Press, 2022).

Donovan, Ken, 'Forum: Slavery and Freedom in Atlantic Canada's African Diaspora: Introduction', *Acadiensis* 43:1 (2014), 109–15.

Douglass, Frederick, *My Bondage and My Freedom* (New York: Miller, Orton & Mulligan, 1855).

Douglass, Frederick, *My Bondage and My Freedom*, David W. Blight (ed.) (New Haven: Yale University Press, 2014).

Doyle, William, *The Oxford History of the French Revolution*, 2nd edn (Oxford: Oxford University Press, 2002).

Drescher, Seymour, *Abolition: A History of Slavery and Antislavery* (Cambridge: Cambridge University Press, 2009).

Drescher, Seymour, 'The Shocking Birth of British Abolitionism', *Slavery & Abolition* 33:4 (2012), 571–93. https://doi.org/10.1080/0144039X .2011.644070.

Drew, Benjamin, *A North-Side View of Slavery: The Refugee: Or the Narratives of Fugitives Slaves in Canada* (Boston: J. P. Jewett & Co., 1856).

Drew, Benjamin, *The Refugee: Narratives of Fugitive Slaves in Canada*, George Elliott Clarke (ed.) (Toronto: Dundurn Press, 2008).

Elgersman, Maureen G., *Unyielding Spirits: Black Women and Slavery in Early Canada and Jamaica* (London: Routledge, 1999).

Epp, Marlene, and Franca Lacovetta (eds), *Sisters or Strangers? Immigrant, Ethnic, and Racialized Women in Canadian History*, 2nd edn (Toronto: University of Toronto Press, 2016).

Equiano, Olaudah, *The Interesting Narrative and Other Writings*, Vincent Carretta (ed.) (New York: Penguin Books, 1995).

Equiano, Olaudah, *The Interesting Narrative*, Brycchan Carey (ed.) (Oxford: Oxford University Press, 2018).

Bibliography 169

Ernest, John, 'Beyond Douglass and Jacobs', in Audrey Fisch (ed.), *The African American Slave Narrative* (Cambridge: Cambridge University Press, 2007), pp. 218–31.

Fagan, Benjamin, *The Black Newspaper and the Chosen Nation* (Athens: The University of Georgia Press, 2016).

Fedric, Francis, *Slave Life in Virginia and Kentucky: A Narrative of Francis Fedric, Escaped Slave*, C. L. Innes (ed.) (Baton Rouge: Louisiana State University Press, 2010).

Ferguson, Moira, *Subject to Others: British Women Writers and Colonial Slavery, 1670–1834* (London: Routledge, 1992).

Fisch, Audrey, *American Slaves in Victorian England: Abolitionist Politics in Popular Literature and Culture* (Cambridge: Cambridge University Press, 2000).

Fisch, Audrey (ed.), *The Cambridge Companion to the African American Slave Narrative* (Cambridge: Cambridge University Press, 2007).

Friskney, Janet, 'Beyond the Shadow of William Briggs Part II: Canadian-Authored Titles and the Commitment to Canadian Writing', *Papers of the Bibliographical Society of Canada* 35:2 (1997), 161–207.

Frost, John and Jim Henson, *Broken Shackles* (Toronto: William Briggs, 1889).

Galarneau, Claude, 'Fleury Mesplet', *Dictionary of Canadian Biography*, www.biographi.ca/en/bio/mesplet_fleury_4E.html (accessed 15 March 2023).

Gardner, Eric, 'Slave Narratives and Archival Research', in John Ernest (ed.), *The Oxford Handbook of the African American Slave Narrative* (Oxford: Oxford University Press, 2014), pp. 36–53.

Gardner, Jared, *The Rise and Fall of Early American Magazine Culture* (Urbana: University of Illinois Press, 2012).

Gates, Jr., Henry Louis, *The Signifying Monkey: A Theory of African American Literary Criticism, with a New Preface by the Author* (New York: Oxford University Press, 2014).

Genette, Gérard, *Paratexts: Thresholds of Interpretation*, trans. Jane E. Lewin (Cambridge: Cambridge University Press, 1997).

George, David, 'An Account of the Life of Mr David George, from Sierra Leone in Africa; Given by Himself in a Conversation with Brother Rippon of London and Brother Pearce of Birmingham', in Vincent Carretta (ed.), *Unchained Voices: An Anthology of Black Authors in the English-Speaking World of the Eighteenth Century, Expanded Edition* (Lexington: University Press of Kentucky, 2004), pp. 336–40.

Gerson, Carole, 'Literature of Settlement', in Coral Ann Howells and Eva-Marie Kroller (eds), *The Cambridge History of Canadian Literature* (Cambridge: Cambridge University Press, 2009), pp. 87–103.

170 Bibliography

Gervais, Jean-Francis, 'William Brown', *Dictionary of Canadian Biography*, www.biographi.ca/en/bio/brown_william_4E.html (accessed 15 March 2023).

Gilroy, Paul, *The Black Atlantic: Modernity and Double Consciousness* (London: Verso, 1993).

Goddu, Teresa A., 'The Slave Narrative as Material Text', in John Ernest (ed.), *The Oxford Handbook of the African American Slave Narrative* (Oxford: Oxford University Press, 2014), pp. 149–64.

Goddu, Teresa A., *Selling Antislavery: Abolition and Mass Media in Antebellum America* (Philadelphia: University of Pennsylvania Press, 2020).

Gould, Philip, 'The Economies of the Slave Narrative', in Gene Andrew Jarrett (ed.), *A Companion to African American Literature* (Oxford: Wiley-Blackwell, 2010), pp. 90–102.

Green, James, 'The Publishing History of Olaudah Equiano's Interesting Narrative', *Slavery & Abolition* 16:3 (1995), 362–75. https://doi.org/10.1080/01440399508575167.

Green, James N., 'The British Book in North America', in Michael F. Suarez, S. J., and Michael L. Turner (eds), *The Cambridge History of the Book in Britain: Volume V: 1695–1830* (Cambridge: Cambridge University Press, 2009), pp. 544–59.

Haas, Astrid, 'Native Bondage, Narrative Mobility: African American Accounts of Indian Captivity', *Journal of American Studies* 56:2 (2022), 242–66. https://doi.org/10.1017/S0021875821000852.

Hanley, Ryan, *Beyond Slavery and Abolition: Black British Writing c. 1770–1830* (Cambridge: Cambridge University Press, 2019).

Hare, John E., 'Samuel Neilson', *Dictionary of Canadian Biography*, www.biographi.ca.en/bio/neilson_samuel_1771_93_4E.html (accessed 15 March 2023).

Henry, Natasha, 'Where, Oh Where, Is Bet? Locating Enslaved Black Women on the Ontario Landscape', in Michele A. Johnson and Funké Aladejebi (eds), *Unsettling the Great White North* (Toronto: University of Toronto Press, 2022), pp. 85–112.

Henson, Jim, *Broken Shackles: Old Man Henson, From Slavery to Freedom*, Peter Meyler (ed.) (Toronto: Natural Heritage Books, 2001).

Henson, Josiah, *The Life of Josiah Henson, Formerly a Slave, Now an Inhabitant of Canada, as Narrated by Himself* (Boston: A. D. Phelps, 1849).

Hodges, Graham Russell, and Alan Edward Brown (eds), *'Pretends to Be Free': Runaway Slave Advertisements from Colonial and Revolutionary New York and New Jersey* (New York: Garland Publishing, 1994).

Bibliography

Hunter, Andrew, *It Was Dark There All the Time: Sophia Burthen and the Legacy of Slavery in Canada* (Fredericton: Goose Lane Editions, 2022).

Innes, C. L., 'Introduction: Francis Fedric's Story: Historical and Cultural Contexts', in C. L. Innes (ed.), *Slave Life in Virginia and Kentucky: A Narrative of Francis Fedric, Escaped Slave* (Baton Rouge: Louisiana State University Press, 2010), pp. ix–xxxviii.

Jasanoff, Maya, *Liberty's Exiles: The Loss of America and the Remaking of the British Empire* (London: HarperPress, 2011).

Johnson, Michele A., and Funké Aladejebi (eds), *Unsettling the Great White North: Black Canadian History* (Toronto: University of Toronto Press, 2022).

Jones, Thomas, *The Experience of Thomas Jones, Who Was a Slave for Forty-Three Years, Written by a Friend as Given by Brother Jones* (Saint John: N. B., J. & A. McMillan, 1853). Library and Archives Canada, E444 J793, 1853.

Jones, Thomas H., Letter to William Lloyd Garrison, February 16 1854, Boston Public Library, https://archive.org/details/lettertodearmrg a00jone_1/mode/2up (accessed 10 August 2022).

Jones, Thomas H., *The Experience of Rev. Thomas H. Jones Who Was a Slave for Forty-Three Years* (Boston: A. T. Bliss and Co., Printers, 1880).

Jones, Thomas H., *The Experience of Rev. Thomas H. Jones, Who Was a Slave for Forty-Three Years* (New Bedford, E. Anthony and Sons, 1885).

Kang, Nancy, '"As If I Had Entered a Paradise": Fugitive Slave Narratives and Cross-Border Literary History', *African American Review* 39:3 (2005), 431–57.

King, Boston, 'Memoirs of the Life of Boston King, a Black Preacher: Written by Himself, during his Residence at Kingswood School', in *Methodist Magazine, for the Year 1798: Being a Continuation of the Arminian Magazine: First Published by the Rev. John Wesley A. M. Consisting Chiefly of Extracts and Original Treatises on General Redemption* (London: printed for G. Whitfield, City-Road and sold at the Methodist Preaching-Houses in Town and County, 1798), pp. 105–10, pp. 157–61, pp. 209–13, pp. 261–65.

King, Boston, 'Memoirs of the Life of Boston King, a Black Preacher, Written by Himself, during his Residence at Kingswood-School', in Vincent Carretta (ed.), *Unchained Voices: An Anthology of Black Authors in the English-Speaking World of the Eighteenth Century* (Lexington: University Press of Kentucky, 2004), pp. 351–68.

Lambert, James H., 'Alexander Spark', *Dictionary of Canadian Biography*, www.biographi.ca/en/bio/spark_alexander_5E.html (accessed 15 March 2023).

172   *Bibliography*

Laurence, Gérard, 'The Newspaper Press in Quebec and Lower Canada', in Patricia Lockhart Fleming, Gilles Gallichan, and Yvan Lamonde (eds), *The History of the Book in Canada, Volume One, Beginnings to 1840* (Toronto: University of Toronto Press, 2004), pp. 233–37.

Leavell, Lori, '"Not Intended Exclusively for the Slave States": Antebellum Recirculation of David Walker's Appeal', *Callaloo* 38:3 (2015), 679–95. https://doi.org/10.1353/cal.2015.008.

Lee, Julia Sun-Joo, *The American Slave Narrative and the Victorian Novel* (Oxford: Oxford University Press, 2010).

Lemay, Therese P., 'Joe', *Dictionary of Canadian Biography*, www.biographi .ca/en/bio/joe_4E.html (accessed 15 March 2023).

MacGregor, Rev. James, *Letter to a Clergyman Urging Him to Set Free a Black Girl He Held in Slavery* (Halifax: John Howe, 1788).

Mackey, Frank, *Done with Slavery: The Black Fact in Montreal, 1760–1840* (Montreal and Kingston: McGill-Queen's University Press, 2010).

MacLaren, Eli, *Dominion and Agency: Copyright and the Structure of the Canadian Book Trade 1867–1918* (Toronto: University of Toronto Press, 2011).

Maclean, Alyssa, 'Canadian Migrations: Reading Canada in Nineteenth-Century American Literature' (unpublished PhD thesis, University of British Columbia, 2010).

MacLean, Alyssa, 'Writing Back to Massa: The Black Open Letter in Transnational Abolitionist Print Culture', in Gillian Roberts (ed.), *Reading Between the Borderlines: Cultural Production and Consumption Across the 49th Parallel* (Montreal and Kingston: McGill-Queen's University Press, 2018), pp. 42–66.

Marrant, John, *A Narrative of the Lord's Wonderful Dealings with John Marrant, a Black (Now Going to Preach the Gospel in Nova Scotia)* (London: printed and sold by Gilbert and Plummer, 1788), *Eighteenth Century Collections Online*.

Marrant, John, *A Journal of the Rev. John Marrant, From August the 18th, 1785 to the 16th March, 1790 to Which Are Added: Two Sermons, One Preached on Ragged Island on Sabbath Day, the 27th Day of October, 1787, the Other at Boston, in New England, on Thursday, the 24th of June, 1789* (London: printed for the Author, sold by J. Taylor and Mr. Marrant, 1790).

Marrant, John, *A Narrative of the Life of John Marrant* (Halifax: J. Nicholson, 1812).

Marrant, John, *A Narrative of the Life of John Marrant* (Halifax: J. Nicholson, 1813).

Marrant, John, 'A Narrative of the Lord's Wonderful Dealings with John Marrant, A Black', in Vincent Carretta (ed.), *Unchained Voices: An*

Anthology of Black Authors in the English-Speaking World of the Eighteenth Century, Expanded Edition (Lexington: University Press of Kentucky, 2004), pp. 110–33.

Mason, Isaac, 'Life of Isaac Mason as a Slave', in B. Eugene McCarthy and Thomas L. Doughton (eds), *From Bondage to Belonging: The Worcester Slave Narratives* (Amherst: University of Massachusetts Press, 2007), pp. 245–85.

McCarthy, Eugene B., and Thomas L. Doughton (eds), *From Bondage to Belonging: The Worcester Slave Narratives* (Amherst: University of Massachusetts Press, 2007).

McGill, Meredith L., *American Literature and the Culture of Reprinting, 1834–1853* (Philadelphia: University of Pennsylvania Press, 2003).

Mckee, Kathryn B., 'Region, Genre and the Nineteenth-Century South', in Sharon Monteith (ed.), *The Cambridge Companion to the Literature of the American South* (Cambridge: Cambridge University Press, 2013), pp. 11–25.

McLeod Hutchins, Zachary, *Before Equiano: A Prehistory of the North American Slave Narrative* (Chapel Hill: University of North Carolina Press, 2022).

Meer, Sarah, *Uncle Tom Mania: Slavery, Minstrelsy and Transatlantic Culture in the 1850s* (Athens: University of Georgia Press, 2005).

Meyler, Peter, 'A Watermelon, a Post Card and the Fate of Old Man Henson', *Northern Terminus: The African Canadian History Journal* 11 (2014), 1–4.

Moodie, Susanna, *Roughing It in the Bush*, Michael A. Peterman (ed.) (New York: W. W. Norton & Company, 2007).

Moynagh, Maureen, '"This History's Only Good for Anger": Gender and Cultural Memory in Beatrice Chancy', in Joseph Pivato (ed.), *Africadian Atlantic: Essays on George Elliott Clarke* (Toronto: Guernica Editions, 2012), pp. 91–133.

Nelson, Charmaine A., *Slavery, Geography and Empire in Nineteenth-Century Marine Landscapes of Montreal and Jamaica* (Abingdon: Routledge, 2016).

Nelson, Charmaine A., '"Ran Away from Her Master … a Negroe Girl Named Thursday": Examining Evidence of Punishment, Isolation, Trauma, and Illness in Nova Scotia and Quebec Fugitive Slave Advertisements', in Joshua Nichols and Amy Swiffen (eds), *Legal Violence and the Limits of the Law* (New York City: Routledge, 2017), pp. 68–91.

Nelson, Charmaine, 'Servant, Seraglio, Savage or "Sarah": Examining the Visual Representation of Black Female Subjects in Canadian Art and Visual Culture', in Nina Reid-Maroney, Boulou Ebanda de B'béri, and

174 *Bibliography*

Wanda Thomas Bernard (eds), *Women in the 'Promised Land': Essays in African Canadian History* (Toronto: Women's Press, 2018), pp. 43–74.

Oldfield, J. R., *Popular Politics and British Anti-Slavery: The Mobilization of British Opinion against the Slave Trade, 1787–1807* (Manchester: Manchester University Press, 1995).

Oldfield, J. R., *Transatlantic Abolitionism in the Age of Revolution: An International History of Anti-Slavery, c. 1787–1820* (Cambridge: Cambridge University Press, 2013).

Olney, James, 'Slave Narratives, Their Status as Autobiography and as Literature', in Charles T. Davis and Henry Louis Gates, Jr. (eds), *The Slave's Narrative* (Oxford: Oxford University Press, 1985), pp. 148–75.

O'Malley, Gregory, *Final Passages: The Intercolonial Slave Trade of British America, 1619–1807* (Chapel Hill: University of North Carolina Press, 2014).

Orwell, George, *Nineteen Eighty-Four* (London: Penguin Books, 1949).

Paquet, Sandra Pouchet, 'The Heartbeat of the West Indian Slave: The History of Mary Prince', *African American Review* 26:1 (1992), 131–46.

Parker, George L., *The Beginnings of the Book Trade in Canada* (Toronto: University of Toronto Press, 1985).

Parker, George L., 'Henry Chubb', *Dictionary of Canadian Biography* http://www.biographi.ca/en/bio/chubb_henry_8E.html (accessed 4 November 2024) .

Pennington, James W. C., 'The Fugitive Blacksmith; Or Events in the History of James W. C. Pennington', in Yuval Taylor (ed.), *I Was Born: An Anthology of Classic Slave Narratives: Volume Two: 1849–1866* (Edinburgh: Payback Press, 1999), pp. 107–56.

Pierce, Yolanda, 'Redeeming Bondage: The Captivity Narrative and the Spiritual Autobiography in the African American Slave Narrative Tradition', in Fisch (ed.), *The Cambridge Companion to the African American Slave Narrative* (Cambridge: Cambridge University Press, 2007), pp. 83–98.

Prince, Mary, *The History of Mary Prince, A West Indian Slave, Related by Herself*, Moira Ferguson (ed.) (London: Pandora, 1987).

Prince, Mary, *The History of Mary Prince, A West Indian Slave*, Sara Salih (ed.) (London: Penguin, 2004).

Reid-Maroney, Nina, 'History, Historiography, and the Promised Land Project', in Boulou Ebanda de B'béri, Nina Reid-Maroney, and Handel Kashope Wright (eds), *The Promised Land: History and Historiography of the Black Experience in Chatham-Kent's Settlements and Beyond* (Toronto: University of Toronto Press, 2014), pp. 62–70.

Bibliography

175

Reid-Maroney, Nina, Boulou Ebanda de B'béri, and Wanda Thomas Bernard (eds), *Women in the 'Promised Land': Essays in African Canadian History* (Toronto: Women's Press, 2018).

Ripley, Peter (ed.), *The Black Abolitionist Papers: Volume II: Canada, 1830–1865* (Chapel Hill: University of North Carolina Press, 1986).

Rowe, Anne E., 'Regionalism and Local Color', in Charles Reagan Wilson and William Ferris (eds), *Encyclopedia for Southern Culture* (Chapel Hill: University North Carolina Press, 1989).

Roy, Michaël, 'Cheap Editions, Little Books, and Handsome Duodecimos: A Book History Approach to Antebellum Slave Narratives', *Melus* 40:3 (2015), 69–93. https://doi.org/10.1093/melus/mlv032.

Roy, Michaël, 'The Slave Narrative Unbound', in Brigitte Fielder and Jonathan Senchyne (eds), *Against a Sharp White Background: Infrastructures of African American Print* (Madison: University of Wisconsin Press, 2019), pp. 259–76.

Roy, Michaël, *Fugitive Texts: Slave Narratives in Antebellum Print Culture* (Madison: University of Wisconsin Press, 2022).

Rushforth, Brett, *Bonds of Alliance: Indigenous and Atlantic Slaveries in New France* (Chapel Hill: The University of North Carolina Press, 2012).

Salih, Sara, '*The History of Mary Prince*, the Black Subject, and the Black Canon', in Brycchan Carey, Markman Ellis, and Sara Salih (eds), *Discourses of Slavery and Abolition: Britain and its Colonies, 1760–1838* (Basingstoke: Palgrave Macmillan, 2004), pp. 123–38.

Sawallisch, Nele, *Fugitive Borders: Canadian Cross-Border Literature at Mid-Nineteenth Century* (Bielefeld: Transcript Verlag, 2019).

Sawallisch, Nele, 'Radical Legacies in Black Nineteenth-Century Canadian Writing', in Ronald Cummings and Natalee Caple (eds), *Harriet's Legacies: Race, Historical Memory, and Futures in Canada* (Montreal and Kingston: McGill-Queen's University Press, 2022), pp. 104–17.

Schama, Simon, *Rough Crossings: Britain, the Slaves and the American Revolution* (London: Vintage Books, 2009).

Shadd, Mary A., *A Plea for Emigration: Or, Notes of Canada West*, Richard Almonte (ed.) (Toronto: Mercury Press, 1998).

Siemerling, Winfried, 'Slave Narratives and Hemispheric Studies', in John Ernest (ed.), *The Oxford Handbook of the African American Slave Narrative* (Oxford: Oxford University Press, 2014), pp. 344–61.

Siemerling, Winfried, *The Black Atlantic Reconsidered: Black Canadian Writing, Cultural History and the Presence of the Past* (Montreal: McGill-Queen's University Press, 2015).

Simmons, K. Merinda, 'Beyond "Authenticity": Migration and the Epistemology of "Voice" in Mary Prince's "History of Mary Prince" and Maryse Conde's "I Tituba"', *College Literature* 36:4 (2009), 75–99. https://doi.org/10.1353/lit.0.0078.

Smallwood, Thomas, *A Narrative of Thomas Smallwood (Coloured Man) Giving an Account of His Birth – The Period He Was Held in Slavery – His Release – and Removal to Canada etc, Together with an Account of the Underground Railroad Written by Himself* (Toronto: printed for the author by James Stephens, 1851).

Smallwood, Thomas, *A Narrative of Thomas Smallwood (Colored Man)*, Richard Almonte (ed.) (Toronto: Mercury Press, 2000).

Smardz Frost, Karolyn, and Veta Smith Tucker (eds), *A Fluid Frontier: Slavery, Resistance, and the Underground Railroad in the Detroit River Borderland* (Detroit: Wayne State University Press, 2016).

Smardz Frost, Karolyn, 'The Cataract House Hotel: Underground to Canada through the Niagara River Borderlands', in Ronald Cummings and Natalee Caple (eds), *Harriet's Legacies: Race, Historical Memory, and Futures in Canada* (Montreal and Kingston: McGill-Queen's University Press, 2022), pp. 41–79.

Smardz Frost, Karolyn, 'Planting Slavery in Nova Scotia's Promised Land, 1759–1775', in Michele A. Johnson and Funké Aladejebi (eds), *Unsettling the Great White North: Black Canadian History* (Toronto: University of Toronto Press, 2022), pp. 53–84.

Smith, Billy G., and Richard Wojtowicz (eds), *Blacks Who Stole Themselves: Advertisements for Runaways in the Pennsylvania Gazette, 1728–1790* (Philadelphia: University of Pennsylvania Press, 1989).

Smith, W. L. G., *Life at the South, or 'Uncle Tom's Cabin' As It Is, Being Narratives, Scenes, and Incidents in the Real 'Life of the Lowly'* (Buffalo: Geo. H. Derby, 1852).

Stauffer, John, 'Frederick Douglass and the Aesthetics of Freedom', *Raritan: A Quarterly Review* 25:1 (2005), 114–36.

Stauffer, John, 'Frederick Douglass's Self-Fashioning and the Making of a Representative American Man', in Audrey Fisch (ed.), *The Cambridge Companion to the African American Slave Narrative* (Cambridge: Cambridge University Press, 2007), pp. 201–17.

Steward, Austin, *Twenty-Two Years a Slave and Forty Years a Freeman* (Rochester: Allings & Cory, 1859).

Steward, Austin, *Twenty-Two Years a Slave and Forty Years a Freeman*, Jane H. Pease and William H. Pease (eds) (New York: Dover Publications Inc., 2004).

Stouck, David, '"Secrets of the Prison-House": Mrs Moodie and the Canadian Imagination', in Susanna Moodie, *Roughing It in the Bush*, Michael A. Peterman (ed.) (New York: W. W. Norton & Company, 2007), pp. 425–33.

Bibliography

Stouffer, Allen P., *The Light of Nature and the Law of God: Antislavery in Ontario 1833–1877* (Montreal: McGill-Queen's University Press, 1992).

Swaminathan, Srividhya, *Debating the Slave Trade: Rhetoric of British National Identity, 1759–1815* (Farnham: Ashgate, 2009).

Sypher, Willie, *Guinea's Captive Kings: British Anti-Slavery Literature of the Eighteenth Century* (Chapel Hill: University of North Carolina Press, 1942).

Taylor, Douglas, *The Nicholson Family: Printers & Publishers* (Halifax: Halifax Antiquarian Society, 1977).

Thwaites, Reuben Gold (ed.), *The Jesuit Relations and Allied Documents, Vol. 5: Quebec, 1632–1633* (Cleveland: The Burrows Brothers Co, 1897).

Tompkins, Jane P., *Sensational Designs: The Cultural Work of American Fiction 1790–1860* (New York: Oxford University Press, 1985).

Tratt, Gertrude, *A Survey and Listing of Nova Scotia Newspapers, 1752–1957: With Particular Reference to the Period Before 1867* (Halifax: Dalhousie University, 1979).

Tremaine, Marie, *A Bibliography of Canadian Imprints, 1751–1800* (Toronto: University of Toronto Press, 1952).

Trudel, Marcel, *Canada's Forgotten Slaves: Two Hundred Years of Bondage*, trans. George Tombs (Montreal: Véhicule Press, 2013).

Turnbull, Mary D., 'William Dunlap, Colonial Printer, Journalist, and Minister', *The Pennsylvania Magazine of History and Biography* 103:2 (1979), 143–65.

Van Die, Marguerite, 'Religion and Law in British North America, 1800–1867', in Stephen J. Stein (ed.), *The Cambridge History of Religions in America: Volume II: 1790 to 1945* (Cambridge: Cambridge University Press, 2000), pp. 46–65.

Waldstreicher, David, 'Reading the Runaways: Self-fashioning, Print Culture, and Confidence in Slavery in the Eighteenth-Century Mid-Atlantic', *William and Mary Quarterly* 56:2 (1999), 243–72. https://doi.org/10.2307/2674119.

Waldstreicher, David, *Runaway America, Benjamin Franklin, Slavery and the American Revolution* (New York: Hill & Wang, 2004).

Walker, James W. St. G., *The Black Loyalists: The Search for a Promised Land in Nova Scotia and Sierra Leone, 1783–1870* (London: Longman, 1976).

Wallace, C. M., 'Edward George Fenety', *Dictionary of Canadian Biography*, http://www.biographi.ca/en/bio/fenety_george_edward_12E.html (acccessed 4 November 2024).

Ward, Samuel Ringgold, *Autobiography of A Fugitive Negro: His Anti-Slavery Labours in the United States, Canada and England* (London: John Snow, 1855).

178   *Bibliography*

Warren, Richard, *Narrative of the Life and Sufferings of Rev Richard Warren (a Fugitive Slave)* (Hamilton: Christian Advocate, 1856).

Weinstein, Cindy, 'The Slave Narrative and Sentimental Literature', in Audrey Fisch (ed.), *The Cambridge Companion to the African American Slave Narrative* (Cambridge: Cambridge University Press, 2007), pp. 115–34.

Wheeler, Roxann, *The Complexion of Race: Categories of Difference in Eighteenth-Century British Culture* (Philadelphia: University of Pennsylvania Press, 2000).

Whitehead, Ruth Holmes, *Black Loyalists: Southern Settlers of Nova Scotia's First Free Black Communities* (Halifax: Nimbus Publishing Limited, 2013).

Whitfield, Harvey Amani, *Blacks on the Border: The Black Refugees in British North America, 1815–1860* (Burlington: University of Vermont Press, 2006).

Whitfield, Harvey Amani, *North to Bondage: Loyalist Slavery in the Maritimes* (Vancouver: University of British Columbia Press, 2016).

Whitfield, Harvey Amani, *Black Slavery in the Maritimes: A History in Documents* (Peterborough, ON: Broadview Press, 2018).

Whitfield, Harvey Amani, *Biographical Dictionary of Enslaved Black People in the Maritimes* (Toronto: University of Toronto Press, 2022).

Whitlock, Gillian, *The Intimate Empire: Reading Women's Autobiography* (London: Cassell, 2000).

Wideman, John Edgar, 'Charles Chesnutt and the WPA Narratives: The Oral and Literate Roots of Afro-American Literature', in Charles T. Davis and Henry Louis Gates, Jr. (eds), *The Slave's Narrative* (Oxford: Oxford University Press, 1985), pp. 59–78.

Windley, Lathan A. (ed.), *Runaway Slave Advertisements: A Documentary History from the 1730s to 1790, vol. 3. South Carolina* (Westport: Greenwood Press, 1983).

Winks, Robin W., *The Blacks in Canada: A History* (Montreal and Kingston: McGill-Queen's University Press, 1997).

Wolfe, John, 'William Wilberforce', *Oxford Dictionary of National Biography*, www.oxforddnb.com/view/article/29386 (accessed 13 March 2023).

Newspapers

'Proposal for the Establishment of a New Gazette', *MG*, British Library, reel BL M.C.270.

'The Printer to the Public', *MG* (25 August 1785), p. 1.

Bibliography

'Run Away on Thursday Morning Last from the Subscriber, a Mullatto Man Named TOM' (29 September 1785), p. 4.

'Such Persons as Are Willing to Subscribe ...', *MG* (6 October 1785), p. 4.

'Ran Away from the Printing-Office in Quebec', *QG* (27 November 1777), p. 3.

'Advertisements. Ran Away from the Printing-Office in Quebec', *QG* (29 January 1788), p. 2.

'From the Gentleman's Magazine ... Epilogue to "The Padlock"', *Pennsylvania Packet and Daily Advertiser* (3 March 1788), p. 3.

'Run Away from the Schooner Lucy', *QG* (5 June 1788), p. 5.

'Eight Dollars Reward. Run Away from the Subscriber on Saturday Morning', *QG* (26 June 1788), p. 2.

'Quebec, March 26', *QG* (26 March 1789), p. 3.

'To Be Sold', *MG* (9 April 1789), p. 3.

'Slave Trade', *Diary or Woodfall's Register* (13 May 1789), pp. 2–4. Burney Newspapers Collection.

'The Diary, London, May 14, 1789', *Diary or Woodfall's Register* (14 May 1789), p. 2. Burney Newspapers Collection.

'To the Printer of *The Diary*: Slave Trade: Letter I', *Diary or Woodfall's Register* (16 May 1789), p. 2. Burney Newspapers Collection.

'Slave Trade, A Card', *Diary or Woodfall's Register* (18 May 1789), p. 3. Burney Newspapers Collection.

'Slave Trade: The Following Petition has been Presented to the House of Commons on Behalf of the Planters and Owners of Property in the Island of St. Christopher', *Diary or Woodfall's Register* (18 May 1789), pp. 3–4. Burney Newspapers Collection.

'Parnassian Flowers. The Negro's Complaint, A Song, To the Tune of Hosier's Ghost:' *MG* (11 June 1789), p. 4.

'From Woodfall's Register, London May 13, House of Commons, Tuesday May 12, The Slave Trade', *QG* (13 August 1789), pp. 2–4.

'Chambre des Communes, LONDRES, Mardi le 12 Mai, 1789. Debat sur le Commerce D'esclaves', *QG* (20 August 1789), p. 4 (27 August 1789), p. 4 (3 September 1789), p. 4.

'Correct and Authentic Copies of the Twelve Propositions Submitted on Tuesday Evening the 12th May last, by Mr Wilberforce ...', *QG* (20 August 1789), p. 3.

'London, May 9: Slave Trade', *MG* (20 August 1789), p. 1–2.

'London, May 13', *MG* (27 August 1789), pp. 1–2.

'Negroes: To the Printer of the St. J. Chronicle', *St James's Chronicle or the British Evening Post* (27–29 August 1789), p. 2. Burney Newspapers Collection.

'Extract at Large from That Part of Mr. Necker's Speech Which Concerns the Slave Trade', *MG* (3 September 1789), p. 2.

180 *Bibliography*

'Il s'enfuit de Québec Lundi dernier matin', *QG* (3 September 1789), p. 3.

'London, June 2 to 10', *QG* (3 September 1789), p. 2.

'Paris, May 11 to 25. His Most Christian Majesty's Speech at the Opening of the States General at Versailles, the 5th of May, 1789', *MG* (3 September 1789), pp. 1–2.

'Paris, May 25', *QG* (3 September 1789), p. 1.

'Extracts from the Instructions of Some of the Bailiwicks Relating to the Abolition of the Slave Trade', *MG* (10 September 1789), p. 1.

'London, May 16: Correct and Authentick Copies of the Twelve Propositions Submitted on Tuesday Evening by Mr Wilberforce …', *MG* (1 October 1789), pp. 1–3.

'The Following Beautiful and Pathetic Lines by Mr COWPER Need No Other Introduction Than the Name of Their Author', *QG* (21 January 1790), p. 4.

'From a Late New York Paper. Advertisement', *The Royal Gazette and the Nova Scotia Advertiser* (26 January 1790), p. 4. Nova Scotia Archives, reel 8163.

'The Negro's Recital', *QG* (16 December 1790), p. 4.

'Sunday, Aug. 28', *QG* (24 November 1791), p. 2.

'Quebec, April 19', *QG* (19 April 1792), p. 2.

'Song. The Dying Negro', *QG* (21 June 1792), p. 2.

Thomas H. Jones, 'Card', *Weekly Chronicle* (13 June 1851), p. 3.

'Narrative of a Refugee Slave', *Wesleyan* (21 June 1851), p. 5.

'The Rev. Thomas Jones', *Presbyterian Witness* (21 June 1851), p. 3.

'Took Her Freedom', *St. John Chronicle and Colonial Conservative* (5 September 1851), p. 1.

'Old Moses', *Wesleyan* (20 September 1851), p. 1.

'Mechanics Institute', *St. John Chronicle and Colonial Conservative* (6 February 1852), p. 2.

'Fugitive Slaves in Canada', *New Brunswick Courier* (3 April 1852), p. 2.

'The Bazaar', *St. John Chronicle and Colonial Conservative* (9 July 1852), p. 2.

'Godey's Lady's Book', *St John Chronicle and Colonial Conservative* (30 July 1852), p. 2.

'Literature: Life in the South – a Companion to Uncle Tom's Cabin', *Presbyterian Witness* (21 August 1852), p. 3.

'Coloured Convention at Baltimore', *St. John Chronicle and Colonial Conservative* (27 August 1852), p. 2.

'Uncle Tom', *Liberator* (27 August 1852), pp. 1–2. Uncle Tom's Cabin and American Culture, http://utc.iath.virginia.edu/notices/noar02qt.html (accessed 10 August 2023).

'Educational Works', *Presbyterian Witness* (11 September 1852), p. 3.

Bibliography

'The New Brunswick Temperance Almanac, for 1853', *St. John Chronicle and Colonial Conservative* (22 October 1852), p. 2.

'A Real "Uncle Tom"', *Presbyterian Witness* (30 October 1852), p. 5.

'Martin's Rose', *Presbyterian Witness* (20 November 1852), pp. 1–2.

'Eustache, the St. Domingo Slave', *Wesleyan* (16 December 1852), p. 1. Nova Scotia Archives, reel 8423.

'Commencement of the New Year', *Presbyterian Witness* (1 January 1853), p. 2.

'The News Boy's Address, Respectfully Presented to the Patrons of the St. John Chronicle', *St. John Chronicle and Colonial Conservative* (7 January 1853), p. 4.

'Uncle Tom's Cabin', *Morning News* (2 February 1853), p. 2.

'Uncle Tom's Cabin', *Morning News* (4 February 1853), p. 2.

'New Books', *New Brunswick Courier* (19 February 1853), p. 2.

'The Old Oak Tree', *Wesleyan* (24 February 1853), p. 1.

[no title], *New Brunswick Courier* (23 April 1853), p. 2.

'Thrilling Narrative', *Morning News* (27 July 1853), p. 1 (29 July 1853), p. 1 (1 August 1853), p. 1.

'Rev. Thomas H. Jones', *Liberator* (19 August 1853), p. 3. *Nineteenth-Century U.S. Newspapers*, www.gale.com/intl/c/19th-century-us-newspapers (accessed 10 August 2022).

'Old Jeddy – There's Rest at Home', *Wesleyan* (20 October 1853), p. 1.

'The Great Plea for Freedom: Read It and You Cannot Resist It: My Bondage and My Freedom', *Frederick Douglass' Paper* (19 October 1855), p. 4.

Manuscript sources

Photographic postcard of James (Jim) Henson, Grey Roots Archival Collection 968.61.15.

Internet sources

A Black People's History of Canada, www.blackpeopleshistory.ca (accessed 2 November 2023).

'"A Black People's History of Canada" Set to Produce a Seismic Shift in Education about Canadian History', www.dal.ca/news/2021/04/09/-a-black-people-s-history-of-canada--set-to-produce-a-seismic-sh.html (accessed 20 June 2023).

Bibliography

Acadian Recorder, Nova Scotia Historical Newspapers, www.novascotia.ca/archives/newspapers/results.asp?nTitle=Acadian+Recorder (accessed 1 January 2023).

Brock, Jared A., 'The Story of Josiah Henson, the Real Inspiration for "Uncle Tom's Cabin"', *Smithsonian Magazine*, www.smithsonianmag.com/author/jared-brock/ (accessed 2 August 2023).

'Charmaine Nelson Leading the Creation of the Institute for the Study of Canadian Slavery', www.ronfanfair.com/home/2020/7/22/a4sv9iwp3m9nm4fuya2q00llz2m75i (accessed 20 June 2023).

'doublethink', *Oxford English Dictionary Online*, https://doi.org/10.1093/OED/6408439140 (accessed 2 January 2017).

The Early Caribbean Digital Archive, https://web.archive.org/web/20220617204426/https://ecda.northeastern.edu/ (accessed 2 October 2023).

'Epilogue to "The Padlock", From the Gentleman's Magazine', www.brycchancarey.com/slavery/padlock1.htm (accessed 1 November 2018).

'experience', *Oxford English Dictionary Online*, https://doi.org/10.1093/OED/5485237439 (accessed 2 November 2024).

Keats-Shelley Association of America, 'Anti-'Racist Pedagogies Teach-In', www.k-saa.org/blog/urgent-belated-imperiled-demanding-dangerous-transgressive-transformative-impossible-imperative-a-report-on-anti-racist-pedagogies-for-18th-and-19th-century-studies-a-teach-in (accessed 2 October 2023).

'R. v. Andrews, 19 May 1801, Shelburne County Special Court of Oyer and Terminer', Nova Scotia Archives, African Nova Scotians in the Age of Slavery in Abolition, https://archives.novascotia.ca/africanns/archives/?ID=61 (accessed 15 March 2023).

'Runaway Slaves in Britain: Bondage, Freedom, and Race in the Eighteenth Century', www.runaways.gla.ac.uk (accessed 15 March 2023).

Index

Angelique, Marie-Joseph 28, 132
anti-*Tom* fiction, depiction of
 Canada in 1–2

Barnes, James (editor of the
 Presbyterian Witness) 108,
 110–13
Bibb, Henry, *The Narrative of the
 Life of Henry Bibb* (1849)
 62–63
the Black Atlantic (Paul Gilroy) 9
 The Black Atlantic Reconsidered
 (Winfried Siemerling) 9, 94
 in relation to Canada 9
Black Loyalists 4, 13
 John Marrant as an advocate
 for 98
 the narratives of Boston King
 and David George 99–100
Briggs, William 133–35
Brown, William (editor of the
 Quebec Gazette 1764–89)
 29–30

Clarke, George Elliott
 bibliography of Canadian slave
 narratives 6
 view that praise of Canadian
 liberty in antebellum slave
 narratives obscured earlier
 accounts of slavery and
 racism in Canada 6, 60
colourism 137–42, 146, 154
Cowper, William, 'The Negro's
 Complaint' 15, 47–48

Crèvecœur, J. Hector St John de
 (*Letters from an American
 Farmer*, 1752) 75–76
culture of reprinting (Meredith L.
 McGill) 104
Cunnabell, William (owner of the
 Wesleyan) 108

Douglass, Frederick 64, 66–68,
 95, 101
Drew, Benjamin (*A North-Side
 View of Slavery: The Refugee,
 or Narratives of Fugitive
 Slaves in Canada*) 59–60, 65,
 67–73, 82, 83, 87
Durant, William (editor of the
 Weekly Chronicle) 105–6
'Epilogue to "The Padlock"' (1787)
 47–49

Equiano, Olaudah 61–62, 100, 145
'exodus' of authors to the United
 States 136

Frost, John 129–30, 132–33,
 136–37, 143, 154
fugitive slave advertisements in the
 Quebec newspapers 14–15,
 28–29, 33–36, 147–48

Garrison, William Lloyd (*The
 Liberator*) 96, 104–5, 110
George, David *see* Black Loyalists,
 the narratives of Boston King
 and David George

184 *Index*

Gilmore, Thomas 29
Glenelg (narrator/amanuensis), *Broken Shackles* (1889) 129–33, 137–47, 151–53, 155

Halifax, Nova Scotia 5–6, 12, 98, 104, 108, 113–15, 118, 134
Henson, Jim, *Broken Shackles* (1889) 129–33, 137–38, 140–47, 149–53, 155
Henson, Josiah 1–2

Joe, enslaved pressman at the *Quebec Gazette* 32–34
Jones, Thomas H.
advertisements for his narrative published in newspapers in Halifax, Nova Scotia (1851) 113–18
card in the *Weekly Chronicle* (1851) 105–6
The Experience of Thomas Jones, Who Was a Slave for Forty-Three Years 101–2, 107–8
New Brunswick reprint of *The Experience of Thomas Jones* (1853) 102–3
salesman of *The Liberator* 101
subversion of the grateful slave trope 119
time in Nova Scotia and New Brunswick 101, 104–6

King, Boston *see* Black Loyalists, the narratives of Boston King and David George

Lake Erie (depiction of crossings in slave narratives) 2, 9
Le Jeune, Olivier 27
Little, John 70–71
Little, John Mrs 70–71

Macleod, Alex W. Rev. (editor of the *Wesleyan*) 108
Marrant, John 97–98
Mason, Isaac 86–88

McMillan, J. & A. (New Brunswick booksellers) 102–3
Mesplet, Fleury
enslaver 32
French and British anti-slave-trade arguments 45–46
reprinting French anti-slave-trade texts 42–47
reprinting letter by La Société des Amis des Noirs in Paris 44
on the specialness of French liberty 45
Montreal 6, 12–14, 28, 30–31, 134, 148
Moodie, Susanna 61, 80–86, 132

Neilson, Samuel
does not reprint pro-slave-trade arguments 38
editorship of *Quebec Gazette* (1789–93) 37
reprinting British anti-slave-trade poetry 47–51
reprinting William Wilberforce's speech to the House of Commons (1789) 37–39
uncertainty around whether he was an enslaver 32–33
view of the Middle Passage 41–43
Nicholson, J. (publisher in Halifax, West Yorkshire, England) 100

Owen Sound (Ontario) 129–31, 153–54

Pooley (nee Burthen), Sophia 16–17
Prince, Mary 61, 80–86, 132

Queen's Bush 16, 65, 86

Rochester, New York 84

Saint John, New Brunswick 102, 104–6
Sayers, Frank, 'The Dying African' (*c.* 1789–90) 47

Index

Shadd, Mary Ann (*A Plea for Emigration to Canada West*) 79, 83, 85
slavery in colonial Canada
  history of 10–15
  textualisation of slavery and significance of Canadian newspapers 26
Steward, Austin
  construction of Canada as a special haven for fugitives from slavery 72
  depiction of the exploitation of Black settlers in Upper Canada 79–80, 82–85
  influence of Susanna Moodie on 80–86
  President of the Wilberforce Colony 65
  writing on the transformative power of the Canadian wilderness for fugitives from slavery 73
Stowe, Harriet Beecher (*Uncle Tom's Cabin*) 1–2, 129

Ward, Samuel Ringgold 4
Wilberforce, William *see* Neilson, Samuel, reprinting William Wilberforce's speech to the House of Commons (1789)

EU authorised representative for GPSR:
Easy Access System Europe, Mustamäe tee 50,
10621 Tallinn, Estonia
gpsr.requests@easproject.com

www.ingramcontent.com/pod-product-compliance
Lightning Source LLC
LaVergne TN
LVHW050046200525
811683LV00004B/23